Workplace Democracy

Workplace Democracy

The Political Effects of Participation

EDWARD S. GREENBERG

Cornell University Press | Ithaca and London

First published 1986 by Cornell University Press.

International Standard Book Number 0–8014–1921–2
Library of Congress Catalog Card Number 86–47641
Printed in the United States of America.
Librarians: Library of Congress cataloging information appears on the last page of the book.

The paper in this book is acid-free and meets the guidelines for permanence and durability of the Committee on Production Guidelines for Book Longevity of the Council on Library Resources.

Contents

Preface

In the late 1960s and early 1970s the political air was filled with talk of direct democracy, participatory democracy, and workers' control. To many on the Left, these various political forms seemed to presage the formation of a more humane, egalitarian, and democratic society; they seemed to many, as well, to be a strategy for an achievable utopia, an alternative to the tired and failed strategies of Marxism-Leninism and Social Democracy.

Of particular importance in the process of social change was the role to be played by a democratized, participatory workplace. Whether under the name of workers' self-management, workers' control, or workplace democracy, such contexts were hypothesized to be rich educational environments in which people would overcome alienation in its many forms; become thoughtful, public-spirited, and engaged citizens; and become transformed into class-conscious members of the working class, willing and able to act politically in accordance with their broad class interests.

I found myself during those years caught up in most of these political and economic currents and very enthusiastic about workplace democracy as a strategy for political change. Being a trained social scientist as well, however, I wanted to know whether evidence could be found to support the claims made for the political effects of workplace democracy. A study of the Pacific Northwest plywood cooperatives, of which this book is in part the final report, was the result of that curiosity. Although my enthusiasm for workplace democracy has been somewhat diminished by the results of this investigation, it has not been entirely erased. I am simply more sensitive now than when I began this study to the complexities of workplace democratic processes and the role played in attitude and be-havior change by the dominant political and cultural environment.

Any project of the duration and complexity of this one is always the product of the efforts and support of many people and institutions. I take this opportunity to thank them and to let them know that their efforts are deeply appreciated. I begin with my first graduate research assistant on this project, Thad Tecza, whose "street smarts" helped immeasurably in gaining access to initially distrustful plywood firms and in identifying and locating subjects in cooperative and conventional companies for the depth interviews. He also proved to be a sensitive and penetrating interviewer, a good companion during our long travels on the rain-slicked highways of the Northwest, and an indispensable colleague in the creation of the final test instrument for the questionnaire stage of the project. Art Ensley, the elected treasurer of one of the plywood cooperatives, was kind enough to spend many hours outside of work describing in great detail how these unique institutions operate as technical, economic, and social institutions. Another graduate research assistant, Farideh Farhi (now on the political science faculty at the University of Hawaii), was the guardian and manager of the various data sets and my guide through the manifold terrors of the valley of the CYBER and SPSS. She was also the person upon whom I would first try out my sometimes outlandish ideas, which she invariably met with good humor and honesty (often painful honesty at that). Lorraine Blank, a doctoral dissertation student at American University, taught me more about confirmatory factor analysis and index construction than I ever thought possible. Christopher Gunn of Hobart and William Smith Col-leges, one of the foremost scholars in the world today working in the field of industrial and workplace democracy, kindly read and commented on virtually every paper I wrote over the years. More than anyone else, he helped me guard against serious errors of evidence and interpretation. Menachem Rosner of the University of Haifa, one of the world's author-ities on the life of the kibbutz, was generous enough, as conference organizer and all-purpose catalyst, to arrange cherished invitations to Israel and Yugoslavia, where I was able to see workplace democracy firsthand and to refine my understanding of the complexities of interaction of work-place democracy and environment. I also appreciate his thorough critiques of several conference papers that eventually became a part of this book. My secretary, Jean Umbreit, turned my often illegible and incomprehen-sible scratchings into polished finished products with dispatch and good humor. Thanks are also owed to the National Science Foundation for its generous research grant support (SOC76–11897 and SES81–10946) and to the Institute of Behavioral Science at the University of Colorado and its director, Richard Jessor, for providing the ideal setting for the conduct of serious scholarship. I am grateful to the University of California Press for giving me permission to reprint substantial parts of my chapter on the plywood cooperatives in *Worker Cooperatives in America* (1984), edited by Robert Jackall and Henry Levin, in Chapter 2 of this book. The journal *Economic and Industrial Democracy* has allowed me to reprint substantial portions of my "Context and Cooperation" in Chapter 7; the article first appeared in vol. 4 (1983) of that journal. My thanks go finally to Peter Agree, my editor at Cornell University Press, and the several anonymous referees of the manuscript whose enthusiasm for this project served to validate all of the years and effort that went into its creation.

EDWARD S. GREENBERG

Boulder, Colorado

Workplace Democracy

· 1 ·

The Democratic Left and the
Appeals of Workplace Democracy

At this very moment, somewhere in the world, an innovation in workplace democracy—decisional participation, job enrichment, worker ownership, or worker self-management—is being put into place. A moment from now, somewhere in the world, an activist, journalist, or scholar of the democratic Left[1] will enthusiastically applaud this innovation, argue for its profound implications for social change, and place it squarely within a growing movement for workplace and societal democratization. This pattern of innovation and response is not new. The French workers' and students' uprising in May 1968, for instance, was interpreted as placing the issue of worker self-management at the center of the political agenda in that country. A similar response was sparked by the wave of factory seizures in northern Italy in the late 1960s in which "bread-and-butter" demands were subordinated to demands for the democratization of the workplace. The democratic Left has enthusiastically greeted the several revolts over the years in Eastern Europe against Soviet domination in which the spontaneous proliferation of workers' councils and other workplace democratic forms have played a prominent role.

Less dramatically, though persistently, activists, journalists, and scholars of the democratic Left in the United States and other countries have celebrated and publicized such exemplars of workplace democracy as the Israeli kibbutz, the Yugoslav system of worker self-management, industrial democracy in Allende's Chile, the flourishing Mondragon cooperatives in Spain, and the vast array of workplace democracy programs in place today in Sweden and Norway.[2] Such publications as the *Nation*, *Dissent*, the *Progressive*, and *In These Times* enthusiastically report to

13

their readers the latest initiatives in job enrichment, workplace participation, self-management, codetermination, and worker buyouts.[3] Almost
every proposal for a transformed political and economic system in the
United States emanating from the democratic Left includes workplace
democracy and worker self-management as integral to an overall reform
program.[4] Typical of this literature is Joshua Cohen and Joel Rogers's *On
Democracy* (1983), Martin Carnoy and Derek Shearer's *Economic Democracy* (1980), Samuel Bowles, David M. Gordon, and Thomas E.
Weisskopf's *Beyond the Waste Land* (1983), and Barry Bluestone and
Bennett Harrison's *Deindustrialization of America* (1982a). Recent efforts
to formulate the outlines of a democratic socialist society, finally, place
democratically controlled enterprises at their center (Howe, 1985; Nove,
1983).

Much of this enthusiasm for workplace democracy is based on a belief
that it anticipates the creation (perhaps in the distant future) of a new,
more democratic, and more egalitarian society.[5] Is such enthusiasm warranted? If it is true, as one scholar has said, that "it is quite clear that
socialists are identified, in part at least, by their support for industrial
democracy or workers' control" (Street, 1983:519), it is worth asking
why this might be the case. It is also important to ask whether the empirical
evidence supports the general belief that instances of workplace democratization, no matter how small or seemingly insignificant, represent necessary building blocks in a social process leading to the full
democratization of social, economic, and political life. In this book, I
make an inquiry into such issues the center of analysis and bring to bear
empirical data gathered from workers in one of the largest, oldest, and
most fully democratic industrial enterprises in the United States: the producer cooperatives of the Pacific Northwest plywood industry.

The Appeals of Workplace Democracy to the Democratic Left

Why is the democratic Left drawn so enthusiastically to virtually every
instance in which workers, whether blue or white collar, gain a voice in
decision making in the workplace? If "socialists are identified . . . by their
support for industrial democracy or workers' control" (Street, 1983:519),[6]
why is it true? What is appealing about workplace democracy? I shall
argue that the appeal of workplace democracy and, in particular, of its
fullest expression in worker self-management,[7] may be located in three

intellectual/political traditions that have long nurtured the democratic Left: that literature addressing the problem of alienation and its alleviation; that which is concerned with the encouragement of participatory democracy; and that which has searched for radical but popular-democratic strategies for the overthrow of capitalism. These three traditions are reviewed briefly below and form the basis for the empirical analyses in the remainder of this book.[8]

The Problem of Alienation

Interest in the subject of alienation and its various effects springs, to a large extent, from a rediscovery of the roots of the socialist tradition and its powerful critique of the Industrial Revolution and market capitalism, and most especially the effects of market-based industrialization upon human beings caught in its throes.[9] Most important in this regard was the contribution made by the giant of the socialist tradition, Karl Marx, in his *Economic and Philosophical Manuscripts*, with its central focus on alienation in industrial capitalism.[10] Here, Marx stressed that under capitalism humankind was alienated in the sense that the conditions of life in such a system, particularly in the area of work and production, separate people from their essence as free, creative beings. To Marx, the abolition of private property through socialist revolution was the essential starting point from which human beings could fulfill themselves by eliminating the conditions leading to their alienation: wage labor, industrial specialization, powerlessness, and passivity. Labor, which to Marx was the expression of human personality and creativity, had become alienated under industrial capitalism because the organization of production had separated the worker from him or herself and from the product; he no longer used creative skills, had no control over what was produced, nor could determine how to produce. Work, in short, had been transformed from a free, creative activity to one of involuntary servitude. As Marx put this issue:

What constitutes the alienation of labor? First, that the work is *external* to the worker, that it is not part of his nature, and that, consequently, he does not fulfill himself in his work but denies himself, has a feeling of misery rather than well being, does not develop freely his mental and physical energies but is physically exhausted and mentally debased. The worker therefore feels himself at home only during his leisure time, whereas at work he feels homeless. His work . . . is not the satisfaction of a need but only a *means* for satisfying other needs.[11]

This concern with the interrelationship of workplace and alienation and the need for their transformation has always been at the heart of Marxism.[12]

To contemporary political philosopher C. B. MacPherson, the concern for alienation, understood as a state of existence that thwarts the development of human capacities, is the central building block of the socialist tradition, both Marxist and non-Marxist. That tradition takes as its starting point the nature and possibilities of human beings. As with all other sociopolitical traditions, the socialist tradition makes certain assumptions about the nature of human beings and their relationships to others. It starts with those characteristics it believes common to all human beings and that entitle all people to equal consideration and respect. Most important, the socialist tradition insists that human beings are more than simple maximizers of utilities and bundles of appetites seeking satisfaction, an assumption basic to the Western liberal tradition. Rather, human beings are, in the eloquent words of MacPherson, "doers, creators, enjoyers of their human attributes. . . . Man is not a bundle of appetites seeking satisfaction but a bundle of conscious energies seeking to be exerted" (1973:5). Humans are purposeful beings who are capable, if given a chance, of making decisions intelligently, who have intentions and purposes, and who can become aware of alternatives and rationally choose among them. People are potentially self-directed and self-determining; and to be placed in settings where others direct all essential aspects of their efforts is to be separated from one's humanness. People also possess the capacity for self-expression and creativity. They are capable of developing excellence in some area of life—intellectual, aesthetic, or moral, theoretical or practical, personal or public (Lukes, 1975:157). Although people do not have equal capability in each and every area, they "share the capacity to realize potentialities that are worthy of admiration" (Lukes, 1975:157).

A just society, in the traditional socialist view, is one in which human beings are "empowered," in MacPherson's terms; they are able to use and develop their essentially human capacities. It is a society organized to transcend alienation. Several impediments to the realization of these potentialities exist in various societies. First, the means to sustain life at an adequate level of health and security may not allow for the expression of human power. Such an impediment is most evident in the less-developed societies, though it also exists to varying degrees elsewhere. Second, a people may not be protected against intrusion by others, and especially by the state, which thus destroys the private space in which much of the development of human capacities necessarily takes place. Such impediments are most evident in presently existing socialist states. Third, and most important for the purposes of this study, a society may not allow adequate access to the means of labor and productive creativity. This is especially the case in capitalist societies, in which the means of labor and production are unevenly distributed and some must sell their labor power to others and must work for purposes and in a manner determined by others. In such a system, according to MacPherson, human powers are continually transferred from one group to another.

Alienation, then, whether understood as an objective situation of powerlessness and thwarted human creativity or as any of a series of subjective psychological adjuncts to that situation, adheres to a set of social relations in which workers are divorced from the control of the production process, the use of their own labor power, and the fruits of their labor. The transcendence of alienation, it follows, is possible, in the socialist tradition, only in a situation in which worker *subordination* is displaced by worker *superordination*. In the call for such a transformation one may locate an important source of the persistent socialist fascination with workplace democracy and worker self-management.

Participatory Democracy

Participatory democracy is the second of the great traditions that help feed the enthusiasm for workplace democracy on the Left both here and abroad. Finding their intellectual and political inspiration in a wide variety of sources—some in socialism, some in anarchism, but most in traditional democratic theory (Pateman, 1970)—participatory democrats are united in their belief that direct, face-to-face, participatory decision making within all major social institutions and with regard to all major societal decisions is both necessary and proper. Participatory democracy, in this view, forms the basis for an educated and efficacious citizenry, represents the fulfillment of the democratic idea, and embodies the essential foundations of the good society.[13]

Participatory democrats insist that their conception of democracy is essentially a return to an older and richer tradition, one that rejects what they consider to be the overly narrow and sterile conception of democracy found in liberal democratic and pluralist democratic theory with their focus on elections, representation, and group bargaining and their deemphasis of the role of participation (Berelson, 1952; Dahl, 1956, 1963; Dahl and Lindblom, 1953; Eckstein, 1966; Sartori, 1962; Schumpeter, 1943). Despite some differences in nuance and emphasis, traditional democratic theorists, they insist, believe that all people have deliberate and moral potential; that, given the proper education and environment, ordinary people can be responsible and reflective (Pateman, 1970; Thompson, 1970). Faith in the capacity of ordinary human beings to govern themselves wisely is at the heart of traditional democratic theory. In the eloquent words of philosopher-educator John Dewey: "The foundation of democracy is faith in the capacities of human nature; faith in human intelligence and in the power of pooled and cooperative experience. It is not belief that these things are complete but that if given a show they will grow and be able to generate progressively the knowledge and wisdom needed to guide collective action" (1927:211). Many contemporary social scientists have mounted a ferocious attack against this hopeful and optimistic formulation of democracy. In the name of hard-nosed, scientific objectivity, they brand traditional democratic notions as naive, unfounded, and impossible to construct in the real world of flawed humanity. The reasons for such a transformation of democratic theory are too complex and involved to pursue here, but the central factors revolve around both the rise of mass totalitarianism (Nazi Germany, the Soviet Union) and the results of post–World War II public opinion research. Both seemed to offer proof that the mass public is characterized by ignorance, irrationality, apathy, emotionalism, and general availability for mass mobilization by demagogues. Interpreting their own systems as democratic, yet observing the poor popular material at its base, many social scientists argued that democratic theory ought to be reformulated in such a way that it no longer required mass participation of the public, aside from occasional exercise of the suffrage in elections to choose between competing, although ideologically similar, elite groups.[14]

Traditional democratic theorists such as John Stuart Mill, Jean-Jacques Rousseau, John Dewey, and G. D. H. Cole acknowledged that human beings do not measure up to their prescriptions. They argued, however, that under the proper circumstances, people could develop in such a direction. Central to traditional democratic thought is the notion that ordinary people are improvable and educable, that they have the potential to become more rational and attentive and, as a result, to govern themselves well.

Mill was concerned with the problem of how people might become more "public-spirited." He concluded that people could reach democratic standards only by living in societies that encouraged them to participate in their own governance at all levels and in all spheres of activity. Further, he proposed that societies be judged by the extent to which they fulfilled this educative function. Traditional democratic theorists have been primarily interested in the relationship between the nature of social institutions and the structure of human personality and character. In the main, they have argued that the emergence of democratic personality is impossible in a setting that does not allow for participatory modes of behavior. In the words of Carole Pateman:

> The theory of participatory democracy is built round the central assertion that individuals and their institutions cannot be considered in isolation from one another. The existence of representative institutions at the national level is not sufficient for democracy; for maximum participation by all the people of that level, socialization, or "social training," for democracy must take place in other spheres in order that the necessary individual attitudes and psychological qualities can be developed. This development takes place through the process of participation itself. The major function of participation in the theory of participatory democracy is therefore an educative one, educative in the very widest sense, including both the psychological aspect and the gaining of practice in democratic skills and procedures. [1970:42]

It must be emphasized that participation, in this view, is not to be confined to what we normally think of as politics, but must encompass the entire society. Or, to put it another way, politics is defined so broadly that it transcends formal government. In truly democratic societies, political participation by ordinary citizens would take place in the total universe of significant institutions, including the family, the school, and the workplace. In short, the emergence of democratic and fully developed human beings is possible only in a fully democratic, participatory society. Participation is thus the central tenet of traditional democratic theory and its rejection by modern revisionist theorists makes the label "democratic" attached to their formulations highly suspect. To the traditional theorists of democracy, participation is the principal social process by which human beings, practicing the arts of self-direction, cooperation, and responsibility, liberate their capacities and thereby become whole, healthy, and integrated persons. As a consequence of participation, the individual develops the attitudes and skills essential to participation in other social spheres including the political. Participation in decision making at the workplace is thus central to the democratic vision and basic to the good society.

Strategies for the Transcendence of Capitalism

The third great tradition that helps form the foundation of enthusiasm for workplace democracy on the Left, both here and abroad, is that which rejects both the anarchy and injustice of market capitalism and the tyranny of Soviet-style socialism[15] in favor of "socialism with a human face"— self-governing socialism. Central to the thinking of the main theorists of this tradition is the need to link means and ends so that change strategies are tied to ultimate goals. Most important, in this view, a society with a human face must use instruments with a human face to achieve its goals; a democratic, egalitarian, and just socialism must be "prefigured" in the change strategies themselves. Theorists in this tradition, for obvious reasons, have concluded that Marxist-Leninist vanguard methods inevitably pervert the ultimate goals of socialism (Horvat, 1982). They also argue that because of their deemphasis on popular participation, the parliamentary, electoral strategies of Social Democracy are both ineffective for the construction of a socialist society and destructive of the ultimate values and goals of self-governing socialism.[16] Out of this twin rejection of Marxism-Leninism and Social Democracy has emerged a search for a new strategy of social change in which workplace democracy, particularly in its most highly developed form—worker self-management—plays a preeminent role.

The literature in this tradition is diverse and of widely differentiated theoretical sophistication. At the simplest level, there is the notion that fully democratized workplaces, to the extent that they bear a striking resemblance to enterprises in socialist theory (to the extent that they encourage cooperative and egalitarian social relations), must be an essential component of a strategy to reach socialism (Bernstein, 1974, 1976; Zwerdling, 1978). The unstated theory seems to be that by building brick by brick, workplace by workplace, a democratic socialist edifice will in time be constructed.

Though not a theory, as such, another approach suggests a linkage between self-management and democratic socialism by noting the historical association of modern social revolutions and spontaneously organized institutions of direct participatory democracy on the model of the soviet (Arendt, 1965; Horvat, 1982). One is reminded of the Paris Commune of

1871, the workers' and soldiers' soviets of the 1905 and 1917 Russian revolutions; the soviets of the failed Hungarian and German revolutions of 1918–19; the factory and neighborhood committees formed in the Republican areas (particularly Catalonia) during the Spanish Civil War; the workers' councils of the factory takeovers in northern Italy in 1919; and the soviets formed in the midst of every popular revolt against (ironically) domination by the Soviet Union in Eastern Europe (Hungary and East Germany in 1956, Czechoslovakia in 1968, and Poland in 1981). Even though such attempts generally failed to sustain themselves, the recurrent coexistence of direct participatory democracy—especially at the point of production— with revolutions for socialism, is an inescapable fact (Horvat, 1982) and has led many to conclude that workplace democratization is an essential tool for the transformation to a system of democratic socialism.

Another approach sees worker control of production within free-market capitalism as a model for other working people of what is possible, a compelling demonstration that production can be managed without capitalists. Several contemporary writers also see fully democratic workplaces, such as producer cooperatives, as an inspirational model. Carnoy and Shearer, for example, in their influential work, *Economic Democracy*, suggest:

> Worker ownership and democratic decision-making in production can spotlight the contradiction between American democratic ideology and capitalist production. Worker-controlled firms act as a model for democratic production even if they are functioning in a capitalist society. Certainly, such firms can operate alongside corporate capitalist firms without necessarily threatening them, particularly when there is no organized movement to channel such experiences into meaningful political action against corporate power. But if there were to be such a movement, the structure and practice of producer cooperatives could very well serve as the beginning of a more democratic economy. [1980:194]

By far the most elaborate and compelling theory of linkage between self-management and economic democracy is one that I label "the theory of escalation." This theory concerns the development of political consciousness—the dynamic growth, both of the working individual and of the working class as a whole—in the belief that workers ought to exercise decisive power in society and that they are capable of doing so. The theory suggests that the experience of democracy in the most immediate work environment is an essential educative tool in the growth of socialist consciousness because in such an environment a person comes to appreciate cooperative and collective efforts, cultivates confidence in productive skills, and develops a sense of power as a member of a class; here, too, human talents and abilities become sufficiently developed that the absurdity of capitalist social relations becomes clear.

The educative effects of full democratic management in the workplace, in this view, cannot be contained within the confines of the lowest level of production. As workers gain a sense of confidence in their abilities through the practice of democracy, the desire to control their own destiny begins to escalate to higher levels, first to the level of the enterprise and eventually to the entire economy. Each conquest of democratic participation and control, instead of satisfying workers, makes them increasingly dissatisfied with the remaining obstacles to democracy. With each victory for democracy in the workplace, whether partial or total, the power of the workers is strengthened and the level of socialist consciousness is raised. As André Gorz has put it, "It is through the struggle for 'industrial democracy' . . . that is to say, the workers' power of control, of management and self-management, rising from the shop floor to the corporation and the industry until it embraces the economy as a whole—that the working class learns to know the value and necessity of socialism and thus grows up to become the ruling class" (Gorz, 1973:95).

The view that self-management at the point of production nurtures within individuals a commitment to communitarian, egalitarian, and democratic values ready to participate in movements for economic democracy is, of course, familiar in the history of political thought. One is immediately reminded of the utopian socialists, Pierre Joseph Proudhon, G. D. H. Cole, and the guild socialist movement (especially as it took form in the shop stewards' movement) as well as such modern proponents as Carole Pateman (1970), David Tornquist (1973), John Case (1973),[17] John Coates (1966), Juan Espinosa and Andrew Zimbalist (1978),[18] and particularly Branko Horvat. As Horvat states the case in his discussion of a strategy of transition,

If universal self-management is introduced to either capitalist or etatist societies, it will gradually resolve the old production relations and eventually the disintegrating system will have to be replaced by something more compatible with the institution. By participating in management, . . . by fighting for a continuous extension of participation until it reaches full self-management, workers learn in their daily lives how to control their destiny, how to overcome fragmentation and decomposition of labor, how to achieve meaningful social equality, how to destroy antiquated hierarchies. They do this without the tutorship of omniscient leaders. . . . The growth of participation from its primitive forms of joint consultation toward full-fledged self-management cannot be antisocialist, in spite of the attempts to misuse it for the preservation of the status quo. [1982:427]

This position is nicely articulated by the editors of the important collection *Workers' Control*: "Workers' control suggests both an ultimate goal . . . and a strategy for reaching that goal" (Hunnius, Garson, and Case, 1973:ix).

The Study

As the above discussion illustrates, much of the democratic Left holds high expectations for workplace democracy, especially in its most fully developed form—workers' self-management. Basing these expectations primarily upon the three great intellectual/political traditions reviewed above—alienation, participatory democracy, and radical but popular-democratic revolution—the democratic Left has enthusiastically welcomed and supported most manifestations of workplace democracy in the Western capitalist nations, even the most seemingly insignificant among them. This book is designed to serve as a partial test for these expectations; it asks whether and to what extent the enthusiasm for workplace democracy (and, especially, self-management) is warranted by the available evidence, based on a detailed empirical study of one case.

The three traditions may be seen not only as a source of inspiration for the democratic Left but as a source for a set of testable claims about the effects of workplace democracy, a set of hypotheses open to methods of scientific inquiry like any other set of hypotheses in the social sciences. The central task of this book is to test these claims against an array of empirical data generated in the Pacific Northwest plywood cooperatives, enterprises that are among the oldest and most fully developed examples of workplace democracy in the United States.

What are these testable claims or hypotheses? In the first tradition, the claim is made that democratic workplaces, settings in which workers jointly decide policy regarding the organization, processes, and purposes of production, will be characterized by significantly less alienation (in both the objective and subjective understanding of that term) than conventional bureaucratic, hierarchical workplaces. The second tradition claims that democratized workplaces serve as schools for democracy, that they help mold an educated citizenry, skilled and confident in the democratic arts, public-spirited, politically informed, and involved in the affairs of community, region, and nation. The third tradition claims that the most fully developed democratic work settings help to fashion political class-consciousness in the working class by enhancing self-confidence, faith and confidence in one's fellow workers, cooperative attitudes and practices, egalitarian relations and sympathies, and the desire to create a new society beyond capitalism in which these qualities might be nurtured. This book is organized as a test of these general claims. In Chapter 3 I turn my attention to the further explication of the problem of alienation in modern industrial life, pose the claims about workplace democracy and alienation in a more testable form, and set them against some relevant empirical evidence. In Chapter 5, I do the same for participatory democratic claims, and in Chapter 6, I consider the relationship between workplace democracy and class-consciousness.

Although the scholarly and journalistic literature has contained many discussions of workplace democracy over the years, the actual number of enduring cases in the United States are surprisingly few. There is no shortage of cases in which workers have been given some role in decision making on the work line—for example, quality circles, participative management schemes, and Scanlon Plans among others. Nor is there a shortage of cases in which workers share in the profits of the firm or partially share in ownership (ESOP's or employee stock ownership plans being the most notable of the latter). But enterprises in which workers are in control, in which decisions about enterprise policy—including the design of production, control of the work process, choice of what to produce, distribution of earnings, and determination of investment—are in their hands entirely, are rare in the United States. An exception is the set of producer cooperatives in the Pacific Northwest plywood industry which are directly owned and managed by working men and women.[19] A lengthy and detailed description of these enterprises will be presented in Chapter 2.

Most of the worker-owned plywood firms were founded in the years immediately following World War II. Several were started by lumber workers worried about the dismal employment prospects in their industry, several were the product of workers seeking to prevent the closing of a privately owned mill, and more than a few were created by promoters who took a healthy slice of initial profits for their efforts. Without exception, studies of the plywood industry indicate that the worker-owned firms, which range in size from 80 to 350 members, are characterized by higher levels of productivity than are conventional firms. These firms account for over 10 percent of all softwood plywood production and are generally agreed to be the source of the industry's highest-quality product.

In general, the plywood cooperatives are impressively democratic enterprises. They are legal entities owned and controlled by their working shareholders. Periodic meetings of the worker-shareholders decide all matters of enterprise policy. Only working shareholders are permitted to vote; each can cast but a single vote. Shareholders elect a board of directors and hire a manager to run day-to-day affairs. Attendance at meetings is high; participation in discussions and debate is widespread; technical and financial information is readily available and the worker-shareholders are well informed. The plywood co-ops are true labor communities, moreover, in that earnings are distributed on the basis of work performed and not on the basis of differential ownership of shares. Social relations in these enterprises are highly egalitarian, equal wage rates are the norm, supervision is loose, job rotation is common, and cooperative problem solving on the job is frequent. The producer cooperatives in the American plywood industry are substantially democratized work settings, as close as we have come in the United States to worker self-management in industrial enterprises. If workplace democracy has the effects that are claimed by the three traditions reviewed in this chapter, it should be evident in the plywood cooperatives. If it is not, we have grounds for rejecting or at least fundamentally rethinking many of these claims.[20]

Full details of data-collection strategies may be found in the chapters that follow, as well as in the methodological appendix. Briefly, however, data were collected in four ways. First, overall descriptions and assessments of the operations of cooperative and conventional (the control group) plywood firms were gathered through interviews with people familiar with both the industry and particular companies. Second, in-depth interviews, some lasting as long as three and four hours, were conducted with worker-shareholders in the cooperatives, hired workers in the same companies, and workers in a conventionally organized plywood firm, all with an eye toward gaining a richly textured sense of the particulars of the work experience, the social dynamics internal to the plants, and the felt effects of such an experience. Third, attitudinal and behavioral data were collected from people working in cooperative and conventional plywood firms by a lengthy mail questionnaire. Finally, a second wave of mail questionnaires was administered approximately five years later to many of the people who had participated in the first wave to generate longitudinal panel data amenable to the analysis of attitudinal and behavioral change. All of the firms involved in the study are in close geographical proximity, are virtually identical in the technical organization of production, and are practically indistinguishable in the demographic characteristics of the work force. Consequently, these cooperative and conventionally organized firms provide an unusually well-defined scientific sample in which the two major categories of plants differ only with respect to the central variable of concern: the degree of workplace democracy. Using such a sample serves to isolate the effects of workplace democracy by diminishing the possibility that any observed differences between workers in cooperative and conventional firms might be explained by differences in the technical division of labor, geographically specific cultures, or demographic characteristics of the work force. Because these cases are so closely matched, the introduction of a long string of controls, common in contemporary survey research, is unnecessary. Rather, controls are built into the analysis through the sampling design.

To determine whether workers in the plywood cooperatives differ from workers in conventionally organized plywood firms on measures of alienation, political orientation and behavior, and class-consciousness, in what ways they differ, and why, the following data-analysis strategy is followed in the book. First, the two samples are directly compared on each of the measures both in cross-section and over time. Second, when statistically significant differences are observed between workers in cooperative and conventional enterprises in either the cross-sectional or longitudinal-panel analyses, demographic control variables (education, age, income, and the like) are introduced to determine whether the observed relationship may be attributed to background or self-selection factors. Third, if the statistically significant relationships between factory type and dependent variables survive the introduction of control variables, the relationships are further elaborated in a multivariate analysis using multiple regression. The focus at this stage of the analysis is on the internal structure and dynamics of the plywood enterprises (relationships with peers, the nature of supervision, participation in decision making, and the like). Further details on the analytic strategy appear in the body of the text and in the methodological appendix.

A Brief Look Ahead

The remainder of the volume is organized around the claims and tests of claims regarding each tradition reviewed in these pages: two chapters on alienation, one on participatory democracy, and two on political class-consciousness. Each chapter will bring to bear a rich and diverse data set, encompassing information gathered by observation, interview, cross-sectional survey, and longitudinal-panel survey, so as to illuminate and make possible judgments regarding the adequacy of these diverse claims as well as the body of theoretical work upon which they are based. Before doing so, however, it is important that the reader come to understand the producer cooperatives in plywood and how their operations and decision-making processes justify my designation of them as democratic institutions.

·2·

The Plywood Cooperatives

The plywood producer cooperatives are among the most fully developed and enduring democratic industrial enterprises in the United States. Other experiments in workplace democracy have come and gone, but the Pacific Northwest plywood cooperatives, most of which have been in existence for twenty-five to thirty years,[1] not only have persisted through the good and bad times characteristic of that industry but have remained enterprises in which those who work also generally decide policy.[2]

In contrast to cooperatives, conventional industrial organizations, whether in capitalist or socialist societies, are more authoritarian than democratic. Their vitality in the work setting is impressive and in vivid contrast to the democratic rhetoric that surrounds and justifies most social systems, East and West. The paradox of enterprise authoritarianism operating within a formally democratic political system is particularly marked in the United States, where surprisingly few advances have been made toward democracy in the workplace and the distribution and practice of formal democratic rights and liberties are theoretically the most widespread. As a condition of earning a living, American workers must give up their accustomed rights and privileges of citizenship upon crossing the threshold of the factory gate or office door. Within the business firm, the rights of free speech, free association, election of leadership, and general control of collective policy—so central to most definitions of the democratic polity—are not generally considered to be in effect. It is widely assumed by all parties concerned—employees and business managers, union and government officials—that the wage relationship that forms the core of economic life in capitalism axiomatically implies an unequal and hierarchical relationship within the firm. In this relationship between an employer and an employee, managers retain the right, subject to relatively minor restrictions and standards set by government and labor unions, to direct and coordinate enterprise production. It is generally understood that hired employees must conform both to the purposes of the enterprise and to its internal order. The only residual right that is retained (and it is an important one) is the right to leave the enterprise and seek other employment. The exercise of choice is external to the life of the enterprise, not internal to it.

That is not to say that all such enterprises are necessarily dismal places in which to work or that employees necessarily feel a sense of loss in such settings (especially in the notable absence of alternative models of work organization in the United States), but only that authoritarian, hierarchical forms are the core of work life for almost all Americans. As we shall see in this chapter, the producer cooperatives in plywood are quite different. In them, working people exercise power over production and distribution, as well as over the particular procedures and arrangements whereby production and distribution are planned, executed, and monitored.[3]

Direct and Indirect Democracy

The producer cooperatives in plywood are notable not for their relative prosperity and productivity (Berman, 1967; Gunn, 1984) but for their self-governing quality, their organization and operation as enterprises in which those who work also manage.[4] This quality distinguishes the producer cooperatives from other firms that share similar technological organization and product mix, and it has attracted the admiring attention of scholars, activists, public officials, and industrial leaders.

Self-governance immediately raises the issue of democracy. What we want to know about producer cooperatives—formal democratic communities in theory—is something about the quality of the democratic life within them and the effects that a self-governing workplace has upon the people who work within it. We want to know what self-governance looks like up close, how people participate in this formally democratic setting, and how this way of life compares with the internal processes of more conventional enterprises. In short, we want to understand the degree to which governance and political interactions in the cooperatives approach standards of what we know, in nonenterprise governance and politics, as democracy.

The main problem in reaching specific and unambiguous conclusions about these issues is that no precise and universally accepted definition of "democracy" exists. Historically, there have existed at least two sharply competing democratic models (Greenberg, 1986: chap. 2; MacPherson, 1962), each of which embodies such sharply divergent sets of social processes, institutions, and value configurations that the common democratic label begins to look more confusing than helpful. It is important, therefore, before undertaking a close examination of the politics and governance of producer cooperatives, to set out the main outlines of these competing models or forms of democracy.

Direct, Participatory Democracy

One democratic model stresses direct, face-to-face, participatory decision making among ordinary people as the basis of a democratic polity.[5] Our initial understanding of this form of democracy comes from the Greeks, who tied the definition of citizenship to the idea of continuous involvement in the public life of the community. To be a passive observer of public life, to be uninvolved, to be separated from community decision making, was to be a noncitizen. To the Greeks, citizenship was not a category to which was appended a set of rights and freedoms over and against the community—that is, a "negative" conception concerning freedom from interference by others, including the government—but a set of obligations and opportunities related to participation in the act of governance. To the Greeks, people were human only to the extent that they were part of and involved in the life of the community, interacting with others in the public arena. In such a public arena, discussion, deliberation, and argumentation would obliterate the distance between ruler and ruled as well as the distance between amateur and professional politician, creating a situation of political equality and mutual respect (Arendt, 1965).[6]

The conception of democracy as "direct" (that is, not mediated through other persons or institutions) or "participatory" represents an important deviation from what has been considered normal and appropriate in political life. To most political practitioners and thinkers through the ages, governance has been understood to be a difficult art requiring the greatest sophistication, intelligence, character, and training, and not an activity to be left to ordinary people. Theorists of direct, participatory democracy, on the other hand, believe that human beings have the ability to reflect, deliberate, and decide about public issues on the basis of morality, reason, and the public interest.

Indirect, Representative Democracy

Central to direct democracy is the notion that government and the governed are identical, that within the boundaries of the political community, ruled and ruler are the same people, designated citizens. From the point of view of the principal competing model of democracy—"representative" democracy[7]—government and the governed are separate and distinct, and therefore, the principal motivation for political involvement is to forge instruments by which citizens might exercise some control over government policy and distant political leaders. In this conception of democracy, the people rule only indirectly through representatives who are authorized to make policy decisions in the name of those who elect them. Citizen participation remains important, but it becomes extremely limited in scope, confined primarily to the periodic elections of persons who act in the capacity of representatives and to the occasional transmission of instructions to them (Sartori, 1962; Schumpeter, 1943).

Why substitute what is essentially a two-step process of political participation for the more unitary one? According to political scientist Robert Dahl, representative democracy is preferable to direct democracy because of the inescapable problems of size and time (Dahl, 1970). First, as to size, it seems reasonable to suppose that there is some upper limit on the number of people who can meet and deliberate face to face. Although we have as yet no scientific method to determine exactly what that limit might be, no one can suppose that it does not exist. Once a certain maximum size is surpassed, the problem of allowing everyone who holds a view or opinion to speak in a meeting becomes unmanageable (Mansbridge, 1980). Second, as to time, it is everywhere the case that ordinary people have other concerns besides public affairs that must be attended to; these concerns include but are not limited to family and livelihood. It follows that a general assembly of the political community cannot sit in continuous session.

Although representative forms of democracy can compensate for certain inherent problems in the direct variant, serious difficulties arise relative to the distance between citizen and representative. First, participation is intermittent, involving mainly the election of representatives and the occasional conveyance of demands or expressions of concern to those representatives. Such limited involvement potentially destroys the capacity of self-governance to be educative and broadening. Second, there is a strong tendency in representative democratic systems to create and consolidate a professional political class that makes life as a representative a full-time occupation. The ordinary citizen tends to assume an amateur status and is only rarely involved in political life. The possibility for this professional class to go its own way and to formulate policy at odds with popular desires and interests is an obvious concern. Third, as the distance between government and governed increases, the central focus of political life becomes one of defining and protecting a private space into which a potentially threatening government might intrude unless limited and constrained. Questions of rights and liberties then come to center stage, and the conception of active self-governance recedes to the wings.

The Politics and Governance of the Plywood Cooperatives

Not without reason, direct, participatory democracy and indirect, representative democracy have been understood to be distinctly contradictory forms of governance; the presence of one has been assumed largely to preempt the other. The producer cooperatives, however, embody a complex and enriching mixing and cross-fertilization of the two forms.[8] We shall see how worker-shareholders choose between them, depending on conditions and circumstances, and how each form of democracy serves to compensate for some of the problems inherent in the other.

Formal Governance

The single most important formal organizational feature of the worker-owned plywood firms is the legal vesting of decisive authority and responsibility for all matters in the hands of the shareholding members of the cooperative, as expressed in the general membership meeting, which gathers, on average, about twice a year. Although the worker-shareholders may choose to delegate many day-to-day concerns and responsibilities to the general manager and the elected board of directors, in a formal sense purview of the meeting is unlimited and responsible for the total governance and direction of the enterprise. Worker-shareholders at these meetings may decide to fire the manager and hire a new one, alter hourly wage rates, build a new plant, or reach any other decision about the enterprise that seems appropriate to them. Traditionally, membership meetings attend to the periodic review of company financial performance, the division of the annual enterprise income between investment (capital equipment, buildings, machinery, timber purchases) and distribution to working members, review of managerial performance, and election of a board of directors. In such membership meetings, each shareholder is entitled to only a single vote even if, as in a few exceptional cases, the member owns more than one share.

At these meetings, an entirely or partially new board of directors is elected from among the worker-shareholders, all of whom are eligible to serve. This board is charged with general policy making in the interim between general membership meetings. The board is not entirely free in policy matters, however, because all of the firms require the board to gain permission from the general membership for any expenditures beyond some specified maximum figure.

Other features are common to the formal organization of the plywood cooperatives. All, for instance, operate on the principle of equal hourly wage rates among the shareholders, regardless of the number of years on the job or skill level. All divide the annual surplus (the amount that remains from total income after hourly wage rates, operating costs, taxes, investment, and savings have been deducted) to the shareholders as workers rather than as dividends on capital. Nonworking shareholders are not entitled to a portion of the surplus. All hire a management team (a general manager and assistants) that is responsible for the day-to-day operations of the firm, subject to the guidance of the board of directors (which usually meets biweekly) and the sufferance of the general membership meeting. All insist that potential new worker-owners spend a probationary period working in the plant and that their membership be formally accepted by either the general membership meeting or the board of directors.

To be sure, some important differences in formal arrangements do exist among the plywood cooperatives. For instance, although all firms hold to the principle of equal hourly wage rates, they tend to vary in their willingness to allow differentials in the total hours worked over the course of the year. Some firms allow their members to work as many hours of overtime as they wish if such work is available, and several firms attempt to limit the differentials in total hours worked among their members. The latter system guarantees a rough equality in annual member compensation, but the former allows very wide disparities because of the time-and-a-half provision for overtime work and the division of the annual enterprise surplus according to total hours worked. In addition, most of the cooperatives hire general managers from the outside who are not shareholders, although a few allow shareholders hold such posts.

Nevertheless, despite these variations, an impressive similarity exists in the formal organization and rules of procedure among the plywood cooperatives. What differences are evident are simply minor deviations in an otherwise relatively uniform picture. When compared with the formal organization of conventional firms, the similarities among the plywood cooperatives are more evident than their differences.

Informal Governing Processes

An understanding of the formal organization of the cooperatives is obviously an important first step in our understanding of them as institutions, but it does not take us very far. It provides only an understanding of the skeleton, but not of the flesh or the dynamic processes at work within the body of the cooperatives. The formal structure is simply the frame upon which the colorful and rich life of human interaction takes place. The remainder of this chapter explores these more elusive yet vital aspects of cooperative life.

In this analysis I shall compare cooperative and conventional firms within the plywood industry, all of which are characterized by an identical technical division of labor within the plant, roughly similar size, location within the same geographical region, and similar work force demographics. Differences that are discovered in the internal political environment and governing processes, given their near identity on all other major variables, will be mainly attributed to differences between the cooperative as against the conventional form of work organization.

Joining a Cooperative

In the decision to join a plywood cooperative political motivations are virtually absent (see Table 2–1). Rather than a calculus based on democratic values, the strongest motivations for deciding to join these enterprises are almost universally financial, with little initial attention given to self-governance, the relatively pleasant work environment, or the unique social relations within the plant.[9] The people who join these cooperatives are working class in origin, many have had periods of economic difficulty

Table 2–1. Reasons for becoming shareholders (1978 cross-section sample)*

Question: "How important were each of the following in your decision to *first* become a shareholder in this cooperative?"

	Percent answering "very important"	Number
Heard that workers in the plant got along well with each other	16.2	185
Heard that supervisors and workers got along well	15.1	185
Thought it would be a good financial investment	69.1	194
Wanted an opportunity help run a company	13.4	187
Wanted a guaranteed job in case times got hard	48.2	191
The wages are good	50.5	194
There were no other jobs available at the time	14.9	179
I liked working with lumber	19.3	195

*When change over time is not at issue, the 1978 cross-section sample, because of a larger number of respondents, will be used in preference to the panel sample. Goodness-of-fit analysis indicates no significant differences between the two samples. The panel is a representative subset of the original and larger cross-section sample. See Appendixes for details of data collection, sample characteristics, and test items.

in their lives, and many have experienced significant periods of unemployment—47 percent reported that they had been unemployed, with 46 percent of these having at least once experienced more than five months of unemployment. The guarantee of a job so long as the firm remains in operation is no small attraction to people who worry about job insecurity. Furthermore, given the limited ability to save and declining opportunities in the small business sector, the producer cooperative is one of the few outlets available to working-class people for making a small financial investment. Jobs and investment are, thus, the recurrent themes in explanations for joining the plywood cooperatives.

Not a single respondent, spontaneously and without prompting, even vaguely suggested political or ideological reasons for joining these enterprises. Most were quick to mention the investment and job security aspects, a surprisingly large number mentioned the desire to escape labor union–company tensions and uncertainties, and not a few seemed to have accidentally wandered in for no premeditated reason.

I thought of it . . . as an investment . . . that shares would go up.

Buying a job . . . it was a job. The plant's running 7 days a week, 12-hour days ever since I've been here. So, if a guy wanted to really get in to work, he could make all the overtime he wanted. So he could actually bring home a pretty good check.

And I was getting a little tired [of seasonal work]. So I came down here. . . . These guys work 365 days a year. . . . And so I thought more or less buying a share was a good security for a job . . . good chance of staying, you know, instead of getting caught in a layoff.

Well, I thought I wanted to buy into a small business . . . be my own boss. And my brother-in-law convinced me that would take too long and.it would be more risky than [this].

These themes are reflected in the figures in Table 2–1, which reports the responses of shareholders when they were asked why they first joined the co-op. The responses emphasize the dominance of investment as a motivation for joining a cooperative, closely followed by good wages and job security, and, conversely, the relatively minor importance of internal governance and political processes of the cooperatives.[10]

Democracy, Involvement, and Sense of Responsibility

If self-governance is less important than financial motivations for joining the plywood cooperatives, it soon catches up. In time, almost all members come to appreciate the special environment that these enterprises offer to those who own and work in them.

This change in the general outlook of worker-shareholders is evident from the figures in Table 2–2, which reports the differences between motivations for first joining and the reasons worker-shareholders remained members of the cooperatives. Investment, wages, and job security remained very high motivations, but an impressive increase occurred in appreciation for factors associated with the special communitarian nature of these enterprises. The most significant changes in linkages of the worker-shareholders to the cooperatives are those having to do with the peer culture and the quality of the supervisory environment, which, we shall see, are closely tied to the democratic character of the cooperatives.

Central to life in the cooperatives is the sense that the worker-shareholders are in charge, that they run the enterprise, are responsible for what goes on in it, and have the opportunity, within certain boundaries, to make of their environment what they will.

If it comes down to it, the stockholders have absolute rule down there. In fact it has happened in this mill before. . . . If things get too bad, the stock-

Table 2–2. Changing worker-shareholder opinions on reasons for cooperative membership (1978 cross-section sample; $N = 206$)

	Percentage reporting very important in decision to first join	Percentage reporting very important in decision to remain member today	Percentage point change
Workers get along	16.2	56.4	+40.2
Supervisors and workers get along	15.1	52.8	+37.7
Good investment	69.1	76.1	+10.0
Can run the company	13.4	–*	–
Guaranteed job	48.2	67.9	+19.7
Good wages	50.5	58.0	+ 7.5
No other jobs	14.9	16.0	+ 1.1
Like lumber	19.3	21.4	+ 2.1

*This option was inadvertently omitted from the final printed form of the questionnaire so no before-after comparison is possible.

holders can just say, "Wait a minute . . . we are going to change this." And if they have enough of them, they can do it, if enough guys get together. I think that's great because there's a lot of companies that take advantage of the workers, and there's nothing that can be done about it.

The contrast to the situation in the conventionally run mills, in which workers are apart from and the objects of the decision-making process, could not be more marked. Employees of the conventional mills feel that they are acted upon by distant and inaccessible decision makers.

[In response to a question about possible layoffs] We asked and tried to find out what they had in mind, but it was all kind of hush-hush, and no one was saying very much. Nobody ever found out.

[About work breaks] It's all set by the company.

But we never see any high level guys that would let us know what's going on. So I don't know where the major decisions come from.

This sense of distance from decision making, of being an object rather than a subject in the workplace, was a constantly recurring theme among workers interviewed in the conventionally organized plywood mill.

The importance of self-governance to worker-shareholders is confirmed by their responses to a question asking what they would look for in their

Table 2–3. Worker-shareholders' preference for participation or ownership (T_2 panel sample)*

Question: "Being a shareholder in a cooperative means that you are both an *owner* of the company and (at least indirectly) a decision-making *manager*. If you had to go to another company where you could only play one of these roles, which type would you choose?"

	Percent	Number
A company where I would own a share but would play no part in decision making	21.2	18
A company where I would take part in decision making but would *not* own a share	36.5	31
I can't say/I don't know	42.4	36

*T_1 and T_2 refer to the longitudinal panel sample. T_1 refers to the data collected in 1978; T_2 refers to the second-stage data collected in 1983. See Appendix I for details. Only T_2 is reported in this table because the test item was not a part of the original 1978 questionnaire.

next job if they had to leave their co-op. Would they look for a company that allowed them to be part-owners but not to participate in governance, or would they look for a company in which they would not be owners but could be practicing members of a democratic institution? The results are reported in Table 2–3. That far more would opt for participation than for ownership is particularly impressive in light of the financial motivations for first joining. The high percentage answering "I can't say/I don't know" seems indicative of a major change in outlook.

Ownership and participation in the co-ops also fosters an extremely strong sense of collective responsibility and mutuality.

You just find it's kind of a big family attitude. Those that can put out, do, and you don't feel too bad about the guys that can't.

[In response to a question asking why he supports the concept of equal wages] I think they all got to equalize out . . . they all got to eat.

It's altogether different here [than in his former job.] It took me a little while to get used to this because where I worked over there, there was a union and you did your job and you didn't go out and do something else. Here you get in and do anything to help. Everybody pitches in and helps. The people stick together, that's the reason we've gone so far and production is so high, cuz everybody works together.

Shareholders' strong commitment to the work of the collective enterprise becomes explicit in a comparison with workers in the conventional plant,

Table 2–4. Workers' responses on work ethic (in percentages; 1978 cross-section sample)

Question: "Which of the following statements best describes your attitude about working here?"

	Cooperatives (N = 202)	Conventional firm (N = 131)
I do as little as possible	0.0	0.0
I do an average day's work	11.9	12.2
I do the *best* work I can for the time I'm paid	32.2	48.1
I not only do the best work I can, but I do whatever extra needs to be done	55.9	39.7

Tau$_c$ = 0.14; p = 0.01.

as shown in Table 2–4. More of the workers in the conventional plant placed themselves in what might be called the "wage-labor" category— that is, they expressed a willingness to work diligently for the time they were paid, but not more, whereas a majority of worker-shareholders indicated a collective responsibility to the enterprise beyond a straight trade of pay for hours worked. This attitude is reaffirmed, and the contrast with workers in conventional plants reinforced, by the responses to questions about sense of responsibility for the work group and the plant as a whole (Tables 2–5 and 2–6).

Participation in Policy Making

Compared to workers in the conventional firm, worker-shareholders are committed to and engaged in the life of their enterprises. Since all of the firms in this study are characterized by identical technical production

Table 2–5. Workers' sense of responsibility for work group (in percentages; 1978 cross-section sample)

Question: "To what extent do you feel responsible for the success of your own work group or production line?"

	Cooperatives (N = 183)	Conventional firm (N = 122)
Hardly at all	0.5	3.3
Somewhat	20.2	29.5
Very much	79.2	67.2

Tau$_c$ = 0.12; p = 0.007.

Table 2–6. Workers' sense of responsibility for the entire plant (in percentages; 1978 cross-section sample)

Question: "To what extent to you feel responsible for the success of the whole plant?"

	Cooperatives (N = 198)	Conventional firm (N = 118)
Hardly at all	5.6	17.8
Somewhat	40.4	47.5
Very much	54.0	34.7

Tau_c = 0.22; p = 0.00.

processes, division of labor, size, and demographic composition of the work force, this difference in collective mood between the plants may be the result of differences in the organization of power and authority within them, one set characterized by self-governance, the other by hierarchical authority and superordinate-subordinate relations. These governing processes must be examined in more detail to observe and explicate the particular processes and interactions that are involved in this self-governing experience and to contrast them with more conventional industrial settings.

Although they are closely linked and interrelated in practice, for purposes of analysis these internal plant processes are divided into two levels of decision making with the plant: general enterprise policy formation and shop-floor decision making. Although in practice they are not sharply separated, the decisions made, the range of implications of those decisions, the number of workers directly involved, the information required, and the necessary implementation machinery do sharply contrast for each level of decision making.

Shop-Floor Governance

In some respects, there is no great variation in day-to-day governance of the work process between the plywood cooperatives and the conventional firms. An example is the pace and manner by which raw logs (or, in several factories, sheets of veneer) are transformed into finished plywood panels. The reason for the similarities is that the technical production processes, the composition of the machinery, the optimal level of operation of that machinery, and the division of labor are virtually identical in all of the plywood plants. Unless one is especially knowledgeable and blessed with a discerning eye, one cannot easily tell the difference in the actual production process between cooperative and conventional firms. Because most of the technical processes of plywood production are repetitious and machine-paced, requiring only semiskilled labor, workers' in both types of firms express similar reactions to and complaints about the work.

> You're doing something that's basically kind of unpleasant in the first place. You're really not too enthused about it and it's a repetition kind of thing. Most jobs are monotony and repetitious once you get the hang of it.

> It's coming constantly. . . . It's always coming.

> But he got up there and it was so automated he [saw] he couldn't handle it. . . . You sit there and the machine's going. . . . It was driving him nuts. . . . It goes so fast. . . . You got to keep going fast all the time.

> It's different than it used to be. It used to be a slow work pace and you had some time to do things and think a little bit. Today, it's just like you're always up against something to be done, that has to be done.

Significant differences are apparent, however, in the informal social arrangements of work performance. As one might expect within firms whose workers own and are responsible for the entire enterprise, worker-shareholders are much more likely to cooperate on production problems than are workers in a conventional plant. Indeed, there is a very strong tendency among the latter to stick to one's assigned job and not to meddle in what is considered the business of other workers or the responsibility of some other production unit in the plant. The boundaries of work responsibility are clearly drawn; workers in conventional plants are willing to put in a hard day's work on their assigned tasks, but they are not likely to move beyond those boundaries and act in ways that will enhance the productivity of the entire process. In the cooperatives, the job boundaries are less rigid and more fluid when, in the opinion of the people involved in production, the situation demands it.

> If the people grading off the end of the dryer do not use reasonable prudence and they start mixing the grades too much, I get hold of somebody and I say, now look, this came over to me as face stock and it wouldn't even make decent back. What the hell's goin' on here?

> [Interviewer: That wouldn't happen if it were a regular mill?]

> That wouldn't happen. . . . [In a regular mill] he has absolutely no money invested in the produce that's being manufactured. . . . He's selling nothing but his time. Any knowledge he has on the side, he is not committed or he is not required to share that.

It took me a little while to get used to this because where I worked before there was a union and you did your job and you didn't go out and do something else. Here you get in and do anything to help. . . . I see somebody needs help, whey you just go help them.

I also tend to look around and make sure things are working right a little more than if I didn't have anything invested in the company. . . . I would probably never say anything when I saw something wrong. . . . I don't know. It gives you a feeling of responsibility.

That's pretty much shared by the rest of the shareholders, you know, the same feeling.

This spontaneous cooperation in the production process extends to the informal rotation and sharing of jobs, which is notable for its absence in the conventional plant, where jobs are assigned through precise and formal agreements made between management and the union, and where, once assigned, workers do not generally make their own informal and alternative arrangements. Such workers tend to stick to their assigned jobs until they apply for some other situation. Job assignments are made in a similar fashion in the plywood cooperatives (a bidding system based almost exclusively on seniority), but there is a greater tendency, when the occasion arises, to share and rotate jobs.

I'm on a three-man crew that edge glues stock . . . and we rotate positions. I have insisted on this. We have a feeder and a joiner and an off-bearer. And we each rotate.

Well, if you're on the dry belt, that machine never stops. You know there are machines that just don't stop. And that's one of them. And you don't just walk off and let the wood go. . . . You holler at somebody, "Come here and give me a quickie." And he comes over there and takes your place, and you go.

They used to have a policy where when the guys went hunting, you could trade around. . . . Hell, you can pretty much take off when you want. You can always get somebody to cover for you.

Although some of the same informal job-assignment processes may occasionally take place in the conventional plants, they were never spontaneously mentioned by any workers from these plants during the interviews. This omission suggests that it is not a regular occurrence, nor is it done with the sense of freedom enjoyed by the worker-shareholders.

Given both the commitment to the success of the overall enterprise and the relative freedom to constitute informal work arrangements in them (within the boundaries set by the technical process), it is not surprising to learn that worker-shareholders in cooperatives are much more likely to suggest and to initiate innovations to work procedures.

[Everybody] should do the job his own way and he'll do it better than if he's forced to do a certain way.... The same way with ... patching equipment; they made their own glue pots.

The greatest differences in shop-floor governance between producer cooperatives and conventional plants were found in the area of supervision. Again, this should not be surprising since supervision is the meeting point between owners of enterprises and the work force. The supervisory hierarchy transmits the desires of the owners (or managers acting in their stead) to those persons who are engaged in production. Besides the technology of production—the machinery and its requirements—control of production in conventional factories is communicated through supervisors and foremen who represent capital and is exercised upon wage laborers. The goal of this hierarchy is to check spontaneous and informal networks of independent action found among workers and to impose order upon the human portion of the production process so as to harness its abilities and energies to the purposes of the owners and managers of the enterprise (Braverman, 1974; Marglin, 1974). The historic political problem internal to the enterprise, therefore, has been the struggle over the control of the work force and how to get it to work willingly, energetically, and smoothly. Reforms and reorganization efforts such as Taylorism, scientific management, humanistic supervision, personnel management, and the like were originated for this purpose (Braverman, 1974; Greenberg, 1975). The continued opposition of purposes between capital and labor—the inherent political struggle within the walls of the plant—is demonstrated by the ubiquitous presence of an elaborate supervisory machinery in most industrial enterprises.

The present sample bears out this observation as suggested by the significant difference in the number of supervisors and foremen found in conventional plants as compared to the plywood cooperatives. The latter are easily able to manage production with no more than two foremen per shift, and often with only one, whereas the former often require six or seven. In one mill that had recently been converted from a worker-owned to a conventional, privately owned firm, the first action taken by the new management team was to quadruple the number of line supervisors and foremen. The general manager of this mill, who had been the manager before its conversion, stated:

> We need more foremen because, in the old days, the shareholders supervised themselves. . . . They cared for the machinery, kept their areas picked-up, helped break up production bottlenecks all by themselves. That's not true anymore . . . we've got to pretty much keep on them all of the time.

This general supervisor similarly characterized the nature of the change when a cooperative is transformed into a conventionally organized company:

> It sure as hell is easier now. Before, I had 250 bosses . . . everybody wanted to put his two cents in. Now I just answer to one man. . . . I like it better that way.[11]

This theme of close supervision and intense control recurred in interviews with workers in the conventional plants:

> I means you're under pressure all the time . . . because the minute that things shut down . . . if something goes wrong, they're over there finding out what's wrong. . . .
>
> They're never completely satisfied. . . .
>
> I think one of the things I notice most about supervisors is their silence. . . . He's looking at you and your work and he doesn't say a word. . . . You don't know whether he's thinking about something else and he just happens to be standing there, or if he's thinking about your work and he doesn't wish to comment on it. . . . What's even worse than one supervisor standing in silence, it's two supervisors standing in silence, who then walk away and talk together and you never hear what it was about. They do a lot of their planning when they're on the floor walking around . . . you can get paranoid.

Almost identical words were used by another coworker:

> On day shift you never know when they're going to pop through there. . . . They might stand there and watch you for awhile and they'll move on. Very seldom that they'll ever speak to any of us. . . . [When they're watching you] you kind of tense up and wonder, geez, am I doing this right, am I doing

that right? Then they'll come through there with three or four guys all dressed up in suits and you don't know who they are. The other day there was some of the big wigs in there. . . . Nobody knew who they were . . . they just walk by there and they might stand there for five minutes and just be talking back and forth amongst themselves and they're watching every move you're making. . . . God, I hope I'm doing it the right way. After they walk away you just kind of relax. He don't say much anyway. He's going to the foreman and say something. When they have their executive meeting that's when that all comes out. They'll tell them what they think the guys are doing wrong. . . . The manager himself never says anything. He goes to your foreman and tells him; he lays it on the line to him and then he comes down there and lays it out to us guys.

In such a hierarchical system of supervision, workers are treated not as autonomous, rational, and responsible people but as persons to be watched, carefully managed, and compelled to work. Workers frequently mentioned that they were treated by the supervisory system as children, a relationship they greatly resented:

They like to treat you like a kid going to school. . . . They act like they're a little better than you are.

[Interviewer: Why wouldn't you like to be a foreman?]

I've never had the practice at telling people what to do . . . so I don't know if that's the direction I'd want. I'm good at telling little kids what to do, but not adults. Sometimes they treat the adults like little kids down at the mill.

As wage earners and not owners of capital, workers in conventional enterprises are forced, on pain of losing their jobs, to listen to foremen and supervisors even when they have little confidence in them, or even if they know a better way to accomplish a certain task. Supervision may be the object of grumbling and complaints in the lunchroom or at the dinner table, but it is to be obeyed (not always enthusiastically) at the point of production.

Well, like I said, every guy grades the way he thinks, and I grade the way I think it should be graded. But if the foreman insists he wants it that way, there's not much you can do. You have to do it the way he tells you to do it. There's no two foremen that'll come by and tell you the same thing. But what is really frustrating sometimes . . . I'm supposed to have the authority to tell my crews what to do and my helper what to do. And then sometimes due to this foreman business, I got . . . there's two or three that come in here and try to be boss. Well, they'll tell somebody something, somebody else something else and all of a sudden my crews will say, well, what are we supposed to be doing? Well, I already told you what to do. Yeah, well so-and-so said so-and-so. And it really irritates . . . if they want to change to tell me and let me tell my guys you know. Because if they think that I'm telling them stuff that's wrong or confusing to them, they're going to lose respect for me. And a couple of times I've made a couple of these frantic changes that the foreman's told me to do. I have to tell my spreader crew and then the press crew cuz after they're glued together they go over in the press to get pressed down. And so I'm telling about six or seven guys what to do and I just no sooner tell them one thing and they want to change something else, so I do that.

I'm not bragging, but I know my job . . . and yet they'll bring a foreman in . . . like we call a 90 day wonder in the army. . . . He don't know nothing, and yet we have to carry him and then he gets all the glory. . . . And it does gall us. It galls me! They don't need near the supervisors they got . . . half of them they got don't know their tail from a piece of wood.

The contrast with the producer cooperatives could not be more marked. Because there are significantly fewer of them, supervisors in the cooperatives are not "on the backs" of the production workers, but are forced to be concerned with broader, plantwide issues having to do with the flow of materials and machine usage. Even when they are in direct contact, the relationship between workers and supervisors is markedly different from that in the conventional mill. This should not occasion much surprise, for being worker-owners rather than wage laborers, shareholders are ultimately responsible for the fates of their supervisors. Supervisors have the formal power to fire and to discipline shareholders (subject to appeal to the board of directors), but they rarely exercise this power. In firms with hired nonshareholders as supervisors, workers are seldom fired because continuation of employment depends on the sufferance of the worker-shareholders as a whole, as expressed either through the board or the general membership meeting. In those firms where the supervisors are themselves worker-shareholders, supervisors must continue to coexist over the long haul with the other shareholders. Thus the shareholder's role as an owner and not a wage laborer transforms the function of supervision from the exercise of control in the name of distant capital and management to coordination of production. The responses, for instance, to the question, "Does your foreman act more as a coordinator or more as a boss? (Table

Table 2-7. Workers' perceptions of the foreman's role (in percentages; 1978 cross-section sample)

Question: "Does your foreman act more as a coordinator or more as a boss?"

	Cooperatives ($N = 204$)	Conventional firm ($N = 128$)
Coordinator	63.2	50.0
Boss	20.6	35.9
Neither	9.8	5.5

$Tau_c = 0.10; p = 0.03.$

2-7), show the different perceptions of the foreman's role. This relationship might have been even stronger with some refinement of the question, since workers in the conventional plants were prone to interpret the item in light of their perception that the real bosses were the plant manager, personnel director, and, most centrally, the parent corporation, and that the supervisors were, in the words of one worker, "nothing but lackeys."

The words shareholders used to describe these relationships are even more compelling, especially compared with the observations of workers in the conventional plant. In contrast to the latter's view that supervision is close, intense, and omnipresent, worker-shareholders gave a much more benign and pleasant characterization of supervision:

[Interviewer: What is supervision like in this mill?]

Pretty loose really. . . . It's probably the most unsupervised place I've ever worked . . . myself, I have little or none supervision . . . on this shift there's only one foreman.

They're there to help us. They're there to make our job easier. They're not there as bosses. . . . They're just hired help. If he wants us to do something, he says, "Would you please? Would you mind?"

My job down there is real good because nobody bugs you. They know you're going to work. Now . . . if I was working there and you'd walk in, I wouldn't hesitate stopping and talking to you . . . and if a boss went by he'd never say anything. . . . They know I was going to go right back and hit the ball and try to catch up what little time I lost.

A handful of shareholders, all with experience in conventional mills, were somewhat bothered by this style of supervision:

[Supervision] is not quite as good as it should be . . . too much laxity and letting people do what they want to and then you fool around.

This complaint is unlikely to be voiced in a conventional mill.

Besides the cooperatives' general looseness and distance of supervision, allowing a great deal of free space for individual initiative and informal cooperation among production workers, there is also a significant difference between cooperative and conventional mills in the style of interaction between supervisor and worker. In the conventional plant, communication is hierarchical and one-way, with orders coming from the top and compliance (whether willing or unwilling, enthusiastic or begrudging) from the bottom. In the producer cooperatives, communication is two-way, open, and relatively freewheeling, characteristic of communications between equals.

But like I say, you have got to realize that you're in a whole different ballgame. Your foreman is still entitled to respect and adherence to and things like that. . . . And if I have an idea that I feel should be instituted or should be called to his attention, I go and see the boss, and I say, "Now look, these are things that I think should be done and there's reason for it and here's the reason and I think that it'd be profitable to get to it." Whereas at a private company, you just don't do this.

Some guys get abusive with the foreman because they know they aren't going to be fired.

How free do I feel to make suggestions? Just as free as I would to be talking to you. No hesitation at all.

For those who had experienced supervision in conventional factories, relative freedom on the line helped compensate for the problems, aggravations, and tensions connected to the job.

You know as far as the job goes it's better than in any other mill because the fact that there's a foreman standing there and you can thumb your nose at him if you want to.

How is it possible to operate a mill in which more than 150 people work on a shift without close supervision? How is this complex production process, using a variety of woods and glues and manufacturing a wide range of grades of finished panel, coordinated? The answer is startlingly obvious, and it cropped up in every one of our interviews in one form or another, yet it is so divergent from "normal" industrial organization assumptions that it gives pause. The shareholders individually manage themselves and each other. Filled with a sense of responsibility for the enterprise as a whole, they work in a manner that is sufficiently diligent and responsible as to require little outside supervision. If coordination becomes necessary, or some members are not contributing in a way that other members consider appropriate, groups of worker-shareholders will tend to act as collective supervisors on the job.

> And if somebody . . . is goofing off . . . you can holler over there and tell him, "Let's get going here." You know, frankly, we're all watching each other so that nobody else is goofing off too much.

> And I also tend to look around and make sure things are working right a little bit more than if I didn't have anything invested in the company.

> If the shareholder sees another one who's not involved and screwing around, well all the shareholders would frown on it. And if it gets bad enough they can make it tough enough for the guy to leave.

> [Interviewer: What would happen if you made a bad mistake on the job?]

> I think I'd probably feel like hell just for general principles. But I think the other shareholders would probably rub it in, you know. The superintendent would come over and let you know . . . and then that's all you'd hear out of him, the one time, you know. But the rest, they can rub it in for weeks. They wouldn't hold it against you, but they'd tease the shit out of you. We got guys make mistakes around here lots of times, you know. Everybody makes mistakes. They razz them.

The attention the plywood cooperatives have attracted in recent years has been focused primarily upon self-governance at the enterprise level of decision making: the processes by which a large group of worker-shareholders democratically formulates company policy through discussions in general meetings, election of a responsible and responsive board of directors composed of working shareholders, the hiring of a general manager, and continuous monitoring of the manager's performance. Little or no attention has been devoted to decisional processes at the point of production. I hope I have demonstrated the degree to which mechanisms, practices, and relationships characteristic of self-governance have invaded this area in the producer cooperatives, an area hitherto considered appropriate mainly to authoritarian forms, whether harsh or benign.

Although it is important to be constantly sensitive to the limits to self-governance placed by the technical, machine process, it is also true that in the spaces and interstices of that process, work is largely self-governing in the direct democratic sense. Work is organized to allow considerable space for individual initiative, informal work cooperation, and self-management, with supervision generally in the background as a nonthreatening and assistance-giving institution. On the job, worker-shareholders are active and informed participants in those informal decisional processes by which work is organized and executed.

Enterprise-Level Decision Making

Enterprise policy on all matters in the cooperatives is lodged in the general meeting of the shareholders. At these meetings, discussions pertaining to raw material purchases, plant modernization and expansion, wages, division of the surplus, vacations, health insurance, managerial and supervisory staff performance, sales, relations with government agencies, and product mix and quality take place and policies are determined. Moreover, elections are held at these meetings to fill positions on the board of directors, a group charged with conducting the general business of the enterprise in the period between regular meetings of the shareholders. The hired general manager is responsible for the everyday business of the enterprise, subject to the direction of the board and of the general membership meeting.

The first question to ask about these discussions is the degree to which worker-shareholders are actually informed, interested, and involved in the mechanisms by which general policy is formulated. The impressively widespread availability of information necessary to develop informed judgment and the high level of continuous discussion about this information and the policy decisions for which it is appropriate became quickly apparent in the interviews. Information is available in the cooperatives in a number of forms. All of the enterprises, for instance, publish the minutes of board meetings and make them readily available, either by putting copies in the lunchroom or posting them on bulletin boards. Furthermore, any shareholder is free to go to the general manager or the treasurer in the business office and ask to see whatever documents or data he desires, a right that is often practiced.

> Oh yeah, the guys are always talking back and forth, this and that, you know
> ... discussing other things and whatnot and how they think and where they

might be pissed off or have you heard this or heard that, you know. Rumors fly fast, you know. And if I'm really interested, if I find something that, a rumor going around that I want to clear up, I'll come straight into the office. I'll talk to the secretary. He'll tell you; he'll clear it right up for you. If there's something I really want to know or find out how things are going on with some particular thing, then I'll go on in and talk to the manager, you know. And express my views on some things. I like to keep informed.

Most important, however, since only a small percentage of shareholders make it a regular practice to examine the books, to read all of the minutes, or to interrogate the manager, information flow is maximized because board members continue to hold their regular jobs in the mill and are continually, often to distraction, required to discuss policy matters with their fellow shareholders.

Well, when I worked with George . . . he was always real active in what was going on in the company . . . he was on the board . . . and I used to always get all the information from him.

Well, we post the minutes all the time. . . . If they are interested, they're up on that and then they ask a lot of questions. After we've had a board meeting, sometimes they jump us the first thing we come in and they want to know why we did this or why we done that. And I don't know how they learn about it so fast; sometimes I think they learn about it before the day's over in the board meeting.

This availability of information is very different, of course, from the norm in conventional mills for which decisions are made by distant persons of authority, and virtually no information is shared with workers. Decisions are made, and workers must simply adapt to them. As one of these workers described the situation when he asked why a certain policy had been implemented in his plant:

I really don't know . . . they merged with a couple of other companies . . . we just had to change our name . . . maybe they're taking their orders from the other one we merged with.

The degree to which matters of company policy are part of the normal, everyday discussions in the plant among the shareholders and the significant degree to which involvement in enterprise affairs remains either

Table 2–8. Worker-shareholders responding "Always" or "Very often" to questions about their knowledge of company policies (in percentages; panel sample)

	T_1	T_2	Number
"Do you talk about decisions of the Board of Directors with other shareholders in the plant?"	72.2	74.4	90
"Among the people you know in this plant, is there much discussion of company policies that have to do with in-plant *production* policies and *working conditions*?"	72.2	81.1	90
"Among the people you know in this plant, is there much discussion of company policies that have to do with *finances*, *sales*, and *investment* policies?"	69.2	71.4	91

stable or even increases over time also become immediately evident to an outsider studying the cooperatives (see Table 2–8).

The only remotely comparable situation found in the conventional plant was the high level of discussion during periods when active contract negotiations between the union and corporation were in process. Fully 78 percent of the workers in the 1978 cross-section sample claimed to have discussed the union contract with their coworkers during this period. Significantly, only 18 percent of such workers reported discussing union affairs at times other than a contract negotiation period. Either standing by itself or in comparison with other workers, then, the level of continuous involvement and discussion by cooperative shareholders is impressive and unique.

Interviews suggest that no single description characterizes the prevalent mood regarding the shareholder meetings. Some meetings are generally routine, with the manager and other officers reading reports and responding to questions. At other times, especially when a major investment policy suggestion has been made by the board, or when business has not been consistent with expectations, or when the performance of the general manager is under attack, discussions can be lively and intense. Attendance is very high (92 percent of the 1978 cross-section sample reported regular attendance) and is encouraged by paying shareholders a day's wage for attendance. Involvement in discussions is significant. Of the worker-shareholder sample, 31 percent reported "often" or "always" participating in discussions at these sessions.

In many respects, the key institution of democratic life in the plywood cooperative is the board of directors, an elected representative institution that is more actively engaged in making policy, formulating alternatives, and monitoring the performance of the hired management team than is the general shareholder meeting. What one needs to know about such a representative institution is the degree to which it is responsive and responsible to its constituency, and, conversely, the degree to which it evolves into a distant institution of quasi-permanent-professional politicians formulating policy not consistent with the wishes and desires of the membership.

Significantly, although only a minority of the shareholders actually served on them, the boards of directors of the plywood cooperatives are universally characterized by regular and significant membership turnover. No tight-knit group of people regularly dominates these positions and imposes its views on the remainder of the membership. This turnover can probably be attributed to two key factors: the active participation of the worker-shareholders in elections for board positions, and the costs and disadvantages involved with board membership.

The active participation of the shareholders can be observed from any number of vantage points. We have already seen the relatively high degree of information held by the shareholders relative to company policy, their continuing interest in the activities of the board, and the continuous discussion in the mill about these matters. Another way to gain a sense of the level of participation is to note that 31.5 percent of all shareholders in the 1978 cross-section sample reported that they had, at one time or another, run for a board position and that 17.5 percent of all shareholders had been elected and served. In comparison, only 10.2 percent of workers in the conventional plants reported having run for union office, and only 7.6 percent had served in such positions. Shareholders exhibited interest in elections to board positions:

> Oh yeah, they're pretty active campaigns. . . . We're having an annual meeting in March, so it's starting in now. You can see that. Some guys run every year for 20 years and never get elected. . . . They don't give up. That's good too.

Finally, turnover in board membership each year is high, a tendency that became so marked in one plant that the membership was forced to place controls on the turnover process so as to gain greater stability in operations.

> Each year we elected all nine members on the board. Now we don't do that. We elect only three and the people serve for three years. You can't have a

company . . . each year elect nine new people . . . you never get nowhere. . . .
It takes a while to learn what it's all about.

With the exception of psychic rewards of prestige, status, and a sense of
involvement, membership on the board of a cooperative does not present
an attractive package of rewards and perquisites. Indeed, with the exception of a company-paid lunch on the day of a board meeting, members
receive no compensation or reward for the long hours they devote to
enterprise business, which probably helps explain why more people do
not run for the board and why turnover is so high.

[Interviewer: You've never thought about running for the board?]

No, I'd rather not. I've been nominated but . . . for one thing, there isn't any
additional pay in it . . . you get your day's pay same as if you was tending
dryer.

[Interviewer: Why did you decide to serve only one term?]

I had that one year and I really didn't like it too well. . . . You get involved
in all the business of the company. You have to make all the decisions.
There's no extra pay for it. There's not even extra thanks for it, hardly.

The pressure on board members from their peers is continuous and can
often reach an intensity that is hard for some board members to bear.

We've had quite a few guys who couldn't take it and had to resign.

We've got some real good people out there and they get nominated and they
decline . . . I think it's just the responsibility. They don't want to be put in
a position where somebody's going to holler at them, and bitch at them.

The board of directors does not become dominated by a professional
political class because turnover is relatively high and the rewards of of-
ficeholding are not only small but, in some cases, negative. Service on
the board is often considered more of a burden than a position of comfort
and largesse, a distraction from other more rewarding activity, and not
inherently attractive. That so many different people serve at one time or
another is unquestionably a tribute to the vitality of democratic life in the
cooperatives.

It is also apparent that the board does not become a distant and separate
institution because board members continue to hold jobs in the mill during

their tenure and are completely accessible to the shareholders. Such access is not theoretical but is a fact of everyday life in the mill.

> If you got something that you want to find out, you go to a board member. "What about this?" Explain what you think should be done and he'll let you take it to the board.

Sometimes the relative ease of access causes problems for board members. It is evident from the interviews that service on the board requires not only a sense of dedication but a thick skin.

> We've had quite a few guys who couldn't take it and had to resign. For years I was the only member of the board to eat in the lunchroom. . . . Yeah, the rest of them would hide out in their car or have a nook and corner where they'd be all by themselves, cuz they didn't want to take the guff.

It is probably safe to conclude that the board does not succumb to the problems of rigidity, distance, and professionalization common to representative institutions. The tendency for shareholders to participate actively in and be well informed about all aspects of the business of the board of directors serves as a powerful guard against such developments. Can the same conclusions be made about the general manager, a position that seems even more prone to tend toward ossification in representative institutions? The potential for ossification and professionalization is strong. First, the manager is almost always a nonshareholder and may have a set of interests and perspectives that are at odds with those of the membership. Second, the manager does not have a production job in the plant and is, therefore, not as immediately accessible to the shareholders as are members of the board. Finally, the manager is hired because of his presumed expertise in matters of business and therefore holds skills that are apart from the direct experience of most of the shareholders.

Most of the shareholders are prepared to give the manager relatively wide latitude in conducting the business of the enterprise.

> When you hire a man and you pay him 35 to 45 thousand dollars a year, you figure he's supposed to know what's he's doing and you're going to listen to him.

> We don't try to interfere with the manager . . . cuz he wouldn't be no good to us. . . . If we had to tell him, interfere with him all the time, why hell, we just as well get rid of him and try to run it ourselves.

Nevertheless, even though shareholders give the manager a generally free hand, the position does not become too distant, too independent, and too "out-of-tune" with the membership because the occupant of the position is a hired hand and is universally so defined. The worker-shareholders are psychologically free to approach the manager about any business matter but free as well to criticize or fire him when the company is not performing as the members believe it should.

> We own it lock, stock, and barrel. . . . I'm not working for that turkey in the office; he's working for me. And when I go into that office and want some information, I demand it and get it!

Although few of the respondents spoke so vehemently, this sense that the general manager is a hired person, without tenure, and subject to the desires of the shareholders is powerful and pervasive, and most important, regularly acted upon. Average tenure for cooperative managers is quite low.

> We hire the manager. Running the mill is up to him. If we don't like the way he's running it, we can fire his butt.

That is not to say that managers do not often prevail on some issues relating to their training and expertise.[12] Managers may be more persuasive in some cooperatives than in others, either by dint of their own personalities or the particular configuration of shareholders serving on the board. Expertise, however, carries limited political power within the plant. Much like a baseball manager, he is often the first to go when the team is not performing in the manner the owners deem appropriate.

On the basis of all of the above observations regarding the politics of enterprise-level decision making, it appears that the shareholding membership is in overall control of the policy of the producer cooperatives. Whether it is manifested in the general membership meeting, in the relationship of the shareholders to the board, or in the relationship of the manager to both the membership and the board, the general direction of activity in these enterprises is lodged, in fact as well as in theory, in the hands of the worker-shareholders as a whole. To the extent that the vast majority of the work force controls the enterprise, the producer cooperatives in plywood stand in vivid contrast to the remainder of American industry.

Some Caveats on Cooperative and Conventional Firms

One of the ways I have attempted to highlight the unique aspects of the cooperatives has been to compare their manner of governance with that of firms considered "normal," a task I have attempted to pursue by making continual references to the internal life of a conventional plywood company. In that comparison, the many contrasts between the democratically organized cooperatives and the conventional firm stand out in bold relief. I would not want to leave the impression, however, that workers in conventional firms are completely without resources in their struggle to carve out a sphere of decision making. Certainly there are means by which they can do so. Workers are completely free to quit and to offer their labor power elsewhere. Furthermore, workers have found that passive compliance—working within the boundaries of rules and expectations but with little enthusiasm and no extra, unpaid effort—is often a way to create free space. It is not unknown, moreover, for workers in such settings to regulate the pace of the production line informally, to set production quotas, and the like. In extreme circumstances, finally, workers sometimes sabotage the production process so as to regain some control over their labor.

In the conventional plant used in this study, all of the above methods have made their appearance at one point or another through the years. Nevertheless, the most powerful instrument available to workers in such "normal" enterprises remains the labor union. As the only collectively organized expression of the labor force, it represents a potentially powerful instrument of worker participation in enterprise governance.

Much like labor unions throughout all of American industry (Aronowitz, 1973), however, the union in the conventional plywood plant acts not as an instrument of governance able to impose the wishes and desires of the work force upon the enterprise, but as an organization for self-defense against the continual impositions of management.

> Without unions we'd be working for peanuts. . . . If it wasn't for the union, we wouldn't have a damn thing.

> Our higher-ups there don't care two cents for the workers, you know. They'd give us as little as possible if it wasn't for the union.

This self-defense role is vital and inescapable when labor and capital stand opposed, but by confining its activities to this narrow arena, the union leaves the work force without an effective voice in those processes of governance by which the policies of the entire enterprise are formulated and executed.

Furthermore, I do not wish to leave the impression that the cooperatives are totally harmonious institutions, without tensions, problems, and irritations. In fact, the cooperatives suffer from a range of bothersome problems: some related to their market position, some to the health of the plywood industry in general, and some to their internal political life. One oft-heard theme in the interviews was the complaint that too many people were active in the governance of the cooperatives:

> There's too many chiefs and not enough Indians in this place.

> Everybody thinks they're boss. . . . Everybody stands around and tells everybody else what to do. You know, if you're part owner, then you think you're shit out of sand.

Another complaint is that cooperatives are torn by constant arguing and bickering.

> But we get to arguing, fighting, and quarreling, and we lose production.

> We got to arguing among ourselves, then we don't do nothing. I think that's a bad thing.

Finally, more than a few worker-shareholders complained that too many people were involved in running the cooperative who lacked the competence and intelligence to do so.

> We don't have the brains. . . . We don't have the business brains, I'll put it that way.

> Each one of those directors feel that they're important although they don't have the ability to do the job. And they want to put their two cents in. Ninety percent of the time they're wrong . . . They've had no education.

> I think a lot of the guys are well meaning, but I think there's a great amount of incompetency. I mean, when you go into a plywood mill, you don't find the more educated group of people.

These are very real problems and not to be taken lightly. They suggest that even a relatively successful democratic enterprise is not devoid of problems and tensions but generates its own unique ones. Nevertheless,

I would submit that these problems attest to the very vitality of these enterprises as democratic institutions, as environments in which amateurs are actively and intensely involved in running an important part of their lives and doing it successfully. That such a complex and intense set of activities is not always conducted so that every member is happy at all times should come as no surprise.[13]

Many of the problems previously considered to be endemic to self-managed firms seem to be relatively absent in the plywood cooperatives. Much of the literature on self-managed enterprises in Yugoslavia, for instance, suggests that these firms are often plagued by problems of false and symbolic participation, the gradual formation of a dominant ruling faction, indiscipline at the point of production, and a growing distance between managerial-technical experts and the rank and file (Adizes, 1971; Horvat, 1976; Obradovic and Dunn, 1978; Vanek, 1975). The plywood cooperatives have serious problems of their own, but they do not seem to be prone to those suffered by the largest self-managed firms, or for that matter, the very smallest ones described in the literature. They seem to be sufficiently large to escape the intense, informal chaos characteristic of face-to-face groups yet sufficiently small to avoid the rigidification of status and technical differentiations within the plant. Ordinary worker-owners, the board, and the hired technical strata are so accessible to each other that these problems tend not to develop.

It is also important that the good fortune of the plywood cooperatives in avoiding most of the problems of large-scale self-managed enterprises may be partially attributed to the relatively compressed skill range found in the plywood industry. The spontaneous cooperation and the avoidance of the formation of a rigid stratum of technical experts may be as traceable to the narrowly constricted range of skills as to the firms' moderate size. It is conceivable that in industries characterized by a complex division of labor and hierarchy of skills, producer cooperatives even of moderate size might find themselves confronted with many of the problems found in the Yugoslav examples. Unfortunately, because of the absence of suitable research cases, the question will have to remain unanswered for the time being.

The Issue of Hired Workers

Based on the extensive description of their internal governing processes, the producer cooperatives in the Pacific-Northwest plywood industry included in this study would seem to be democratic institutions and suitable sites for an examination of the effects of workplace democracy. They are not perfectly democratic, however, for they contain pockets of workers who do not participate in enterprise or shop-floor decision processes. Much as Greek democracy was flawed by the presence of many noncitizens, so too is democracy in the cooperatives flawed. Economist Christopher Gunn, noting these features, has argued that the plywood cooperatives "cannot be considered fully self-managed" (1984:131). Sociologist Leon Grunberg goes so far as to suggest the existence of a class system of exploitation within them (1985).

Gunn and Grunberg are perfectly correct in pointing out that the enterprises in this study are not fully worker self-managed, but they are almost so. Although flawed in their democratic character, they are not flawed fatally for, unlike the Greek polis, noncitizens remain a distinct minority, but one not without influence and perquisites. As such, they must be seen as more than exploited and powerless wage labor though, to be sure, the possibility and the occasional occurrence of exploitation (layoffs during hard times, lower benefits, and the like) in the plywood cooperatives must be admitted.

Hired workers make up from 16 to 36 percent of all workers in the enterprises studied here. Though not insignificant, they represent a clear minority of workers. They are diverse in the extreme and though mostly outside of the decision-making process, not entirely devoid of power and influence. Who are they? First, in all but one of the cooperatives, there are the hired plant manager and his supervisory team (production supervisor, foremen). Second, there is the hired office staff, ranging from clerk-typists to accountants and sales managers. Third, there are workers who staff ancillary operations in subsidiaries far from the main plant (logging, veneer production, outlet stores). Fourth, many hired workers are newcomers who are planning to buy a share and become members when they have put aside sufficient capital, and many others are sons of present members working for a time until they either join or move on. Fifth, a few of the hired workers are highly skilled (and highly paid) such as electricians and machine maintenance people whose skills are essential to the cooperatives but not available among the members. Finally, there are hired workers who are members of itinerant "spreader" or "busheling" teams (one team spreads the glue on sheets of veneer, the other builds the plywood by crisscrossing layers of veneer). These jobs require skill, speed, and unflagging energy and are usually filled by young, unattached

Table 2–9. Hired workers' opinions about working in the cooperatives (in percentages; 1978 cross-section sample; $N = 97$)

	Agreed	Disagreed
Hired workers are treated pretty well in this plant	68.7	15.6
Shareholders are *not* very easy to get along with	13.5	64.5
Shareholders treat hired workers pretty much the same as they treat other shareholders	66.6	18.8
Hired workers like me should have a larger role to play	31.6	33.7
Hired workers in this plant should organize a union	33.0	42.5

workers who move often between plywood plants, both conventional and cooperative.[14] Because they are involved in the most important single step in the production of plywood and they work in teams able and willing to offer their services elsewhere, they retain considerable bargaining power and are treated with unusual respect.

Hired workers in this set of cooperatives, then, are not only a distinct minority but also a group that cannot be said to exist in unrelieved subordination. Many are supervisors or highly skilled and essential workers whose needs and interests are attended to continuously; others intend and will one day become shareholders; still others are employed in distant sites apart from the immediate work community and do not adversely affect the mood or milieu of the democratic community.[15] Many, being central to the production process, are very well paid, compensated at a level that is often equal to or in excess of worker-shareholders.

> The fact is we paid our nonshareholders more than we were paying our shareholders. But they're key men. You have to have them.

Some shareholders think that hired workers have it too good, and this feeling creates certain problems. For instance, one complained about the sacrifice that shareholders had to take during hard times, a fate not shared by those hired workers essential for production.

> We gave up our paid holidays when the crunch came. We put in a thousand dollar share which they didn't. We took a dollar an hour pay cut which they didn't.

Hired workers give favorable reports on their own situation in the cooperatives, as shown in Table 2–9.

These conclusions are not meant to suggest that hired workers in the cooperatives are universally satisfied with their lot, that all hired workers receive pay that is equal to or exceeds that of stockholders, that those who are not essential are not laid off during hard times, or that hired workers, even important ones, are full citizens of the work community. I mean only to suggest that hired workers are a minority in the cooperatives, that they are a highly diverse group many of whom exercise considerable influence and receive considerable benefits, and that their presence does not substantially damage the standing of cooperatives as democratic workplaces. They remain among the most fully democratic, enduring, industrial enterprises in the United States.[16] As such, they are important research sites for an investigation of some of the effects of workplace democracy.[17]

Producer Cooperatives and Democratic Theory

At the beginning of this chapter, I suggested that theorists of democracy have conventionally posited the existence of two distinct and opposed conceptions of democratic governance. The first and oldest form is generally known as direct or participatory democracy and stresses the direct participatory experience of ordinary people in their own governance and the capacity of that experience to act as an educative medium for the molding of interested, active, informed, and rational citizens. The second form is generally termed representative democracy and stresses how problems of size and limited time, as well as the limited capacities of ordinary citizens, make it reasonable to create a class of individuals, selected through open and universal elections, to act as intermediaries for a mass population unable to rule itself directly.

These conceptualizations of democratic governance are characterized by opposed notions of the most appropriate form of governance, the evaluation and expectations of the capacities of ordinary people, and the values to be served by the act of governance, and consequently, have usually been understood to represent competing and incompatible democratic forms. This analysis of the plywood cooperatives amply demonstrates, however, not only that these historically competing forms can in certain cases coexist but that they can mutually reinforce the most positive qualities of the other model and soften the most negative ones. In a sense, each of the democratic forms covers for and fills the problematic spaces of the other.

The producer cooperatives are without question examples of direct democratic institutions in which the rank and file generally makes the decisions that give direction to overall enterprise policy and develops informal arrangements through which the social processes of production are carried out in the workplace. These policy decisions are formulated by the worker-shareholders, in a variety of contexts, ranging from the annual or semi-annual meeting to the complex processes of self- and mutual supervision at the point of production. Such arrangements, however, are not sufficient to manage enterprises as large and as complex as those found in plywood, and representative institutions are also required. Most shareholders find, for instance, that the time available to them for matters of formal governance is extremely limited, mainly because of the very long hours devoted to production. Most shareholders in the plywood industry work ten-hour days and six-day weeks. Adding family obligations, recreation, and the like, the time available for frequent and extensive meetings is not abundant. For these reasons, a representative institution like the elected board of directors is a very useful device for easing the burdens imposed by limited time. Furthermore, although the plywood cooperatives are notable for their constricted skill range, some activities require expertise (mostly relating to business affairs—raw material acquisitions, relations with government agencies, product sales, taxes, and the like), which the shareholders, in general, do not have, and which they are willing to lodge in the hands of a hired (or elected) general manager.

Representative institutions thus cover or help compensate for some of the problems endemic to direct democracy. The coexistence of these two democratic forms is not only possible but attractive because of the pervasive participatory democratic milieu and behavior in the cooperatives which helps prevent the development of those tendencies in representative democracy that have made it problematic in other contexts. Almost all of these problematic tendencies are related in one way or another to the distance and lack of communication between a professional political class intensely engaged in governance and a largely uniformed, irrational, and apathetic mass population. Because the plywood cooperatives use representative institutions, these problematic tendencies do not develop.

We might trace this happy state of affairs to the intensely participatory milieu of these firms, which results from a complex combination of worker ownership of the enterprise, its human scale, and its formal locus of final decisional power in the general membership, all of which serve to minimize the distance between representatives and the represented. We have seen, for instance, both that board members are accessible, often painfully so, to the shareholders who work next to them in the mill. We have also seen the easy flow of information and the frequency of policy discussion among the worker-shareholders, which contribute to a well-informed and reasonably rational membership able to hold its own against both the board and the general manager. Whereas representative democracy almost always moves toward rigid stratification, the embedding of representative institutions within a rich participatory environment in the plywood cooperatives allows these institutions to make their positive contribution without decreasing the reality of self-governance.[18]

If this examination of the governance of producer cooperatives tells us anything about some of the central issues of democratic theory, it is that under certain conditions direct and representative democracy not only can exist together but that they can enrich each other. It is also reasonable to suggest that some combination of these two forms is probably necessary to any sizable work institution that is seriously committed to self-governance.

· 3 ·

Alienation in the Cooperatives

Virtually everyone on the democratic Left is agreed that industrial capitalism breeds alienation and that the creation of a society characterized by extensive workplace democracy is an essential step toward a nonalienated society that would allow human beings to realize their capacities.[1] As John Street has pointed out in his review of socialist arguments for industrial democracy, "[what] we have is a . . . common acceptance that the workers are to run their own factories, to organize their work, and to design their products. It is assumed that if these opportunities are denied them, the workers will remain alienated, powerless, and unfulfilled" (1983:519). Following Marx, but also the utopian socialists (Owen, Fourier, Saint-Simon), the anarchists (Proudhon and Kropotkin), the Council Communists, and the guild socialists, among others, the democratic Left has long assumed the existence of an inescapable linkage between capitalist relations of production and worker alienation and has advocated the full-scale democratization of the workplace as part of a program for the transformation of such relations of production. The democratic Left not only holds to particular theory concerning the roots of alienation but also maintains a vision of a possible concrete process of dealienation[2] in which workplace democratization and worker self-management play central roles.

Are these hopes and expectations of the democratic Left supported by the weight of the evidence? Does the democratization of the workplace set in motion a process of dealienation, a reversal of the tendencies so commonly found in industrial capitalism for the human being to become merely a constituent element of the division of labor, without autonomy or control, devoid of purposeful and creative activity, isolated from his or her peers and from control over the very purposes of production? These questions will be addressed by bringing to bear a broad range of data generated in the plywood cooperatives. I shall establish in this chapter that dealienation is only partially realized in the cooperatives, meeting theoretical expectations on a broad front yet missing the mark in some important areas. Before undertaking such an analysis, however, it is important to define the particular meaning of alienation used here.

Alienation

"Alienation" is a term whose popularity and consequent imprecision in usage renders it almost useless for purposes of social scientific analysis. Since 1945 it has become one of the most commonly encountered terms in both serious scholarship and popular culture, appearing in learned philosophical treatises and pop therapies, sociological surveys and best-selling novels, industrial psychology and popular music, ad infinitum. There is no commonly accepted meaning for the term, or worse yet, the usages are often contradictory. Richard Schacht (1971), reports the following scholarly and philosophical usages: as loneliness, lack of solidarity, dissension in social relations, job and life dissatisfaction, feelings of powerlessness, distrust, apathy, incomprehensibility of events, meaninglessness, absence of choice, estrangement from the prevailing culture and social values, anomie, inauthenticity, objectification, estrangement from self, and more.

Almost without exception in contemporary usage, moreover, alienation is understood to be psychological state of being, a *feeling* about something. Thus alienation understood by inauthenticity is conceptualized not as being inauthentic or acting inauthentically but feeling inauthentic; alienation as powerlessness is not understood as being in an objectively powerless condition but rather as a state of feeling powerless (Seeman, 1961); work alienation, in most contemporary social science usages, is about feeling alienated and not about some objective quality in the social relations of production. The problem with such an approach is obvious: it makes it impossible to identify and examine cases in which people may reasonably be said to *be* alienated but do not *feel* alienated. A strict focus on the social-psychological dimension of experience, in such cases, serves to remove from the view the sociological and social structural dimensions.

Comparison with the Marxian approach to alienation highlights the central problem: "The crucial consideration for Marx is that of whether or not one's productive activity is spontaneous and self-directed, and has no end other than the expression and development of one's personality. But it is quite possible for this not to be the case, and yet for one to be quite content with one's job. Indeed, cases of this sort would seem to be quite common today" (Schacht, 1971:169).

Although in its conventional uses the term "alienation" is almost worthless as an instrument of social scientific analysis, in the Marxian conception it remains a powerful analytical instrument to the extent that it brings order to the many diverse meanings of the term, offers a relatively clear standard by which some meanings are included and others excluded, and serves to bridge the yawning gap between the social psychological and the social structural.[3] In this chapter, I organize the consideration of alienation and dealienation processes in the plywood cooperatives along the lines defined by this approach.

Alienation, in the Marxian view, is about the alienation of labor in historically specific conditions and not about the alienation of a transhistorical human being. It is about the problems of producers caught in identifiable social structural settings and not about the "human condition." More specifically, it is about the objective situation of human beings in their roles as producers under relations of production in which they lack autonomy, spontaneity, freedom, or creativity.[4] It is not about "an inescapable and irremediable curse of mankind" (Novack, 1970:6) but about objective situations brought into existence by human activity and subject to change. It is about productive activity that makes it impossible for human beings, a species characterized by historically specific possibilities for working in an autonomous, conscious, social, and creative fashion, to act in a genuinely human fashion and to develop their uniquely human capacities. As Yugoslav social theorist Branko Horvat puts the issue: "A Marxist would [say] . . . that man is a being of praxis. As such, he is free since he can choose consciously among different courses of action that are objectively given. And if he can be free, he ought to be free, for otherwise he loses his essential human property" (1982:84). To act in production in an unalienated way, it follows, is to act in such a way that the entire process of production is brought under the conscious control of the producer and not the control of some blind process or power. Unalienated labor, then, is "the return of the process of production itself to the control of the workers" (Braverman, 1974:446).[5]

Alienation, then, is a concrete social fact rooted in the actual social relations of production, a state of being and not a feeling (though certain subjective states of mind may accompany particular states of being). This state of being in which the producer finds him or herself in a set of conditions that restricts the use or development of the full range of human capabilities is lodged, in the Marxian view, in the basic defining qualities of industrial capitalism: "First, [there is] the fact of private property and, especially, of private ownership of means of production, second, the process of division of labor . . . ; third . . . is that human labor is changed into a commodity on a par with all other commodities" (Israel, 1971:41). In the Marxian view, the alienation of labor is rooted in the institutions of private property in which the producer loses control over his activity because these institutions assume the right and power of the propertyholder to appropriate the surplus product of the worker who has nothing but labor to sell and to control the content and purposes of the production process.[6] Since Marxists generally assume that "work as purposive action, guided by the intelligence, and accomplished in social interaction with others, is the special product of human kind" (Braverman, 1974:49), industrial capitalism causes workers to "forfeit control over their lives, their liberties, and their means of development" (Mandel, 1970:67).

The discussion of alienation to this point is too abstract to be useful for empirical analysis. It is necessary to translate these concepts into a more concrete specification of the objective and subjective dimensions of the Marxian understanding of alienation and to indicate precisely what forms the loss of control over means of production and the process of production take in the real life of workers in industrial capitalism. It is necessary to specify how the overall social relations of production in society at large become articulated as alienation in the setting of the social relations in production (the actual relations between labor and capital in the workplace). The following discussion will be organized around the concept of estrangement or separation from four essential elements: from product, from production, from other workers, and from the self.

Estrangement from Product

To sell one's labor is essentially to lose control over the product of one's labor. Being without control may be understood in a triple sense: as being unable to determine what is to be produced, how to dispose of what is produced, or to enjoy the full fruits of one's labor after the product is sold or transferred. Being without property rights in the means of production, the worker cannot claim the product as his; the product neither represents the interests, aspirations, personality, or conscious choice of the worker nor returns its full value to the worker. The product as well as the rewards attached to it belong to another for the sale of labor power means, by virtue of both law and the realities of social power, that the products of labor are appropriated by the employer as surplus value.[7]

All of this is put rather nicely by (non-Marxist) sociologist Robert Blauner, who in *Alienation and Freedom* points out that "the very nature of employment in a large-scale organization means that workers have forfeited their claims on the finished product and that they do not own the factory, machines, or often their tools. Unlike the absence of control over the immediate work process, ownership powerlessness, for workers, is a constant in modern industry" (1964:17). Blauner blithely accepts as given that which is problematic—that workers choose to be powerless; that all modern industry requires loss of control over the product—but he does summarize one of the essential yet often unrecognized attributes of industrial capitalism.

Estrangement from the Process of Production

When a worker sells his or her labor power, he not only relinquishes control over and enjoyment of the full fruits of the product but also control over decision making in the process of production. This includes decisions concerning overall enterprise policy (investments, product line, technology, and the like) as well as decisions concerning matters at the immediate point of production. Labor for the worker in this context is no longer free and self-directed. By virtue of law, custom, and unequal power, it is understood that the wage relationship that forms the core of economic life in capitalism axiomatically implies an unequal, hierarchical relationship within the firm. In this relationship between employer and employee, managers and owners retain the right, subject to relatively minor restrictions and standards set by government and by labor unions, to direct and coordinate the work of the enterprise. In selling one's labor, one agrees in effect to do the work as stipulated by the employer. It is generally understood that hired employees must conform both to the purposes of the enterprise and to its internal order. The only residual right that is retained in industrial capitalism is the freedom to leave the enterprise and seek other employment. That is, the exercise of choice is external to the life of the enterprise, not internal to it. In the end, the worker plays little part in making decisions about what is to be done at the point of production or how to do it.

As Harry Braverman has brilliantly pointed out, workers who have lost control over the purposes and processes of production have generally lost, as well, their enthusiasm for work and their willingness to use their capabilities to the fullest. The overriding response by management has been to attempt to control ever more closely the use of labor power at the point of production by escalating the intensity of supervision, by honing the directorial qualities of precise bureaucratic procedures (Edwards, 1979), and by further separating the functions of hand and brain (or execution and planning—see Braverman, 1974) in production. To labor under such a set of conditions, to be powerless in the act of labor, to be denied the use of one's conscious, free, and creative capacities, is to be separated, in Marx's view, from the real-life activity of human beings, that is, to be alienated.

Loss of independent decision-making power by the worker is enhanced, furthermore, by the advance of the minute division of labor and the consequent deskilling of labor. Perhaps no better statement of the effects of that advance may be found than that of Adam Smith in his classic, *The Wealth of Nations*: "The man whose life is spent performing a few simple operations . . . has no occasion to exert his understanding or to exercise his invention in finding out expedients for removing difficulties which never occur . . . and generally becomes as stupid and ignorant as it is possible for a human creature to become. And if such work be widespread, all the nobler parts of the human character may be, in great measure, obliterated and extinguished in the great body of people" (1937, 2:264). Since Adam Smith's day, science and technology have accelerated the pace of advance of the division of labor through mechanization and automation, further rendering the worker an appendage of the machine. Although scholars such as Blauner deny that science and technology are transforming the work process, in the Marxian view, the melding of science, technology, and capitalism has the effect, in the end, of forcing the worker to become a being who reacts and responds to the rhythms of the production process and to lose the ability to act as an autonomous, rational being. It is not so much that the worker has lost control of decisions regarding the choice of technology and production methods (which is also true) but that his or her behavior has become barely distinguishable from that of the other mechanical instruments of production; the worker has become "machinelike."

Estrangement of labor in the production process is, then, at least two-fold. In the first place, it implies the loss of autonomous decision-making power in the face of the power of other persons or institutions, submission to the dictates of others as the price of employment. In the second place, it implies an even more profound loss of autonomy and the distortion of human capacities and possibilities to the dictates of technological, auto-mated production.

Estrangement from Others

In industrial capitalism, where everything is for sale, where everything is, in effect, a commodity, including labor power, people face each other as competitive and egoistic beings. Trust, community, and cooperation, though not absent, become less frequently observed forms of behavior than those that are atomistic in character. In such a commodified society, commitment and a sense of belonging are difficult to attain; isolation, self-interest, and loneliness prevail (Bellah et al., 1985; Slater, 1970). In the Marxian view, the essence of human existence is social because all that is necessary for human existence and happiness is socially produced, yet capitalism, it is argued, submerges this incipient cooperation under inex-orable waves of egoism and competition. In capitalism natural cooperation is diluted by competition and the social nature of human beings remains stunted and underdeveloped. Each person becomes the means to an end for other persons.

To Marx, the opposition of one human being to another is rooted in production: "In the relationship of alienated labor every man regards other men according to the standards and relationships in which he finds himself placed as a worker" (*Frühe Schriften*, quoted in Schacht, 1971:103). By this he means, I believe, that the formation of a civil society that requires human beings to be selfish and competitive as the price for survival is itself the creation of a specific set of social relations of production defined by private property, accumulation, commodification, and wage labor.

This all-embracing egoism, one must suppose, is carried into the work-place, where it finds itself in perpetual struggle with the inherent social character of production. The individual worker in industrial capitalism becomes a carrier of both an egoistic ethic, in which fellow workers are considered rivals to be used for one's own ends, and a social ethic, in which fellow workers, similarly exploited and united in cooperative productive activities, are considered to be brothers united against a common foe. The issue of class-consciousness, of course, is tied to the process by which the social ethic comes to prevail over the egoistic ethic.

Self-Estrangement

The notion of self-estrangement in the Marxian view involves separation from what is truly and fully human—the capacity to engage in productive activities in a manner that is rational, conscious, purposive, and social.[8] An alienating context is one in which the prevailing social relations of production do not allow human beings to develop the full range of their capabilities. Thus social relations of production in which workers lack control over the products of their labor, control over the process of production is in the hands of others, the technical division of labor turns workers into automatons, and workers are separated into isolated, atomistic units causes human beings to be separated from that which is human.[9]

Marx used several metaphors to characterize this alienated existence. The first is that of *animal*, alienation being a state in which human beings become animallike, producing not to develop and use their unique capacities for freedom, rationality, and creativity but "under the compulsion of direct physical needs." Their activity becomes mere animal production; they lose their advantage over the animal kingdom, joining, in effect, the other species of the animal kingdom. The second is that of *slave*, alienation being a state in which human beings surrender their capacities for autonomous and conscious behavior to another person who directs their activity. In industrial capitalism, in particular, the necessity for human beings to sell their labor power to another creates a field of power in production in which one set of people orders, directs, and manages and another must, perforce, obey. The third is that of *machine*, alienation being a state in which human beings become unthinking, nonautonomous appendages of the machine-based production process. The worker is "reduced . . . to the condition of a machine." All that is required of him or her is "simple mechanical motion." To be animallike, slavelike, and machinelike is to be dehumanized.[10]

Estrangement from self is thus an objective state of being that has obvious psychological and subjective referents as well. When a human being is objectively estranged, feeling states relevant to that situation are usually also developed. In the production process, the alienation of labor is likely to be expressed by the individual by apathy, detachment, lack of commitment, boredom, dissatisfaction, and more (Israel, 1971:55). This close linkage between objectively alienated situation and subjectivity was described by Marx: "In his work, therefore, the worker, does not affirm himself but denies himself, does not feel content but unhappy, does not develop freely his physical and mental energy but mortifies his body and ruins his mind. The worker therefore only feels himself outside his work, and in his work feels outside himself. He is at home when he is not working, and when he is working he is not at home" (*Economic and Philosophical Manuscripts*, quoted in Blauner, 1964:27).

Workplace Democracy and Dealienation

Having specified the meaning of alienation that will inform this analysis, we can now ask whether workplace democracy helps diminish the alienation of labor so characteristic of industrial capitalism. Do democratic practices in the plywood cooperatives help set in motion a process of dealienation or does the location of these enterprises within a larger system of market-capitalism relations cause the potentially dealienating effects of democracy to remain underdeveloped or even stillborn? Does democratic work life in these enterprises allow workers to overcome their estrangement from product, process, self, and others or are more fundamental social and political transformations in the larger society required to effect these profound changes?

In some respects, it would seem that the question of the nature of the relationship between workplace democracy and alienation has already been decisively answered and that no additional research findings are required. Sociologist Paul Blumberg, for instance, after painstakingly reviewing the research literature on workplace democracy and alienation (which he defines in terms of "satisfaction"), concluded: "There is hardly a study in the entire literature which fails to demonstrate that satisfaction in work is enhanced or that other generally acknowledged beneficial consequences accrue from a genuine increase in workers' decision-making power. Such consistency of findings, I submit, is rare in social research" (1973:123). Compared with autocratic organization, in which workers' mental capacities are underdeveloped or mutated, democratic organizations, he claims, demonstrably develop psychological maturity (1973:131). Ronald Mason, the author or the most authoritative review of scholarship on this subject since the publication of Blumberg's landmark book, concludes that "the contention that workplace participation is linked to satisfaction . . . is strongly supported in the research literature" (1982:133). Such research is enormously suggestive and relevant to the present study, but the prevailing literature on the alienation of labor reported in these volumes is almost entirely directed to the examination of subjective feeling states (especially satisfaction) and not to actual social relations in production and their derivative subjective orientations. It is to the consideration of this complex set of social relations and mental states that I now turn my attention.

Estrangement from Product in the Plywood Cooperatives

To sell one's labor power is to lose control over the product of one's labor; one is unable to decide what to produce, how to dispose or use what is produced, or to enjoy the full fruits of one's labor. The alienation of labor is rooted in the wage relationship and in the property relationship that opposes labor and capital. In producer cooperatives, however, as Marx pointed out, "the antithesis between capital and labor is overcome"; that is, the alienation of labor is overcome to the extent that worker-shareholders both own and control the enterprise. In the U.S. plywood cooperatives, for instance, the members, acting in a democratic assembly, decide what to produce and how to produce it. They are free to decide, and do decide, whether to produce their own veneer or to buy it from another firm; whether to produce construction-grade plywood, high-quality specialized marine plywood, exterior siding, or interior paneling; or whether to produce some mix of these products as a hedge against market uncertainties. Worker-shareholders must and do decide for themselves how to market their plywood products: sometimes they sell to the larger wood products companies; at other times they hire their own sales force and market directly to product users. They are also free, of course, within the constraints posed by prevailing market conditions and their own resources, to decide to move into some entirely different line of production, whether wood products or otherwise. In the end, they may even decide to close down operations, liquidate the enterprise, or sell it to an outside bidder. As a worker-shareholder commented:

> It's a unique thing, this company. What it is really, is a utopian idea, it really is. Everybody gets together, pools their money, decides to make a

particular product, and markets it . . . and with no outside interference, nobody telling them what they have to do.

Worker-shareholders are no longer separated from the product of their labor. They know the products, they know how it is produced, they know what happens to it when it leaves the mill, and they know how it is used by the consumer. The worker-shareholder is not a wage laborer. This situation is recognized and deeply valued by worker-shareholders:

> I don't work for nobody else, I work for myself.

Because they partake in ownership, worker-shareholders do not produce surplus value to be appropriated by others; they are able to retain for themselves any surplus that they realize from the sale of the products of their labor.

> Hey, nobody walks off with what I produce. Nobody can use what we make to go off and buy condos and speculate on Wall Street . . . we get what we make . . . we keep it, we decide what to do with it.

The members of the cooperatives decide what to do with the surplus after the bills are paid. How much should go to wages and bonuses? How much to new equipment? How much to timber purchases? Such choices may not always be rational, but they belong to the worker-shareholders.

> Some of them don't know what it takes to run this place . . . they think the money flows out of a bottomless well with no end to it . . . it just keeps rolling out. I know a company where the members sucked it dry . . . they went under . . . it was just their own ignorance.

Worker-shareholders do not act in an environment free of constraints, of course. To survive, they must respond to market signals. They are dependent on financial institutions for loans when the need arises. They must pay their bills, bid on scarce timber, compete with other small firms, and submit to environmental pollution laws. In regard to decisions concerning their product and the use of the surplus generated by the sale of their product, worker-shareholders are in precisely the same situation as the conventional capitalist. Their constraints are qualitatively different from those suffered by wage laborers.

Estrangement from the Process of Production in the Plywood Cooperatives: Decision Making

The alienation of labor also refers to the loss of autonomy and power to other persons in regard to the decision-making processes by which production is organized and set in motion. Alienation in this sense refers to a situation in which a person is the receiver of orders and instructions, an object of direction, and not a free, autonomous actor, defining the objectives and detailed procedures of the labor process on his or her own or in cooperation with peers. For most workers in market-capitalist societies, especially in the industrial sector, alienated labor in this sense is the prevailing reality even if, for some of their number, working conditions are pleasant and compensation is reasonably high (Berg et al., 1979; Blumberg, 1973; Braverman, 1974; Edwards, 1979; Kornhauser, 1965; Mason, 1982; Sheppard and Herrick, 1972; Terkel, 1974). In producer cooperatives in general and in the U.S. plywood cooperatives in particular, however, enterprise policy is formulated by the general membership. Objectively, then, it cannot be said that worker-shareholders are alienated in the sense of being estranged from the the decision-making process, although their participation in decision making is not entirely unambiguous and unproblematic.

General enterprise policy is formulated in annual or semiannual membership meetings and, in the periods between meetings, by an elected board of directors. This combination of direct, participatory democracy and indirect, representative democracy, buttressed by the ready availability of information and the existence of diverse channels of informal decision making, provides a structure of worker influence over enterprise and production that is notable for its virtual absence anywhere else in American industry. One way to demonstrate the widespread availability and use of these democratic instruments is to note worker-shareholders' responses to a set of questions designed to document participation in formal policy-making institutions. The first of these questions asks worker-shareholders whether they attend general membership meetings. Ninety percent of the panel sample replied that they did. Since attendance is encouraged by payment of a day's wage, however, these responses do not help in evaluating actual participation. Respondents were also asked whether they participate in discussions at the shareholders' meetings, talk with other members about the decisions of the board of directors, or have ever run for or served on the board. The results are reported in Tables 3–1 through

Table 3–1. Worker-shareholders' participation in discussions at meetings (in percentages; panel sample)

Question: "Do you participate in discussions at the shareholder meetings?"

	$T_1 (N = 85)$	$T_2 (N = 88)$
Always	9.4	19.3
Very often	14.1	13.6
From time to time	40.0	33.0
Seldom	23.5	19.3
Never	12.9	14.8

Significance of association between T_1 and T_2 measures:
$Tau_B = 0.615; p = 0.000.$

3–3.[11] It is evident that participation by worker-shareholders is relatively high and tends to increase over time.

We can gain a more parsimonious picture of the degree of participation and changes over time by combining the items in Tables 3-1 and 3-3 into a single index of participation in formal enterprise decision making[12] (see Table 3.4). What is most interesting about this summary measure is the small yet statistically significant increase in the level of worker-shareholder participation over the years of this study.[13] This finding, though not very

Table 3–2. Worker-shareholders' participation as candidates for the board of directors (in percentages; panel sample)

Question: "Have you ever run for the Board of Directors?"

	$T_1 (N = 89)$	$T_2 (N = 88)$
Yes	36.0	48.9
No	64.0	51.1

Significance of association between T_1 and T_2 measures:
$Tau_B = 0.657; p = 0.000.$

Table 3–3. Worker-shareholders' participation as members of the board of directors (in percentages; panel sample)

Question: "Have you ever served on the Board of Directors?"

	$T_1 (N = 89)$	$T_2 (N = 88)$
Yes	18.2	26.1
No	81.8	73.9

Significance of association between T_1 and T_2 measures:
$Tau_B = 0.791; p = 0.000.$

Table 3–4. Index of participation in formal enterprise decision-making (panel sample)

Mean score at T_1*	8.3
Mean score at T_2	7.8
$p = 0.001$[†]	
$N = 86$	

*Possible scores range from 4 to 12. The higher score represents a *lower* level of participation.
[†]Significance of difference between means is measured by the T-test (2-tail probability).

powerful, is entirely consistent with the theoretical literature, which suggests that participation tends to breed more participation and that the act of participation plays an educative role stimulating further participation (Pateman, 1970; Mason, 1982).

When we consider supervision at the point of production, we again find that practices within the co-ops encourage the development of less alienated relations than those in conventional industrial settings. At the objective level of relations of production, of course, the nature of supervision in cooperative and in conventional firms stands in vivid contrast. In the cooperatives, as we learned in Chapter 2, the supervisory touch is light: there are few foremen on the job, their communications with worker-shareholders tend to be two-way as in communication between equals, and their oversight of the specific actions of worker-shareholders is quite loose. We also learned that worker-shareholders are free of the fear of supervisors and foremen found in conventional firms (since the employment of supervisors and foremen depends on the wishes of those being supervised) and that they solve many production difficulties among themselves without recourse to the intervention of superiors. Recall some of the comments from the interviews:

I have little or no supervision.

They're not there as bosses, they're just hired help.

Too much laxity.

Some guys get abusive with the foremen.

You can thumb your nose at him [the foreman] if you want to.

I'm my own boss. I plan my own work.

The relative lightness of touch of the supervisory system in the co-operatives and its burden in the conventional firm is reflected in a ques-

Table 3–5. Workers' responses on optimal number of supervisors (in percentages)

Question: "Thinking about supervisors and foremen in this plant, do you think that there should be *more* of them, that there are about the *right* number, or that there should be *fewer* of them?"

	Cooperatives ($N = 88$)		Conventional ($N = 51$)	
	T_1	T_2	T_1	T_2
More	8.0	6.6	2.0	2.0
About right	79.5	72.7	47.1	39.2
Fewer	12.5	20.5	51.0	58.8
	Significance of change T_1 to T_2 = n.s.		Significance of change T_1 to T_2 = n.s.	

Significance of differences between co-op and conventional plants at T_1, $p = 0.000$ (Kolmogorov-Smirnov [hereafter K.S.] test); at T_2, $p = 0.000$ (K.S.).

tion that asks respondents whether there should be more or fewer foremen on the job. The unsurprising results, with conventional workers strongly supporting a decrease in the weight of supervision, are reported in Table 3–5.

Similar and entirely predictable results are evident in respondents' reactions to a question asking them whether their foremen act more as bosses or as coordinators (Table 3–6). By a wide margin, worker-shareholders in the co-ops are more likely than those in the conventional mill to understand supervision as part of a pattern of cooperative production and not as part of a hierarchical system of control.

The patterns of change over time, however, are slightly surprising.

Table 3–6. Workers' responses on role of foremen (in percentages; panel sample)

Question: "Does your foreman act more as a coordinator or more as a boss?"

	Cooperatives ($N = 76$)		Conventional ($N = 46$)	
	T_1	T_2	T_1	T_2
Coordinator	75.0	65.8	43.5	52.2
Boss	18.4	30.3	54.3	41.3
Neither	6.6	3.9	2.2	6.5
	Significance of change T_1 to T_2 = n.s.		Significance of change T_1 to T_2 = n.s.	

Significance of differences between co-op and conventional plants at T_1, $p = 0.01$ (K.S.); at T_2, $p = $ n.s. (K.S.).

Table 3–7. Workers' perceptions of supervisors' attitudes toward their suggestions (panel sample, in percentages)

Question: "Does your supervisor or foreman take into account your opinions and suggestions when you make them?"

	Cooperatives ($N = 85$)		Conventional ($N = 45$)	
	T_1	T_2	T_1	T_2
Never	5.9	5.9	6.7	6.7
Occasionally	47.0	40.0	46.7	55.6
Often/always	47.0	54.2	46.7	37.7
	Significance of change T_1 to T_2 = n.s.		Significance of change T_1 to T_2 = n.s.	

Significance of differences between co-op and conventional plants at T_1, p = n.s. (K.S.), at T_2, p = .05 (K.S.)

Each set of respondents moved in the opposite direction with conventional workers coming to appreciate the coordinating qualities of supervision a little more and the worker-shareholders' positive evaluations of supervision declining slightly, though, the differences between co-op and conventional workers remain great.

Similar conclusions are warranted with regard to other evaluations of questions regarding supervision in the attitude survey. Respondents were asked whether their supervisors took into account their opinions and suggestions and treated them with respect (see Tables 3–7 and 3–8). Consistent

Table 3–8. Workers' feelings of being treated with respect (panel sample, in percentages)

Question: "Do you feel that your supervisor or foreman treats you with respect?"

	Cooperatives ($N = 89$)		Conventional ($N = 50$)	
	T_1	T_2	T_1	T_2
Never	3.4	3.4	4.0	12.0
Occasionally	22.5	15.7	16.0	22.0
Always	74.1	80.8	80.0	66.0
	Significance of change T_1 to T_2 = n.s.		Significance of change T_1 to T_2 = n.s.	

Significance of differences between co-op and conventional plants at T_1, p = n.s. (K.S.); at T_2, p = n.s. (K.S.).

with both the theoretical literature and common-sense expectations, the worker-shareholders increased their positive evaluations of their supervisors and foremen over time. The evaluations of workers in the conventional firm, however, experienced slippage. The end result of these divergent developments is a significant difference in the subjective evaluation of supervision in the two types of mills. But though the results are in the expected direction, the size differences, in my view, are not. One might have expected much greater differences in subjective evaluations in light of the striking differences in the objective social relations of supervision. Surely it is surprising, in enterprises where worker-shareholders have the power to hire and fire their own supervisors, that more worker-shareholders do not feel that their views are respected and acted upon.[14]

Estrangement from the Work Itself

If the experience of the plywood cooperatives supports, if somewhat weakly, the expectations of the theoretical literature concerning the linkage between workplace democracy and dealienation in the loss of decision-making power, the same cannot be said for the work itself. Plywood production is a mix of automated, continuous-process, and assembly methods. It involves stripping sheets of veneer from logs (except in plants that buy veneer from other companies), cutting the veneer into appropriate sized pieces (done by machine), building plywood sheets by crisscrossing and glueing veneer pieces (mostly hand operations), making the structure permanent by feeding unfinished plywood into a hot press (combination hand and machine process), trimming the plywood to size, patching the 4' x 8' plywood sheets if they are damaged or have unacceptable knotholes (trimming and patching are both combined hand-machine operations), and preparing the finished product for shipping. The production process in cooperative and conventional mills is indistinguishable; it is universally noisy, dirty, dangerous, monotonous, and relentless. Production workers in both types of firms are appendages of the machine process. Workplace democracy in the co-ops has not made a dent in this reality. Production workers described and evaluated the work they do, day in, day out, six days a week, ten hours a day (in "good times").

There is, first, the sheer monotony of the job.

The work? It's boring, I mean, that's the first thing that pops into anybody's mind that works there. That's the worst fight down there is fighting not to get bored. [a worker-shareholder]

It's like being a zombie. . . . They're intelligent guys but they're completely lost in their own thoughts. . . . When I go over to make a change they look at me blank. . . . They might have been running for four hours and never once stopped to look and read the tag to find out what kind of wood they've been running. [supervisor, conventional mill]

You're doing something that's basically unpleasant. . . . Most jobs are monotony and repetition. It can drive you nuts. [worker in conventional mill]

The rapid pace of the automated process makes production workers act and feel a bit like the Charlie Chaplin character in the classic film *Modern Times*.

The drier down there is really fast . . . it puts out three times the wood of our old dryer. I don't complain but everybody else . . . oh God, they put them on there and they just cry. [a worker-shareholder]

There are times when it's so fast you can't hardly keep up . . . times when I want to just cry so I can go drink a coke or take a smoke. [a worker-shareholder]

It comes out of the dryer. It comes onto the table . . . you got to figure you got four rows coming at you or some of the dryers have five rows coming. So within a few minutes you've got eight to ten pieces of things coming at you on that table and you have to keep that table cleared or try to because the next batch is coming right after it. It doesn't wait for you to clear the table. [a worker-shareholder]

Overwhelmed by the deadly combination of monotonous repetition and relentless pace, production workers in both kinds of plants admit to feeling anxious and trapped:

I go through times when I get so depressed. But like I say, it's the only god damn thing I'm programmed for right now. It's too late for me to go back to school at 45 years old. It's just that I was stupid when I was young. [a worker-shareholder]

You have to grin and bear it no matter what job you're doing. There are times when you get disgusted and there are times when you grin and bear it and just overlook it and just keep on plugging. [worker in conventional mill]

Finally, this work, even in the plywood cooperative, does not fully or even significantly use the capacities for creativity and autonomy that Marx, at least, believed to be central to the human species. With a few exceptions the jobs that produce plywood require very little skill. Almost any job in a plywood mill can be mastered in a day or two. The work is machinelike, the worker a nonautonomous part of the automated machine process.

I don't think there's a job down there a man can't do . . . it ain't too hard to learn any of them. [worker in conventional mill]

There's no skilled labor. . . . I mean anybody can lay four pieces of core down there. [worker-shareholder]

You can ask any person you interview, can your boy handle your job? And he'll say, better. [worker-shareholder]

This impression is confirmed by responses to two questions designed to tap the range of skills involved in plywood production. The first asked how many different jobs the respondent could do in the plant without additional training. Almost 80 percent of the worker-shareholders claimed they could do either more than half or most of them, and almost 70 percent of workers in the conventional mill made the same claim. The slight difference (which is not statistically significant) may perhaps be attributed to the greater propensity to rotate jobs in the cooperatives. The second asked respondents how many different jobs they had worked at in the mill. Almost two-thirds of the production workers in both types of mills reported working on at least seven different jobs. These responses might at first glance be seen as confirmation that workplace democracy encourages the development of a broad range of skills. The lack of significant differences between cooperative and conventional mills, however, when combined with data from the interviews and direct observation of the production process, convinces me that what is at work here is the easy transfer of personnel between jobs that require little skill or training.

The situation seems to be anomalous: worker-shareholders in the cooperatives go about producing plywood in almost exactly the same mind-

and body-numbing ways as workers in conventional mills. Such a finding flies directly in the face of all theoretical expectations. Especially on the Left, it is generally assumed that workers labor under alienated conditions because the mobilization and control of the production process is lodged firmly in the hands of capital. Were workers in control, it is further assumed, they would move decisively to transform their conditions of labor as mere interchangeable machine parts. At least in the case of the democratically run plywood cooperatives, this is not the case.

To be sure, worker-shareholders reported an enduring interest in transforming a not too compelling form of work. Seventy-one percent of them reported, for instance, that they had taken part in discussions about how to make work in the plant more interesting. Forty-one percent had talked about the issue in general shareholder meetings. And yet, despite these sentiments, little changes in the mills. The work stays the same; the production process continues to set the rhythm of labor for all concerned. Why is there a contradiction between desire for change in the labor process and the reality of its fixedness? The questionnaire data give few clues. Interviews with workers, managers, and industry officials suggest, however, a preliminary twofold answer. First, there is a palpable sense among virtually all observers, including the worker-shareholders themselves, that the nature of technology is given and that human beings, if they are to reap the material rewards of automated and assembly production, must "grin and bear it." They believe in a technological imperative to which human beings must adjust and which allows only for tinkering around the edges. Second, even when one occasionally encounters a respondent who acknowledges the possibility that production might be organized in a fashion that develops rather than stifles human capacities, there is a belief (probably based on fact) that the costs of creating such a technical production process are prohibitive, certainly beyond the capacities of the small firms in this study. Since most worker-shareholders came to cooperatives with strongly instrumental motives (financial and security) and since such motives remain strong (even if cooperative motives gain strength over time), there is a tendency to ignore work reform in the interests of an assured paycheck.[15]

There is here a hint of self-exploitation as workers do to themselves what capitalists do to hired labor. The hint becomes more pronounced on the issue of workplace safety. The findings here are stunning, completely contradictory to theoretical expectations about the effects of workplace democracy: the plywood cooperatives are by far the most dangerous places

to work in the entire plywood industry. The American Plywood Association (APA), the principal trade organization for the western plywood
industry, collects monthly data on the incidence rate of injuries in its 145
member plants. Over the span of years covered in this study, the cooperative member firms of the APA ranked 128 in safety. In 1982, the two
most financially successful cooperatives in the industry (including one
firm in the present study) ranked 143 and 145 in safety.[16]

These startling and theoretically unexpected findings are buttressed by
the direct reports of the plywood workers. During the many hours of
interviews with worker-shareholders, not once did the issue of company
safety policies and concerns spontaneously arise. When asked directly,
not a single respondent could mention a specific set of mechanisms or
company policies directed toward making the workplace safer. As strange
as it may seem, the conventional company in this study seemed to show
much greater awareness of safety than did the cooperatives, no doubt
because of concern about oversight by the Occupational Safety and Health
Administration (OSHA). Apparently, OSHA, under the impression that
a mill whose workers are in control will be attentive to safety issues, does
not spend much time regulating and inspecting plywood cooperatives.

Any man in the plant can, if he sees an unsafe situation, get a hold of his
supervisor and show it to him. (Interviewer: Do you have a right to stop and
say I'm not going to do it?) Well, yes. If you see something where you
know you're going to get hurt, you don't have to do it. But there's not very
many of them conditions that ever materialize . . . mainly bad spots on the
floor, oil on the floor, oil on the floor from the bulls, holes in the floor, bare
wiring or anything that could be unsafe. Any man that sees it can report it
to his foreman. And then they get it fixed if it don't cost them too much
money. [worker in conventional mill]

But with these new laws, I find they're trying [the company]. I mean, they
take time out and, of course, we pay a guy too, his regular wage to go around
on these inspection tours and check the mill. If you see something unsafe,
report it to your foreman. Now he's supposed to put it down in writing and
send it into the millwright, you know, the mechanics and that department.
And then it's followed through on paper until it's been fixed. [worker in
conventional mill]

These impressions are confirmed by the responses to two questions
asking about the incidence of work-related accidents in the plants. The

Table 3–9. Workers' reports of witnessing work-related accidents (in percentages; panel sample)

Question: "Have you witnessed any accidents in this plant during the past five years in which a person has been seriously injured (causing him or her to stay away from work for at least a week)?"*

	Cooperatives ($N = 95$)	Conventional ($N = 58$)
Yes	38.9	27.6
No	61.1	72.4

$p = 0.07$ (X^2).

*This item was included only in the second wave of questionnaires at T_2.

first, reported in Table 3–9, asks respondents whether they have personally witnessed any serious injuries in the mill. Worker-shareholders witnessed more injuries in their plants than did workers in the conventional plant. The differences are small but significant because they are exactly the opposite from what one would expect from the theoretical literature and consistent with the impressions from the interviews and data from the American Plywood Association.[17] Furthermore, when respondents who reported personally witnessing serious injuries in the plant were asked how many they had witnessed over the past five years, worker-shareholders in the cooperatives reported a significantly higher incidence rate than workers in the conventional mill. Thirty-four percent of the former reported three or more serious injuries; only 16 percent of the latter reported as many. In light of the figures, it is hardly surprising that worker-shareholders are less likely than other workers to see their plants as safe places to work (Table 3–10).

Table 3–10. Workers' perceptions of the safety of the plant (in percentages; panel sample)

Question: "Please rate how safe you think this plant is."*

	Cooperatives ($N = 90$)	Conventional ($N = 57$)
Safer than most plywood plants	26.7	38.6
About as safe as other plywood plants	67.8	57.9
More dangerous than most plywood plants	5.6	3.5

$p = 0.06$ (K.S.).

*This item was included only in the second wave of questionnaires at T_2.

Table 3–11. Workers' perceptions of reasons for injuries (percent responding "very important" [V.I.] or "somewhat important" [S.I.]; panel sample)

Question: "To what do you attribute injuries in your plant?"

		Cooperatives	Conventional	Significance of difference (K.S.)
Worker carelessness	V.I.	81.5	85.7	n.s.
	S.I.	17.4	8.9	
Poorly designed	V.I.	25.6	48.1	
machines	S.I.	33.7	40.7	0.006
Pace of work	V.I.	24.7	53.7	0.008
	S.I.	36.5	33.3	
Fatigue	V.I.	37.2	37.7	n.s.
	S.I.	29.1	34.0	
Lack of manage-	V.I.	36.8	54.7	n.s.
ment concern	S.I.	24.1	13.2	

*For reasons of parsimony, only a part of the data is reported. The test of significance is for the entire table in each case.

An inquiry into workers' interpretation of the causes of accidents is also revealing (see Table 3–11). Workers in both plant settings acknowledged the important role played by individual carelessness in the incidence of injuries. People aren't always attentive to the automated saws, presses, and fast-moving forklifts that fill their environment; they do not always wear gloves or eye-protectors; all too often they set aside safety helmets in the interest of comfort. Worker-shareholders, as compared to other workers, confined their causal analysis to this individualistic level; other workers gave great weight as well to the design of machines, the pace of the production process, and management behavior in their interpretation of the causes of workplace accidents. As one co-op worker put it, "people make safety, not machines." This individualistic outlook not only adds another refinement to our understanding of the safety record of the plywood cooperatives but hints at the strong individualistic political orientations of the worker-shareholder to be explored in Chapter 5.

Estrangement from Others in the Plywood Cooperatives

The dealienation effects of workplace democracy in the cooperatives are essentially nonexistent with regard to the work process itself; a plywood cooperative is in some respects a more alienating production environment

Table 3–12. Workers' socialization patterns outside of work (panel sample, T_1, in percentages)

Question: "If you think of the people you spend time socializing with outside of working hours, about how many of them are people from this plant?"*

	Cooperatives (N = 90)	Conventional (N = 50)
Nearly all	3.3	2.0
Great many	8.9	4.0
Only a few	61.1	56.0
None	26.7	38.0

*This item was included only on the first wave of questionnaires. At T_1, p = n.s. (K.S.).

than is a conventionally owned and operated mill. Although the same cannot be said about alienation understood as estrangement from others, the record of the plywood cooperatives is hardly impressive. In the Marxian view, overcoming the alienation of labor involves, in part, transcending the competition and egoistic individualism of market capitalism that sees (and uses) one's peers as means to one's ends, and coming to enjoy working in community, solidarity, and cooperation with one's peers. At one level, and as we have seen in Chapter 2, the plywood cooperatives are, by definition, unalienated places to the extent that cooperative self-management is the basis for the existence of the enterprise. In such firms, production is possible only through voluntary cooperation, group decision making, and shared effort and sacrifice. At another level, however, community and solidarity remain underdeveloped and deeply elusive.

Let us consider, first, the degree to which the cooperation inherent in the production and decision-making processes in the plywood co-ops carries over into informal friendship networks. Respondents were asked to indicate whether they tend to socialize with their fellow workers outside of work. Because both worker-shareholders and workers in the conventional mills tend to commute by car from all geographical directions to their place of work on trips that average about twenty minutes (a few even commute over distances of sixty miles or more on the freeway system), it is perhaps not surprising that only a few reported that fellow workers constituted a significant proportion of their friendship circle outside of work. No significant differences were apparent between co-op and conventional workers in this regard; community and sociability at work were not carried over the walls of the cooperative enterprise by worker-shareholders (see Table 3–12). Even more surprising, worker-shareholders, in comparison to workers in conventional mills, tended to act as social iso-

Table 3–13. Workers' socialization patterns at lunch time (panel sample, T_1, in percentages)

Question: "When you eat lunch at work, do you generally"*

	Cooperatives (N = 83)	Conventional (N = 50)
Eat alone?	30.1	12.0
Eat with one or a few close friends?	38.6	64.0
Eat with a large group of co-workers?	28.9	22.0
Other	2.4	2.0

*This item was included only on the first wave of questionnaires. At T_1, p = n.s. (K.S.).

lates even at work. In their only off-the-job time in the mill, during lunch breaks, worker-shareholders showed a much greater tendency to be alone, apart from their fellows (see Table 3–13).

The differences in socialization between co-op and conventional mills are small, yet exactly contrary to theoretical expectations. Cooperation and self-management do not enhance general solidarity either away from the plant or, apparently, inside its walls, at least as indicated by these very simple measures. Further evidence of the failure of self-management in the plywood cooperatives to enhance solidarity is provided by a series of questions designed to tap evaluations of the talents and capacities of peers. A reading of the theoretical literature would suggest that workplace democracy should have the following effects: (1) workers in cooperatives should be more confident about the talents and capacities of their fellows than workers in conventional work settings because of their positive experiences with cooperative and egalitarian labor and decision making, and (2) this confidence should increase over time as these experiences accumulate. The data reported in Table 3–14 do not support either one of these expectations. Not only were worker-shareholders' evaluations of their peers indistinguishable from those of other workers, but these evaluations tended either to remain stable or to deteriorate over time. Again, although the changes are not very great, they are (with the exception of "capable of doing a good day's work") contrary to expectations.

Finally, in considering the question of whether self-management creates a sense of solidarity, initiating a process of dealienation in which competition and separation among workers are transcended, one might ask whether worker-shareholders enhance or diminish their general commitment to cooperation as a way of organizing work life over time. To tap

Table 3–14. Workers' perceptions of coworkers' capabilities (percentage answering "almost all" or "over half of them";* panel sample)

Question: "About what number of your fellow workers in this plant are capable of the following activities?"

	Cooperatives ($N = 88$)		Conventional ($N = 49$)	
	T_1	T_2	T_1	T_2
Capable of doing a good day's work	92.1	96.4	87.7	81.7
Capable of working without close supervision	80.7	73.8	77.6	65.4
Capable of being a foreman	8.0	3.4	6.3	8.4
Capable of making a positive contribution at shareholders' or union meeting	30.7	18.2	32.6	17.4
Capable of performing as a member of the board of directors or as a union officer	20.5	10.3	10.9	13.0
Capable of managing the plant	1.2	1.2	2.1	0.0

*For reasons of parsimony, only a part of the data are reported. The K.S. test shows no significant differences between cooperative and conventional workers for any of these questions.

this dimension, respondents were asked whether they would look for an another cooperative to work in if they were to leave their present enterprise. The results, reported in Table 3–15, are not only surprising; they are stunning, for 9.6 percent of worker-shareholders said they would definitely not look for another cooperative to work in at T_1; at T_2 the figure escalated to 26.8 percent. Over 60 percent at T_1 said they would not look for another co-op or that whether a firm was a co-op would not make much difference; at T_2 that figure increased to 65.8 percent. Only 34.2 percent at T_2 said that joining a cooperative would be very important to them. Clearly, they felt no lifelong commitment to cooperation as a way of life or of a stable solidarity with their fellows.

Self-Estrangement

In some sense, the issue of alienation of labor understood as estrangement from the self has already been considered in full in these pages. In the Marxian sense, self-estrangement is about separation from that which

Table 3–15. Worker-shareholders' responses as to whether they would work in another cooperative (in percentages; panel sample)

Question: "If I were to leave this company today,"

	$T_1 (N = 83)$	$T_2 (N = 82)$
I would definitely look for another cooperative to work in.	14.5	17.1
Finding another cooperative would be *one* of the most important considerations in choosing where to work.	25.3	17.1
It wouldn't make much difference to me whether or not a place was a cooperative in choosing where to work.	50.6	30.0
I would definitely *not* look for another cooperative to work in.	9.6	26.8

is fully human, considered as a set of tangible and observable social relations in production. To the extent that people are unable in production to act in ways that are rational, conscious, purposive, and social, they are unable to nurture and develop their uniquely human attributes. We have seen so far in this discussion that productive life in the producer cooperatives only partially meets these conditions.

In our discussion of alienation to this point, the main focus of attention has been the objective social relations of production and not subjective states of mind. Although occasional references have been made to worker-shareholders' interpretations of and feelings about these social relations, the discussion has focused mainly on their relationships to the commodity they produce, the complex decision-making process, the technical production process, and their peers. Even in the Marxian view, however, feeling states or subjective-psychological orientations are part and parcel of the overall concept of alienation and particularly relevant to an understanding of self-estrangement. Again, and fully cognizant of the dangers of repetition, it may be illuminating to quote Marx on this point: "In his work, therefore, [the worker] does not affirm himself but denies himself, does not feel content but unhappy, does not develop freely his physical and mental energy but mortifies his body and ruins his mind . . . labor in which man alienates himself, is a labor of self-sacrifice, of mortification" (*Economic and Philosophical Manuscripts*, quoted in Blauner 1964:27). Two general and widely accepted measures of psychological well-being were used to round out the examination of alienation and dealienation in the plywood cooperatives by considering subjective feeling states.

I begin with work satisfaction, a concept that has proved to be one of the most powerful in the social sciences for explaining the development of a wide range of attitudes, personality characteristics, and political and social behaviors. Recent research has shown work satisfaction to be a significant variable, for instance, in explaining overall judgments about life satisfaction and happiness (Andrews and Withey, 1976; Campbell, Converse, and Rodgers, 1976; Lacy, Hougland, and Shepard, 1982); work motivation and productivity (Bardo and Ross, 1982; Lawler, 1973; Locke, 1970; Mitchell, 1974; Vroom 1964); alienation (Seeman 1954, 1967, 1972); feelings of powerlessness (Duffy, Shiflett, and Downey, 1977; Tudor, 1972); the use and quality of leisure time (Kemper and Reichler, 1976); the content of central life interests (Dubin, 1956, 1979); general mental health (Gardell 1977; Kasl, 1974; Kornhauser, 1965); longevity (Palmore, 1969); and participation in nonworkplace institutions and organizations (Elden, 1981; Karasek, 1976).

The research literature is replete with alternative definitions of work satisfaction and its measurement. Following Kalleberg (1977:126), however, I take work satisfaction to be "an overall affective orientation . . . toward presently occupied work roles." I make no distinction between either intrinsic or extrinsic work satisfaction (Elden, 1981), nor do I consider the effects of specific, distinguishable aspects of work role and particular jobs on work satisfaction. I use work satisfaction as a broadly conceived affective stance toward the overall work situation. To operationalize this concept, I constructed an index of work satisfaction based on four Likert-type questions which asked plywood workers how satisfied they were with their jobs as a whole. The index, on the surface, seems to combine felt satisfaction with aspects of the job and with the place of work, but confirmatory factor analysis suggests the existence of a strong unidimensionality among the questions. The index is a simple additive one, using the following items:[18]

1. If I had it to do over again I'd probably go to work here again.
2. When I start off for work in the morning, I'm generally enthusiastic about going.
3. This plant is *not* as good a place to work as most other plants around here.
4. I get a great feeling of satisfaction from the work I am doing.

From the social relations of production in cooperatives and conventional plywood plants, one would expect that the general level of work satis-

Table 3–16. Index of work satisfaction (panel sample, mean scores; possible range of scores = 3–15)

	Cooperatives ($N = 95$)	Conventional ($N = 58$)
T_1	11.3	9.6
T_2	10.7	9.8

T_1 to T_2 change: For co-ops, t-test, mean difference scores, $p = 0.022$; for conventional firms, $p =$ n.s.

Significance of differences between cooperatives and conventional firms at T_1, one-way analysis of variance, $p = 0.0002$; at T_2, $p = 0.08$.

faction would be higher in the former. I make that claim even though, as we have already seen in this chapter, the objective conditions in the co-ops are not as fully dealienated as one might have expected. Nevertheless, and despite some serious shortcomings already noted, the co-ops remain enterprises in which the worker-shareholders, in contrast to other workers, are in control of their product and of the overall decisional processes by which production is organized. This decisional participation has already been shown by researchers to be strongly related to work satisfaction (Greenberg, 1980; Marrow, Bowers and Seashore, 1967; Morse and Reimer, 1956; Shepard, 1969).

Comparison of workers in the cooperative and conventional plants over time on the index of work satisfaction is generally consistent with these expectations, though there remain some surprises (see Table 3–16). If one compares mean scores on the index, for instance, it is evident that the worker-shareholders are generally more satisfied with their lot than are their peers in the conventional firm. Two qualifications must be added, however. First, the differences between the two groups are not very great; indeed, at T_2 the difference is not statistically significant (though it is almost so). The vast differences in the organization of work life in the two settings, as well as the prevailing literature on the subject, would lead one to expect a more marked contrast. Second, the level of work satisfaction among worker-shareholders declined significantly over time, a finding that is also contrary to expectations. The explanation might be growing disenchantment with the tedious monotony of plywood production, which is not entirely counterbalanced by decisional participation.

Work satisfaction should be examined more closely with an eye toward understanding its relationship to the special work environment of the plywood cooperatives. The first question is whether the observed differences between the cooperative and conventional firms on the index of

Table 3–17. The impact of work setting and background on work satisfaction: Dependent variable = index of work satisfaction* (1978 cross-section sample; $N = 311$)

	Beta weight	F	Probability
Work in cooperative or conventional firm	0.18	8.06	0.01
Education	0.08	1.79	n.s.
Age	0.25	23.64	0.00
Income	0.00	0.42	n.s.
Job tenure	−0.06	0.68	n.s.

*Since the purpose of this research is to explain the relative impact of cooperative and conventional forms of work/organization on a range of politically relevant dependent variables and not to explain the dependent variables themeselves, adjusted R-square values and significance levels for the regression equations are not reported.

work satisfaction hold when the effects of other independent variables are considered, that is, whether the observed differences between co-op and conventional workers is better explained by characteristics workers bring with them to the job. The most powerful and parsimonious way to address this question of the relative impacts of multiple independent variables on a dependent variable (the index of work satisfaction) is use of multiple regression and beta weights. Table 3–17 shows the results of an equation that measures the relative contribution of work setting, certain background demographic factors,[19] and time on the job.[20] The table indicates that age is the most powerful independent variable (a finding consistent with the theoretical literature), but membership in a cooperative as compared to working in a conventional plywood firm also remains significantly related to a sense of work satisfaction.[21]

Having established that the overall distinction between cooperative and conventional work settings holds even when considering the effects of other independent variables, the next question is about the way the operation of the cooperatives shapes attitudes about satisfaction. Four domains may be considered as the principal independent variables in a regression equation with the index of work satisfaction as the dependent variable. First, we know from the literature that most advocates of workplace democracy assume that the act of participation serves as the main educative instrument in the transformation of workers' attitudes and behavior. To measure the degree of decision-making participation by worker-shareholders, I use the index of co-op participation described above. We also know from the literature that work satisfaction is generally related to the supervisory climate and the workers' interpretation of that climate.

Table 3–18. Explaining work satisfaction within the cooperatives (1978 cross-section sample; $N = 164$)

	Beta	F	Significance
Index of participation	−0.05	0.36	n.s.
Friendship	0.14	3.41	0.06
Supervision	0.29	12.92	0.00
Why joined co-op:			
Good investment	0.10	1.81	n.s.
Heard workers got along	0.13	0.78	n.s.
Wanted to help run a			
company	−0.08	0.74	n.s.
Wages were good	−0.08	0.95	n.s.
Heard workers and			
supervisors got along	0.10	0.56	n.s.
Have/have not owned a			
business	0.10	0.56	n.s.

To measure this domain, I use an index of supervision based on the following two Likert-type items: (1) Does your supervisor or foreman take into account your opinions and suggestions when you make them? and (2) Do you feel that your supervisor or foreman treats you with respect?[22] It is reasonable to assume that social solidarity and friendship networks are likely to affect subjective evaluations of work. Working in an environment suffused with a strong sense of fellowship should contribute to a sense of well-being. To tap this dimension of work life, respondents were asked to rate on an ordinal scale "about how many of the people you spend time socializing with outside of working hours are people from this plant?" Finally, it is possible that working in a cooperative has no discernible effects and that the differences in satisfaction between workers in cooperative and conventional firms may be best explained through a process of self-selection. That is, people who join cooperatives may bring with them a unique set of attitudinal and behavioral attributes related to work which they retain while there. To tap this domain in the regression analysis, a series of Likert-type questions regarding motivations for first joining the cooperatives (see details concerning these questions in Chapter 2) was used. Additionally, respondents were asked whether they had ever owned a business based on the possibility that workers with an entrepreneurial interest tend to join cooperatives and that they carry with them a special attitude toward the life of work.

    Table 3–18 reports the results of the regression analysis. Expectations about the role of supervision and friendship networks are fulfilled (though

Table 3–19. Explaining T_2 work satisfaction among worker-shareholders (panel sample; $N = 66$)

	Beta	F	Significance
Work satisfaction at T_1	0.62	32.78	0.00
Index of particiption at T_1	−0.17	2.54	n.s. (0.11)
Supervision	0.11	1.01	n.s.
Friendship			
Why joined			
Good investment	0.00	0.12	n.s.
Heard workers got along	−0.02	0.10	n.s.
Wanted to help run a company	0.01	0.54	n.s.
Wages were good	0.02	0.42	n.s.
Heard workers and supervisors got along	0.03	0.20	n.s.
Have/have not owned a business	0.02	0.46	n.s.

weakly for the latter). Expectations about the role of participation are unfulfilled. Participation in co-op affairs and decision making, surprisingly, in my view, plays no significant role in worker-shareholders' sense of work satisfaction, either positively or negatively. This finding is contrary to the main drift of theoretical expectations. Finally, business background and reasons for joining a cooperative are statistically unrelated to a sense of work satisfaction. Self-selection, then, does not seem to be a factor in shaping this aspect of work attitudes.

Another regression equation was calculated to examine the factors that might be related to the change in worker-shareholders' sense of work satisfaction over time (recall that work satisfaction declined slightly but statistically significantly among worker-shareholders over the course of this study). The results are reported in Table 3–19. Work satisfaction at T_2 is best explained—not surprisingly—by work satisfaction at T_1. Participation in co-op governance plays a slight (though statistically nonsignificant) role, and supervision, friendship networks, and self-selection are not relevant at all.

My second subjective, feeling state measure of alienation understood as self-estrangement is self-esteem. Self-esteem is measured in an index constructed with the following six Likert-type questions.[23]

1. How well do you handle important decisions in your life?
2. How much respect do you feel for yourself as a person?

Table 3–20. Index of self-esteem (panel sample, mean scores; possible range of scores = 6–$N24$)

	Cooperatives (N = 85)	Conventional (N = 53)
T_1	19.51	19.04
T_2	19.07	18.68

Significance: One-way analysis of variance indicates no significant differences between co-ops and conventional categories at either T_1 or T_2. T-test of mean difference scores indicates no significant differences between T_1 and T_2 for either co-ops or conventional categories.

3. How confident do you feel about your potential for self-development in the next few years?
4. How interesting do you feel you are to other people?
5. On the whole, how satisfied are you with yourself?
6. How competent do you feel you are to do the things you're really interested in doing?

The literature of the democratic Left suggests that workplace democracy would be strongly predictive of self-esteem. Indeed, to a very great extent, it is the expected salutary effect of participation in decision making at the workplace on this aspect of mental health that motivates reformers of various political and scholarly persuasions to call for the democratic transformation of American industry (Argyris, 1965; Bachrach, 1967; Blumberg, 1973; Carnoy and Shearer, 1980; Dahl, 1970; Mason, 1982; Pateman, 1970; Sheppard and Herrick, 1972; U.S. Department of Health, Education and Welfare, 1973; Zwerdling, 1978). These almost universal expectations, however, are not met in the present study. A comparison of workers in cooperatives and conventional plywood firms on the index of self-esteem shows no differences between them and no change over time (see Table 3–20). To work in a democratically run enterprise, to determine the essential outcomes of enterprise policy collectively and in an egalitarian fashion, does not give worker-shareholders any greater feelings of self-esteem than those experienced by other workers examined in this study.[24]

Workplace Democracy and Dealienation

The achievements of the American plywood cooperatives in creating conditions for dealienation are decidedly mixed. Theoretical expectations about the linkages between workplace democracy and dealienation are largely met when considering those aspects of the Marxian concept of alienation having to do with the products of labor (choice of products, enjoyment and control of the surplus), the formal decision-making processes within the enterprise (including enterprise-level and point-of-production decisions), and felt satisfaction with work. Theoretical expectations about dealienation are radically disappointed, however, when considering issues like control over the technical division of labor, self-exploitation as seen in the terrible co-op record on safety, relationships with one's peers, and overall mental health. Taken as a whole, evidence from the plywood cooperatives seems to suggest that the linkage between workplace democracy and the process of dealienation is tenuous at best. It may well be, however, that the plywood cooperatives are not suitable cases for the scientific evaluation of that linkage. The unexpected results may be specific to the plywood industry in the United States, a nation not notable for its support of innovations in workplace democracy. Do self-managed enterprises in other societies with friendlier environments for cooperative labor do a better job than the American firms in minimizing the alienation of labor? I turn to a consideration of this question in the next chapter.

·4·

Alienation: The Comparative Record

Do self-managed enterprises in other societies do a better job than the American plywood cooperatives in minimizing the alienation of labor? To shed light on this issue and to better specify the complex linkages between workplace democracy and dealienation, this chapter considers three cases generally thought by scholars to be the most fully democratic industrial work settings in the modern world: Israeli kibbutz industry, the Yugoslav system of self-management, and the Mondragon cooperatives of Spain. I will attempt to determine whether patterns of alienation and dealienation found in the U.S. cooperatives are also evident in these diverse cases. If such patterns are found, it would suggest that my findings with regard to the American plywood cooperatives are general and enduring. If such patterns are absent, it would suggest the special and limited nature of the American case.

Several caveats are in order. First, as is true of any secondary analysis, the scholarly literature on kibbutz industry, the Yugoslav system, and Mondragon consists of information and evidence generated with other issues and questions in mind than the illumination of the Marxian concept of alienation and its permutations. The availability of data concerning product, process, self, and others, therefore, is highly uneven. As a result, I will be forced to extrapolate and infer more than I would like in making the relevant comparisons. Second, much greater attention has been paid by scholars to the kibbutz and Yugoslavian cases than to Mondragon (though there has been much activity on this front in recent years), so I will perforce have much less to say about the latter. Third, the literature on Yugoslavia and the kibbutz is so extensive that I will only report the highlights and central tendencies of that research literature.[1] Finally, although much empirical data have been collected on these three cases, the greater part of the literature remains descriptive and anecdotal in character so it must be interpreted cautiously. Nevertheless, this literature is rich, suggestive, and useful for placing the main findings of Chapter 3 in their proper context.

The Israeli kibbutz is a small, typically rural community organized on the principles of direct, participatory democracy, voluntarism, cooperation, and strict egalitarianism. It is a "total" community in the sense that work life, family life, and social life are closely integrated. It is a collective and cooperative village that, in the words of Menachem Rosner, seeks the "complete identification of the individual with the society" (1965:1). Decision making is generally face to face, leadership positions elected and rotated, and hierarchy is actively discouraged. Ultimate authority on all matters is lodged in the general assembly of all members which meets once a week, though many of the details of kibbutz life are handled by a complex network of elected committees. Industrialization of the once strictly agricultural kibbutz has been advancing rapidly in recent years (by 1980 there were more than three hundred industries among the kibbutzim with more than fifteen thousand worker-members). This industrialization has posed several problems for the kibbutz ideal that have caused widespread concern among its members, including tendencies toward dependence on hired labor, specialization, and hierarchy. Nevertheless, being acutely aware of these emergent possibilities, kibbutz members have attempted to preserve such basic principles as direct democracy and equality within their industrial plants.

The Mondragon group is a collection of more than eighty-five manufacturing cooperatives with in excess of eighteen thousand worker-members located in the Basque region of Spain. It is closely aligned with a large cooperative bank, the Caja Laboral Popular, which provides the major part of necessary financing and technical support, a cooperative educational system, housing cooperatives, and consumer cooperatives. Mondragon is organized on the principles of shared ownership, egalitarianism (a maximum three-to-one spread on wages and salaries), and democratic control on a one-person, one-vote basis. Formal authority in each of the cooperative enterprises is located in a general assembly of all members which meets once a year to decide on general enterprise policies and to elect a board of directors. Top managers are also elected; they in turn appoint middle managers and supervisors. Membership in the cooperatives allows each member to share in the enterprise surplus on the basis of wage rate and total hours worked. The Mondragon cooperatives are one of the most vigorous sectors of the Spanish economy and have enjoyed a much greater than average rate of growth and steady profitability over the years. Unlike the plywood cooperatives, the Mondragon industrial enterprises tend to be capital- rather than labor-intensive.[2]

The only nationwide system of worker-managed enterprises is found in Yugoslavia. Yugoslav leaders have stated their intention to make worker control a reality in virtually every economic enterprise in the nation. By law, overall policy in every enterprise with more than ten workers must be formulated by workers' council, which elects (and may remove) the management board and plant director. Rather than being the private property of the members, as in the U.S. plywood and Mondragon cases, each enterprise is considered social property temporarily in the care of its workers. The director and the board run the enterprise on a day-to-day basis within the overall policy guidelines set by the workers' council. The council is empowered to make policy in all areas of enterprise activity (product lines, financial planning, technological innovation, marketing, and so on) including the division of the surplus into bonuses for members, investment, and modernization. In very large enterprises, smaller units of direct democracy exist at what is called the level of the "working unit." Each of these working units is relatively autonomous, runs its own affairs, and elects delegates to the workers' council of the entire enterprise.

The literature on these comparative cases can inform us about the linkage between workplace democracy and dealienation and enable us to draw conclusions about the generality or particularity of the U.S. plywood cooperatives.

Estrangement from Product

Control over what is produced and over the disposition of the surplus realized in the market is, within certain constraints peculiar to each of the societies in question, located in the hands of the direct producers. Alienation from product is therefore transcended in each of them. These enterprises are not, of course, entirely free agents, operating without restraints or limiting conditions. All of them must respond to market signals if they are to remain viable as economic institutions and to be able to create a surplus for their membership.[3] All must pay taxes and be sensitive to government regulations and guidelines. All must attend to the wishes of other powerful social institutions, whether it be banks, the League of Communists, the commune government, or the unions in Yugoslavia; the Caja Laboral Popular and the Catholic church in Mondragon; or the kibbutz federations, the Labour Alliance, and Jewish National Fund in Israel. In the choice of products and in the control of the surplus realized in the sale of products, the decisions of each of the enterprises under consideration are constrained. Nevertheless, workers within the enterprise may be said to have transcended that form of alienation from product that is typical of wage labor in capitalism. The constraints they suffer are no different, in the main, from those suffered by the owners and managers of privately held businesses and corporations.

Although the similarities regarding alienation from product is the main point here, there are some interesting differences that are worthy of note. In the kibbutz, for instance, although worker-members in the industrial branches run their own day-to-day affairs, basic decision about whether to establish an industrial plant in the first place, what product lines to pursue, what forms of technology and labor to employ, how to distribute and use the surplus, and who should be appointed manager are made by the general assembly of kibbutz members. Workers in the industrial branch are voting members of the general assembly, of course, and their positions on plant issues carry much weight in the assembly's deliberations. Nonetheless, their control over the product is neither direct nor total.

The kibbutz is only partly a profit-seeking community because the market and the search for profit have not come to dominate the industrialization process in the kibbutz. As industrialization moves forward, the preservation of central kibbutz values retains priority. To be sure, in the beginning, industrialization was all too frequently accompanied by tendencies toward specialization, hierarchy, and the use of hired labor. In recent years, however, greater attention has been paid and much has been done to reverse these tendencies. Product lines and technologies have been consciously selected and new organizational forms have been invented to encourage rotation of managerial roles, enhance the autonomy of the work force, and decrease dependence on wage labor. Each of the three kibbutz federations has agreed that its member kibbutzim would not be allowed to start any new industry for which they could not supply labor from among their own membership (Fine, 1973:258). Menachem Rosner reports that the kibbutz movement in recent years has become strongly committed "to a choice of industrial technologies that are more responsive to the human, work related aspirations of kibbutz members" (Rosner, 1984:11).

In the Mondragon cooperative, the disposition of the annual surplus is not entirely open to the wishes of its membership. Under the organizational guidelines of the movement, 10 to 15 percent of the profits of each firm is mandated for the Mondragon community as a whole (mainly for social programs and educational institutions), 15 to 20 percent is directed toward a reserve fund for the firm, and the remainder is mandated for a co-op operating fund in which each worker holds a share.[4] These contributions to the operating fund are treated as loans from the worker-members, who receive a minimum of 6 percent interest on their accounts, which they may withdraw upon leaving or at retirement.

Estrangement from Process: Decision Making

At a formal level, worker-members of Mondragon and Yugoslav industrial enterprises are in complete control of their enterprises and worker-members of kibbutz enterprises are indirectly, if strongly, in control through the plant assembly and their participation in the kibbutz general assembly. Worker-members in all three cases may be considered the active subjects of their work lives rather than the objects of persons, institutions, and forces beyond their control. All are free to decide all policies concerning the enterprise.[5] All are, therefore, in a formal sense, objectively unalienated with respect to control over decision-making in their work lives. Strikes in Yugoslavia and at Mondragon demonstrate that the actual state of the social relations of production are not as clear-cut (Johnson and Whyte, 1976; Jovanov, 1971; Thomas and Logan, 1982; Oakeshott, 1973; Pateman, 1970; Shabad, 1978). Although the incidence rates and duration of strikes are dramatically lower than in the industrial capitalist countries, their very existence suggests that worker-members of theoretically self-governing institutions do not exercise the level of control articulated in the formal rules of governance.

At Mondragon, despite their formal organization as cooperatives, almost all of the industrial enterprises are organized and operate along the lines specified by conventional modern management theory and "Taylorite"-oriented industrial engineering. Almost all of them operate on a day-to-day basis as conventional top-down organizations with managers as givers and workers as takers of orders. The top manager and the board of directors are elected annually by the worker-members, but the remainder of the management and supervisory staff is appointed by top management and acts very much like managers and supervisors everywhere (Johnson and Whyte, 1976:188). One reason for the absence of more direct influence from the rank and file is that the general assembly meets only once a year (as compared to once a week on the kibbutz). At this meeting, moreover, the agenda is largely controlled by management. Opposition to management has few resources at its disposal and has traditionally found it difficult to organize and present an alternative set of policies or to create a political coalition capable of carrying the day. Management control is so complete that, once in office, it alone is responsible for job evaluation, job design, and formulation of pay standards. The elected Social Council has only advisory powers and is seen by most worker-members as a one-way communications arm of management (Johnson and Whyte, 1976:189).[6]

Opportunities for participation are few and far between at Mondragon amounting, in the end, to little more than plebiscite-style elections once a year to approve or disapprove the current leadership team. It is little wonder, then, that most empirical studies show a marked absence of a participatory culture at Mondragon: few worker-members ever speak at the annual assembly, few are informed, and few have any contacts with management (Thomas and Logan, 1982:183), though they *feel* closer to management than do workers in conventional enterprises in the Basque region (Bradley and Gelb, 1985a).

Participation in Yugoslav self-managed firms is much higher, it seems, than at Mondragon, though there are no directly comparative data. The existence of strikes again suggests that less than complete decision-making power is in the hands of the worker-members. Nevertheless, there are at least three features of the Yugoslav system that give it a participatory edge over Mondragon. First, there is the existence and the occasional use of the "recall" against management, the managing board, and the workers' council. Second, the locus of many important decisions in recent years has been radically decentralized to the level of the work unit at which most point-of-production decisions are made. Third, members of the workers' council continue to hold their production jobs in the plant, ensuring the existence of two-way communication. The machinery is in place in Yugoslavia, it would seem, for a lively participatory institutional life. Whether actual participation matches this potential, whether existing forms of participation are authentic, and whether the system is moving away from or toward the ideal as specified by Yugoslav doctrine is another matter. The evidence is mixed and the jury remains out on all of these issues (Dunn and Obradovic, 1978:16–17). The research literature is in agreement on a number of points, however. First, participation in the self-management system is highly biased toward the educated, the skilled, and the white-collared. Such groups are likely to participate in the selection of the workers' council, to serve on the council, and to exercise influence at all levels of decision making (Baumgartner, Burns, and Sekulic, 1979; Comisso, 1979; Hunnius 1973:299; Obradovic, 1978; Obradovic and Dunn, 1978; Rus, 1965, 1978; Zupanov, 1972). The literature is also generally agreed that the manager and the technical staff exercise more influence than any other institution or set of individuals in Yugoslav enterprises, including the workers' council and the councils of work units. Influence is from the top down, not the bottom up. Proposals originate at the management level. The workers' council reacts to proposals. Discussion in meetings is dominated by the managerial and technical staff. Milos Vejnovic, in summarizing this literature, says that the "results of research demonstrate that the distribution of influence is unconditionally oligarchical, even autocratic" (1978).[7] It is not surprising, then, to see in Yugoslavia an increase in the incidence of strikes and a higher participation rate in strikes by production workers (Jovanov, 1971). The relative powerlessness of workers is demonstrated by the members of the councils and the management board often joining the strikers (Jovanov, 1971).

Participation in the Yugoslav system of self-management, then, is not as great as it seems on the surface. To a degree often not recognized in the vast laudatory literature on Yugoslavia, work life is controlled by others. Nevertheless, two important qualifications to this observation can be made. First, the shortcomings of democratic decision making in Yugoslavia are apparent mainly in regard to workers' own hopes and aspirations; compared to industrial workers in the Western capitalist countries, their system is a model of democratic participation. It has been estimated, for instance, that in any given year since 1951, an average of 15 to 20 percent of industrial workers has participated in some self-managing activity (Dunn and Obradovic, 1978:11). Second, the Yugoslavs themselves are acutely aware of the gap between ideal and reality and have been making serious efforts to narrow its size. Since the constitutional changes in 1974, there has been a reemphasis on socialist norms and values, especially those of participation and equality, and a restructuring of institutions to encourage their practice. Most important were the attempts to "dehierarchize" enterprises through the introduction of "basic units of associated labor'' (BOAL) with broad powers over the organization of production and of health and social services; to increase blue-collar and unskilled representation on workers' councils; and to give the reconstituted workers' council access to better technical and business services, thereby enabling them to deal more effectively with management as equals (Baumgartner, Burns, and Sekulic, 1979; Comisso, 1979).

The dealienation of labor, understood as the process whereby the direct producers gain control of enterprise decision making, is not as far advanced at Mondragon, in the U.S. plywood cooperatives, and in Yugoslav self-managed enterprises as one might have predicted based on their formal rules of organization and procedure. In the Israeli kibbutz, however, the reality of democratic, egalitarian participation very nearly matches theoretical aspirations.[8] The typical factory on an Israeli kibbutz is organized so as to integrate it into the overall kibbutz community and to attempt to ensure equality and democracy within it. The factory is run by a director, elected by the kibbutz general assembly, and by a plant management board composed of the director, the chair of the worker assembly, other rank-and-file representatives elected by the assembly, and elected kibbutz officers. The kibbutz general assembly sets overall factory policies very often on the recommendation of the worker assembly and plant management committee. Ordinary rank-and-file workers enjoy multiple avenues of influence both within the factory and within the kibbutz community of which they are members. With the exception of the plant director, all managerial and supervisory positions within the plant are elected by the plant assembly and rotated. Kibbutz worker-members, furthermore, are highly educated and technically trained. Deference to a higher office is nearly nonexistent. Plant management cannot hire, fire, promote, or punish worker-members. The result is the virtual absence of a permanent managerial and technical elite capable of exercising independent control or undermining rank-and-file power.

Although some scholars suggest a tendency toward the growth of inequality, specialization, and hierarchy in the production branches of the kibbutz (Stryjan, 1983), the overwhelming weight of the evidence suggests that the kibbutz has adjusted to industrialization while keeping its central values intact. Research by Arnold Tannenbaum and his associates demonstrates that the kibbutz, as compared to other factory settings including those of the United States and Yugoslavia, enjoys very high levels of rank-and-file participation in decision making, egalitarian relations between workers and supervisors, rapid advancement on the job, and work commitment unrelated to monetary rewards (Tannenbaum, 1974). In the most extensive empirical examination of kibbutz industry extant in the literature, Uri Leviatan and Menachem Rosner demonstrate that the percentage of hired labor in kibbutz production branches has been diminishing, top leadership positions continue to rotate freely,[9] rank-and-file participation in factory assembly and general assembly remain impressively high, first-line supervisors continue to engage in production work, and an impressively high percentage of worker-members hold plant and kibbutz offices or serve on plant and kibbutz committees (Leviatan and Rosner, 1982; also see Palgi and Rosner, 1983).[10] The most important point, perhaps, is that any tendencies toward hierarchy, inequality, and specialization in kibbutz industry are counterbalanced by the rich participatory, democratic, and egalitarian life of the kibbutz community. If minor inequalities of power and prestige appear in the plant, they cannot be reproduced in the larger kibbutz community; that is, inequalities are noncumulative.

Estrangement from Process: The Work

One of the most important and surprising findings reported in Chapter 3 is that worker self-management in the U.S. plywood cooperatives has failed to make a dent in alienation understood as the minute division of labor. Work in the cooperatives remains boring, relentless, and dangerous. The technical process of production seems to the worker-shareholders to be inevitable and beyond human control. Work in the plywood cooperatives is no different than work in privately owned and hierarchically managed plywood plants. Although very little empirical data directed to these issues exist in the literature, much the same conclusion appears warranted with regard to Yugoslavia and the Mondragon cooperatives.

The Mondragon cooperatives nicely demonstrate that formal ownership by workers does not necessarily mean workers' control of production. At Mondragon workers exercise little control over technical production. At the task and work group levels, in particular, workers are objects of the production process, no different from workers without ownership rights. Mondragon has, from the beginning, been strictly organized and operated along the lines of established industrial engineering principles and scientific management. The result, in addition to the exercise of control from the top, has been an extreme division of labor, mechanized, assembly-line operations with little regard for human needs, and extensive routinization (Johnson and Whyte, 1976:188; Keynes, 1982:83). After a series of strikes at Ulgar, the largest industrial cooperative in the Mondragon group, plant managers began a belated but nonetheless real program of job enrichment. The assembly line in a handful of plants has been eliminated; quality circles have been introduced and have been growing in number since 1979; autonomous work groups have been formed at others. Despite these efforts at improvement, however, the work remains surprisingly dehumanized at Mondragon (Thomas and Logan, 1982:68, 70).[11]

Similar conclusions can be made for Yugoslavia. Mihailo Markovic, one of the leading students of the Yugoslav self-management system, has observed that "in Yugoslav society, we dream of developing productive forces, raising productivity, raising the national income per capita, assuring a higher standard of living, but hardly any thought is given to the humanization of work or, if you like, raising the quality of working life" (Cherns, 1982:2780). Veljko Rus, another leading student of the system, points out that scientific management has always been central to the Yugoslav conception (1975:102). Ellen Comisso makes the same point in her important study *Workers' Control under Plan and Market*, suggesting that this course of development was consciously chosen by the nation's leadership and was not an unanticipated by-product of industrialization: "Workers' councils were not established as an alternative to the division of labor. Rather than eliminating the highly specialized character of modern technology and labor, workers' councils, in the eyes of Yugoslav leaders, were to be mechanisms through which the workers themselves were expected to adopt and perfect a more rationalized and narrower division of labor" (1979:55). The results of this international approach to industrial organization are entirely predictable: a rapid advance in the minute division of labor and the further separation of the functions in production of hand and brain (Baumgartner, Burns, and Sekulic, 1979; Comisso, 1979:150–53).

The Israeli kibbutz seems to be the exception that proves the rule.[12] Unlike Mondragon, where the cooperatives were founded to revitalize a depressed region of Spain, and Yugoslavia, where self-management was part of a strategy for rapid economic growth and national autonomy, the Israeli kibbutz was envisioned from the beginning as a place in which to establish an entirely new and nonalienating form of work. These aspirations, not always fulfilled, of course, have been nicely summarized by Menachem Rosner:

For the kibbutz the quality of working life is not limited to improving working conditions or increasing work satisfaction. The desire to improve the quality of working life is part of an overall desire for a *liberated labor*. Liberation means overcoming all forms of alienation which modern society inflicts on working man through technological systems of work, bureaucratic organization and the status of one who must sell his labour. Overcoming alienation within the kibbutz framework should open the way to full actualization of the worker's abilities in all areas of life and the constant development of his talents. [1982:132]

Such aspirations are perhaps impossible to achieve, yet the kibbutz seems to come close. Although the nature of work is not unproblematic in kibbutz industry, work alienation and its alleviation are of constant concern to kibbutz members because work "has a social and collective meaning, not mainly one that is economic" (Blasi, 1978:197). This concern is expressed in constant job rotation within plants and between plants and other production branches, the deliberate pacing of work so as to overcome its relentless quality (Blasi, 1978:192–93), and, most important, the deliberate selection of product lines and technical processes that will maximize the development of human capacities. The latter is often forced upon the kibbutz by a desire not to use hired labor from outside of the kibbutz and by the necessity of persuading a highly trained and educated work force to work in industrial plants in an entirely voluntary setting. Social pressure and collective commitments play a role, of course, but making the work itself attractive is a strategy that most kibbutzim follow with great care. The assembly line and the minute division of labor have not been eliminated, but their elimination is a central goal of the kibbutz movement and strenuous efforts have been and are being made to substitute capital-intensive industrial processes that use a full range of human knowledge and skill. That the kibbutz often falls short is less important, it seems to me, than its impressive efforts in this area.

Estrangement from Others

In the U.S. plywood cooperatives a strong sense of community, deep commitment to cooperation as a way of life, and confidence in one's fellows were notably absent. The same cannot be said for the other cases under consideration. At Mondragon, there is evidence, for instance, that worker-members feel that they belong to a community in which they take great pride. Thomas and Logan report that worker-members have a high degree of trust for their fellows, hope that their children will work in a cooperative some day, and, despite the largely unfulfilling qualities of the production process, come to work each day in much higher proportions than workers in privately owned companies (Thomas and Logan, 1982:49, 183, 189). Other researchers point to the very low turnover at Mondragon despite alternative employment opportunities and the commitment to co-operation over profit maximization when considering whether to start a new company (Johnson and Whyte, 1976:187, 195).

There is also scattered yet suggestive evidence that a sense of community and solidarity exists in Yugoslavian self-managed enterprises. Tannenbaum and his associates report that Yugoslav workers are highly sensitive and attentive to the opinions of peers in the workplace (Tannenbaum et al., 1974:73, 84). Howard Wachtel demonstrates that wage differentials in plants are very narrow and that Yugoslav workers evince strong support for an egalitarian reward structure (1973). Comisso summarizes a wide range of research findings on this subject by concluding that the sense of solidarity, commitment, and community among Yugoslav workers, though falling far short of theoretical aspirations and expectations, is nevertheless impressive (1979:61–64).

Not surprisingly, the strongest sense of solidarity and community may be found in the kibbutz. The kibbutz is organized as a total community in which work, family, and social life are integrated and people join and choose to remain members voluntarily. These communities are small in size; operate on an informal, face-to-face basis; and are almost entirely egalitarian. They are the only successful and enduring case in the world that organizes all of life on the principle "from each according to his ability; to each according to his need." The sense of community and solidarity is strong. The evidence is impressive and almost too extensive to cite: it includes the cohesiveness and mutual loyalties of kibbutz units in the armed forces; the extensiveness of friendship and acquaintance networks; rejection of competition with one's peers; age peer solidarity; commitment to the kibbutz as a chosen way of life; high morale and life satisfaction; involvement in community and workplace decision making; and more (see among others Blais, 1979; Elon, 1981; Fine, 1973; Leviatan and Rosner, 1982; Palgi and Rosner, 1983; Rosner, 1981, 1982; Tannenbaum et al., 1974). I must reiterate the central point: the kibbutz is a solidaristic community in which all aspects of life are integrated and done in relationship to others. Since it is voluntaristic, moreover, those who fail to become integrated into the community and satisfied with its lifestyle invariably leave the kibbutz.

Self-Estrangement

Like many other aspects of alienation considered in Chapter 3, my investigations of the effects of self-management on self-estrangement showed very mixed results. It was evident that worker-shareholders in the U.S. plywood cooperatives were slightly more satisfied with work than their peers in a conventional mill, but no significant differences between them were found on the measures of self-esteem or general mental health. Similar overall assessments regarding Mondragon and Yugoslavia are difficult if not impossible to make because the research findings available in English are so slim. Nevertheless, some findings are worthy of note. In studies at Mondragon conducted by both management and outside researchers, worker-members have been shown to feel more satisfied with work than workers in firms outside of the cooperatives, although the differences are not great (Johnson and Whyte, 1976:187; Thomas and Logan, 1982:189). Moreover, absenteeism and turnover are very low in all of the Mondragon cooperatives, suggesting, at least indirectly, that the level of work satisfaction there is higher than the norm in the Basque region. Arnold Tannenbaum and his associates found very little difference in work satisfaction between Yugoslav workers and those in other industrial nations. They also report that the patterning of work satisfaction in Yugoslavia is best explained in terms of opportunities "to use one's ideas and skills, to learn new things and to set the pace of one's work" (Tannenbaum et al., 1974:133), suggesting that participation in decision making might be less important than technical processes of production in determining levels of satisfaction. Similarly, Obradovic reports extensive work alienation in Yugoslavia tied, in particular, to work in mechanized and automated industries (1970). There is almost no research literature available in English about self-esteem or general mental health in the Mondragon and Yugoslav cooperatives that would allow us to reach definitive conclusions.[13] Nevertheless, what there is is quite interesting and suggestive. Tannenbaum and his associates report that Yugoslav workers, as compared to workers in the other nations in their study, score surprisingly high on measures of depression, resentment, and lack of self-esteem (Tannenbaum, 1974:157). The authors also measure what they call self-estrangement in their study by asking respondents whether they feel that they have an opportunity to use their true abilities: Yugoslav workers, by a wide margin over workers in Italy, Austria, the United States, and Israel, feel the absence of such opportunities (Tannenbaum, 1974:160–62). At Mondragon, Bradley and Gelb report lower levels of estrangement than in conventional capitalist firms (1985a).

Once again the most impressive results are found in Israeli kibbutz industry. These results should not come as a great surprise for the kibbutz movement has consciously and conscientiously directed a major portion of its attention and efforts to the creation of conditions conducive to dealienation understood in terms of mental health. Central to this commitment has been the desire to create the all-around person in the sense of Marx's familiar "hunter, fisherman, and philosopher." To further that objective, and because the abundant leisure time created by the high productivity of collective, cooperative, and egalitarian labor makes it possible, the kibbutz movement has always tried to provide its members with rich and diverse activities, including sports, education, political participation, and culture, as well as democracy in the workplace, which might allow them to overcome the separation of hand and brain, of physical and mental production. Close observation of this way of life moved Jean-Paul Sartre to observe: "On the kibbutz I found the realization of the vision which Marx once expressed—that the day would come when the difference between the man who labors with his hands and the intellectuals would disappear. We saw in the kibbutz farmers who are one and the same time intellectuals and workers. They are shepherds and are informed in literature, sociology and politics" (Goldy, 1977:15).[14]

This observation is strongly if less eloquently supported by the available empirical research literature on mental health in the kibbutz. In a study of a single kibbutz, Joseph Blasi reports remarkably high levels of work satisfaction even among those who, because of the practice of rotation, are not working in the field for which they were trained (1979:224–26). This finding of high satisfaction is generally confirmed for a wide range of kibbutz workers by other research reports (Lindenfeld and Rothschild-Whitt, 1982:48). Tannenbaum and his associates report, moreover, that the satisfaction gap between managers and workers in kibbutz industry is narrower than in any other country in their study (1974:132); other research demonstrates higher satisfaction among worker-members than among managers and supervisors, which is highly unusual (Yuchtman, 1983:186).

There is more evidence to suggest dealienation in the kibbutz. From the perspective of an American, the virtual absence of crime in general and violent crime in particular is striking.[15] Blasi points out that the kibbutz movement does not keep very sophisticated crime statistics and then examines possible reasons: "When one homicide occurs in a population of 100,000 persons in fifty years the reason is obvious. Crimes are petty in nature and social events which occupy the realm of gossip and speculation for months or even years. There is no police force" (1978:402).[16]

There were only four admissions to mental hospitals in forty years on the kibbutz studied by Blasi (1978:403). Tannenbaum and his associates report results that suggest why this might be representative of the general situation among kibbutzim: member-workers in kibbutz industries outscore workers from all nations in their study by a considerable margin on measures of overall psychological adjustment and self-esteem and score the lowest on their measure of self-estrangement. The available evidence is unambiguous. Although mental health problems have not disappeared from the kibbutz and kibbutz industry, the kibbutz community has traveled a considerable distance on this part of the road to dealienation. No other work setting of which I am aware anywhere in the world can make such claim.

Conclusion

I return to the question raised at the beginning of Chapter 3: does the democratization of the workplace set in motion a process of dealienation that reverses estrangement from product, process, self, and others? The evidence presented in this and the previous chapter suggests that a simple, straightforward answer is not warranted and that a particular sensitivity to a historically specific context is inescapable. The specific linkage between workplace democracy and dealienation seems to be dependent not only upon the specific form of workplace democracy but upon the political, cultural, ideological, and economic setting within which democratic workplaces operate. It remains inescapably the case that self-management in the U.S. plywood cooperatives, at Mondragon, and in Yugoslavia has fewer beneficial effects on the diminution of alienation than is conventionally assumed by advocates of the democratic reform of the workplace.

The most powerful effects of workplace democracy on dealienation, apparent in all of the cases examined in these two chapters, are those having to do with control over the product and the surplus realized after its sale, formal decision-making processes concerning the enterprise, and work satisfaction. Without exception, each of the self-managed enterprises or systems reviewed in these pages has made solid advances in these areas. People working within them appear to have moved a great distance away from the alienated state of most industrial workers. It would not be unreasonable to conclude, at least tentatively, that workplace democracy, in most places and at most times, will likely enhance worker control over the product and the formal decision-making process and will make workers more satisfied with their work situation. Workplace democracy, in and of itself, however, seems unable significantly to alter those aspects of alienation having to do with the tyranny of the technical production process, the persistence of hierarchy and specialization, the lack of community and solidarity, and stunted mental health. In this respect, then, one must conclude that workplace democracy is an important but limited instrument of dealienation and that the theoretical expectations of the democratic Left are severely disappointed.

Limited does not mean totally ineffectual, however. It does mean that if workplace democracy is to fulfill the high hopes of its advocates, it must be practiced, as the Israeli kibbutz vividly demonstrates (and which shows great signs of promise at Mondragon), in a larger participatory democratic, egalitarian, and nonhierarchical environment suffused with an ideology committed to community and the development of the whole person. Such an environment is most certainly absent in the case of the U.S. plywood cooperatives and helps to explain the disappointing results found in them.

· 5 ·

Participation in Normal Politics

In this chapter, I test some of the claims that have been made about the possible contributions of workplace democracy to a revitalized and enriched democratic political life. In an age of growing cynicism and declining interest in American politics, some have suggested that the democratic workplace might be an educational setting in which people could become familiar with forms of social interaction more appropriate to genuine democracy than those in the distant, impersonal, and highly abstract system of electoral, representative politics that characterizes our society. Direct democracy in the workplace, participation in decisions that are close and meaningful to those involved, in this view, might help to foster values and skills that make participants more knowledgeable, interested, and socially responsible citizens in the political arena outside of the workplace and advocates for a richer and more profound form of political democracy. In this chapter, I examine these claims in light of empirical materials gathered in the worker-owned plywood cooperatives of the Pacific-Northwest.

Participatory and Workplace Democracy

Claims about the salutary effects of workplace democracy made by the democratic Left are, of course, derived from the larger historical tradition of participatory democracy. Indeed, the interest in workplace democracy that surfaced during the past several decades was but a small part of the vital resurgence of participatory democracy as an issue in the 1960s and

1970s in all the industrialized countries. In virtually every European country, for instance, schemes for worker control of industry, consumer participation in business decisions, and local community involvement in major economic and social policy making have been proposed, advanced, and seriously debated in recent years. The demand for participatory democracy was an integral part of the May 1968 workers' and students' strikes in France, the factory seizures and industrial strikes in northern Italy in the early 1970s, the Portuguese revolution, and the various anti-Soviet revolts in Hungary, Poland, and Czechoslovakia over the years. In our own country, the attraction of direct democracy proved compelling to the New Left of the 1960s (see the "Port Huron" statement of the Students for a Democratic Society), and the civil rights movement in particular, and continues to demonstrate its appeal in the present proliferation of "grassroots associations" directed toward issues as diverse as housing and neighborhood revitalization, utility rates, energy development, health care delivery, social and sexual discrimination, services for senior citizens, a nuclear freeze, tax reform, and environmental pollution.

In the participatory democratic tradition, the practice of direct, face-to-face deliberation and decision making is understood to be the essential core of democratic society for it is thought that only through such intimate and continuous involvement the people may be said to rule. To proponents of such a view, as political scientist Ronald Mason points out, the term "participatory democracy" is redundant in the sense that participation is the fundamental element of democracy and, without direct participation, democracy cannot be said to exist (1982:30).[1]

Advocates of participatory democracy vary widely about why such a form of social intercourse is desirable. To Martin Buber and Hannah Arendt, the desire to form genuine human communities characterized by fraternity, egalitarian social relations, and widespread popular deliberation has been one of the primary aspirations of human beings throughout their history and, as such, represents an expression of human nature (Arendt, 1965; Buber, 1949). Similarly, to Yugoslav social theorist Branko Horvat, participatory democracy is the most desirable form of political life because it is an expression of the most basic human needs. Following a long line of thinkers from Karl Marx to Abraham Maslow, Horvat claims that human beings are creatures who strive for self-actualization, which, in turn, can be attained only through processes of engagement and participation (1982:420). To many other thinkers, direct, participatory democracy is the form of governance which best allows the full development and flowering of human capacities.[2] Thus Carole Pateman argues that participatory democracy is to be preferred not only because it results in better decisions—to the extent that it incorporates a wider range of preferences and information—but because it develops the social and political capacities of each individual (1970:43). Philosopher John Stuart Mill preferred such a form of governance because of its great and salutary influence on the human mind, particular its nurturance of virtue and intellect ([1861] 1958). As political scientist Peter Bachrach, a modern proponent of this position, puts the issue: "Man's development as a human being is closely dependent upon his opportunity to contribute to the solution of problems relating to his own actions" (1967:99). To many others, finally, such a form of political society is an end in itself, requiring no elaborate justification, for it helps define the very nature of the good life and the good society. Thus, in the words of democratic theorist Robert Dahl, "the freedom to help determine, in cooperation with others, the laws and rules that one must obey . . . and the right to govern oneself in conjunction with others is a fundamental first principle and the most basic of human rights" (1985:5).

Workplace democracy, in the view of most of the advocates of participatory democracy, is an essential component of this form of democracy. Participatory democracy at the national level, it is generally argued, requires a participatory society at its base, a society filled with associations in which members are directly and fully engaged in self-governance. To be sure, more limited conceptualizations of industrial democracy exist. To Robert Dahl, for example, industrial democracy has an important role to play in taming the power of giant corporations.[3] Peter Bachrach, after arguing for the contribution that direct democracy can make to human growth and enhanced self-esteem, yet reluctantly acknowledging that critics of this form are largely correct in asserting its impossibility in the political system as a whole, turns to the democratization of the workplace as an imperfect and limited alternative (1967:chap. 7). Modern theorists of industrial democracy such as Carole Pateman and G. D. H. Cole, however, have posited this institutional form as a necessary instrument for the enrichment of democratic citizenship, as a vehicle for teaching those skills, attitudes, and behaviors most appropriate to a fully democratic society. Through the practice of democratic social relations at places of work, it is suggested, people gain the confidence, knowledge, and perspectives that enable them to be effective citizens at the national level. The more they are involved in local participatory forms, the more imbued they become with citizenship attributes. Furthermore, the experience of direct participation in workplace decision making helps people to transcend mere private interest and to expand their sympathies to include others. In the practice of the arts of democratic citizenship in everyday life, it is argued that individuals come to learn to reconcile the private and public interest.[4] Carole Pateman puts the issue in its most convincing form:

> The theory of participatory democracy is built round the central assertion that individuals and their institutions cannot be considered in isolation from one another. The existence of representative institutions at the national level is not sufficient for democracy; for maximum participation by all the people at that level, socialization, or "social training," for democracy must take place in other spheres in order that the necessary individual attitudes and psychological qualities can be developed. This development takes place through the process of participation itself. The major function of participation in the theory of participatory democracy is therefore an educative one, educative in the very widest sense, including both the psychological aspect and the gaining of practice in democratic skills and procedures. [1970:42]

Specifying the Claims about the Political Effects of Workplace Democracy

It is thus generally argued that participatory democracy requires a participatory society at its base. It is further argued by most theorists that workplace democracy is among the most important component parts of a fully participatory society. A few theorists, including Pateman and Mason, consider workplace democracy the single most important element of such a participatory democratic society. To Pateman, "it seems clear . . . that the argument of the participatory theory of democracy that an individual's (politically relevant) attitudes will depend to a large extent on the authority structure of his work environment is a well-founded one" (1970:53). To Mason, the world of work and the world of government and politics are proximate, and the learning experienced in the former is naturally and easily transferred to the latter: "The workplace has more than its presence in adult life . . . recommending it as the *key* community linked to government. Participation in the workplace provides an organized social setting that approximates government in terms of its interaction patterns . . . participation in the workplace is likely to approximate participation in government in terms of the mode, quality, and even intensity of participation" (1982:48–85).

Is workplace democracy, in fact, a school for self-governance? Do people in such settings become better candidates for operating in a fully democratic political life by concretely practicing the arts of democracy in their everyday lives? Are people who are so engaged likely to be not only "pleased" as in "satisfied" with work but "empowered" by their participatory experiences?[5] I shall attempt to answer these questions by using the data from the plywood cooperatives to address four specific claims made by advocates of participatory democracy that workplace democracy encourages participation in other social institutions outside of the workplace; helps create citizens who are endowed with a sense of their own political efficacy; increases participation in normal democratic political life; and creates a sense of political community and cooperation as well as a commitment to the public interest.

Workplace Democracy and Participation in Other Social Institutions

Participation, it is generally argued, is habit-forming. Participation in one social setting—in this case, the workplace—tends to encourage participation in other settings. Much as exercise develops the body and whets the appetite for more exercise, so the practice of democracy develops the aptitude and taste for more democracy. Enjoying the vigorous practices of democratic participation in one association, people are prone, it is suggested, to seek democratic participation in other associations. Much empirical evidence in the literature supports this claim. Menachem Rosner finds that the participatory experience of the Israeli kibbutz encourages widespread participation in other Israeli and kibbutz federation associations outside of one's own kibbutz (1981). Stephen Smith, in a recent study using fifty-five U.S. firms, shows that decision-making participation within the firm is strongly related to participation in community political affairs (1985). Ronald Mason reviews a range of empirical research in American industry and clearly demonstrates a positive relationship between increased participation in the workplace and increased participation in community organizations (1982:100–101). J. Maxwell Elden demonstrates that the level of self-determination and self-governance at work is strongly associated with a more active social life, a finding that holds for all countries studied. He concludes that "the results of the research study reported here and all other empirical evidence which has become available since Pateman (1970) validate her contention that a democratically designed work environment induces the development of the type of political

Table 5–1. Workers' regular attendance at the meetings of organizations (in percentages; 1978 cross-section sample)

Number of organizations	Cooperatives	Conventional
0	47	26
1	40	48
2	10	20
3	3	6
4	0	0

p (K.S.) = 0.01.

resources necessary for participation in and beyond the workplace'' (1981:55).

Worker-shareholders in the plywood cooperatives do *not* fulfill theoretical expectations in this regard. When compared with workers in a conventional plywood mill, worker-shareholders were significantly less likely to participate in the activities of organizations outside of the workplace. Table 5–1 reports the number of organizations for which respondents in the cross-section sample said they regularly attended meetings.[6] That 47 percent of worker-shareholders reported participation in no organizations is particularly noteworthy.[7] Over time, however, as reported in Table 5–2, worker-shareholders significantly increased their level of participation in outside organizations and reached parity with workers in conventional firms. Although this change is encouraging, it does not meet the high hopes found in the theoretical literature that work in a democratic setting as compared to work in a hierarchical-authoritarian setting will result in a participatory spillover effect into a wide range of other organizations.

Although the overall dimension of participation by worker-shareholders in organizations outside of the workplace is somewhat disappointing, the explanation for the increase in such participation over time is perfectly consistent with the expectations of proponents of participatory democracy. The results of a regression equation with outside organizational participation at T_2 as dependent variable and outside organizational participation

Table 5–2. Workers' regular attendance at the meetings of organizations (mean number; panel sample)

	Cooperatives	Conventional	K.S. significance of difference between co-op and conventional
T_1	0.63	1.06	< 0.000
T_2	0.96	0.96	n.s.

Table 5-3. The impact of co-op participation on the change in organizational involve-ment for worker-shareholders (panel sample)*

Independent variables[†]	Beta	F	Significance
Mean number attended at T_1	0.55	28.99	0.000
Index of co-op participation at T_1	-0.29[‡]	6.70	0.012

*Regression equation where dependent variable = mean number of organizations whose meetings respondent regularly attends at T_2.

[†]All other independent variables measuring supervisory climate, social networks, and self-selection are statistically nonsignificant.

[‡]The index of co-op participation has the peculiar quality of relating low participation to high scores and high participation to low scores. This accounts for the negative Beta weight.

at T_1, index of co-op participation, supervisory climate, social networks, and self-selection (for explication of the latter three domains see the discussion of work satisfaction in Chapter 3) as independent variables is summarized in Table 5-3. We see that active involvement in co-op political affairs serves as an instrument of education for involvement outside the walls of the firm. Rather than distracting from outside involvement, democratic activity in the firm does serve to enhance democratic citizenship away from work.

Workplace Democracy and Political Efficacy

Theorists of participatory democracy have long assumed that participation in decision making at work enhances the confidence of individuals in the world of politics beyond the factory door; that is, participation helps to shape what might be called the democratic character. John Stuart Mill, for instance, believed that political participation, as well as the prerequisites for political participation on the national level—knowledge, interest, efficacy—could be nurtured only in small participatory associations, including industry. Guild socialist G. D. H. Cole, as well, believed that a participatory society consisting of small participatory associations, mainly in the workplace, played a great role in shaping the personality and character necessary for engagement in the wider political environment. Carole Pateman, in her classic work *Participation and Democratic Theory*, extensively reviews the theoretical and empirical literature on workplace democracy and argues for the existence of strong, positive linkages between workplace participation and political knowledge, interest, and efficacy. She suggests that people learn to participate by participating and that they develop feelings of personal political efficacy and engagement in such activities. She concludes that ''recent investigations into political socialization have shown that the theorists of participatory democracy were on firm ground when they suggested that the individual would generalize from his experiences in non-governmental authority structures to the wider, national political sphere. . . . All the evidence indicates that . . . participation has a favorable effect on the individual in relationship to the development of a sense of political efficacy'' (1970:47, 66). Pateman's position is supported by the review of the research literature produced since her book by Ronald Mason (1982) and by the empirical research findings of political scientist J. Maxwell Elden, who studied a worker self-managed paper products company on the West Coast (1981).[8]

Contrary to expectations, worker-shareholders in the U.S. plywood industry proved to be no more politically efficacious than workers in conventional companies. Efficacy in this study is measured by a single Likert-style item that asks respondents whether they agree or disagree with the statement ''there is almost no way people like me can have an influence on the government.'' Differences between co-op and conventional workers on this item were statistically nonsignificant ($Tau_C = .00$, $p = $ n.s.). Nor was there any change over time in the sense of political efficacy for workers in either setting, at least as measured by this somewhat inadequate item. Work setting, considered at a single point in time or over a five-year span had no observable effect on political efficacy. Egalitarian and democratic life in the plywood cooperatives does not seem to contribute significantly to growth in a sense of personal mastery in the political realm.

Workplace Democracy and Political Participation

The claim that workplace and political participation are linked is universally shared among advocates of participatory democracy. Participatory democracy on a regional and national scale, it is argued, requires a broadly participatory society and, most especially, participatory workplaces, in which people learn the skills and habits of participation. Conversely, nonparticipatory settings and associations that encourage passivity and apathy are thought to nurture passivity and apathy in political life. The guild socialists are particularly noteworthy in advancing this position and for proposing institutional reforms that would vastly increase the political participation of ordinary working people. G. D. H. Cole was an especially active and influential spokesperson for this position. Cole believed that modern representative democracies were deeply flawed to the extent that everyday occupations trained working people for subservience and powerlessness. By creating institutions that "empowered" people in their work settings, in his case, the "guild system," Cole believed that people would become politically empowered as well and would enter political life outside of the workplace as self-confident and active citizens.

Ronald Mason best summarizes the contemporary case for the workplace–political participation connection.[9] He starts by positing in his "proximity thesis" that attitudes and behaviors at work and in politics will be closely related to each other because the structural conditions and social relations of the workplace are similar to those of politics and government. He states that "participation in the workplace provides an organizational social setting that approximates government in terms of its interaction patterns . . . [and] in terms of the mode, quality, and even intensity of participation" (1982:84–85). He concludes that "with so many Americans experiencing the workplace at one time or another, and with the very close approximation of the workplace and government, there is good reason to believe that participation in the workplace will have a powerful effect on participation in government" (1982:85).

The empirical linkage between workplace participation and political participation, though plausible, is supported only by meager and indirect research. Many proponents of participatory democracy try to establish the linkage by citing the strong empirical association between voluntary group involvement and heightened political participation (Alford and Scoble, 1968; Almond and Verba, 1963; Lipset, Trow, and Coleman, 1956; Burstein, 1972). Another line of argument tries to establish the linkage by showing that the degree of autonomy at work is associated with level of political participation. Thus people in low-status and assembly-line jobs tend to participate less than people in white-collar, professional, and high-status jobs (Form, 1973; Lipset, 1962; Sheppard and Herrick, 1972). Ronald Mason cites the extensive evidence showing the strong association between political efficacy and political participation as support for the workplace democracy–political participation literature because of the evidence that workplace democracy contributes to the nurturance of a sense of political efficacy (Elden, 1981; Mason, 1982:88–90). Finally, there are bits of anecdotal evidence which demonstrate significant increases in civic participation after the introduction of participatory reforms at General Foods in Topeka and Procter and Gamble in Lima, Ohio (Mason, 1982:100).

The evidence from this study is largely consistent with theoretical expectations about the linkage between workplace democracy and participation in normal democratic politics outside of the factory gates. Political participation is measured along four dimensions in this study: voting, campaign activity, involvement in community affairs, and attendance at government hearings. For each area of political activity, an additive index was created from items once factor analysis had confirmed the unidimensionality of items first selected on the basis of their face validity (Table 5–4).

Table 5–5 reports the results of a comparison between co-op and conventional workers using the 1978 cross-section sample. It shows that, consistent with most of the research literature, the respondents were relatively uninvolved in American political life. Mean scores on each political participation index hover around the lower end of the scale. Additionally, and most pertinent to this study, worker-shareholders were consistently more involved in normal democratic politics than were conventional workers though the differences are relatively small and statistically significant only with respect to involvement in community affairs and attendance at public hearings.[10]

This impression of greater political involvement by worker-shareholders is given added weight when the longitudinal dimension is considered. The results are reported in Table 5–6, which shows that with the exception of voting, on which no differences are evident, worker-shareholders in both time periods were consistently and significantly more politically involved than conventional workers. Respondents in both work settings increased the level of their participation over time, but the rate of increase was greater for worker-shareholders. The increase in political participation for co-op workers seems to be a combination of a secular trend common to these respondents in general and an increment traceable to membership in a democratic work organization. In this respect, then, theoretical expectations are met.

Most important for the subject of this chapter, however, is evidence that it is the actual experience of participation in the affairs of the cooperatives that is most associated with political activity outside of the enterprise. Table 5–7 shows the simple zero-order Pearson correlations between degree of involvement in the internal political life of the cooperatives and the degree of involvement in the three main areas of external political involvement in which differences were found to exist between

Table 5–4. Index of political participation

Index	Questions	Range	Reliability (Cronbach's alpha)
Voting*	Did you: (1) Vote in the 1976 (1980) presidential election? (2) Vote in the 1974 (1982) congressional election? (3) Vote in the most recent school board election?	3 (low) to 6 (high)	$T_1 = .74$ $T_2 = .87$
Campaign activity[†]	Have you: (1) Tried to get your friends or neighbors to vote for the candidate you support? (2) Been a volunteer worker during a political campaign?	2 (low) to 6 (high)	$T_1 = .79$ $T_2 = .70$
Community involvement	Have you: (1) Contacted a public official about some public issue? (2) Written a letter to the editor of a newspaper about some public issue? (3) Worked with others in your community to try to solve some community problem?	3 (low) to 9 (high)	$T_1 = .82$ $T_2 = .78$
Attend government hearings	Have you: (1) Attended meetings of your city or town council? (2) Attended a public hearing of some government agency such as a school board?	2 (low) to 6 (high)	$T_1 = .76$ $T_2 = .87$

* A "yes," "no," "don't remember" format was used. "Don't remember" responses were coded as missing values.
[†] A "No, never," "yes, once or twice," "yes, often," "yes, often," format was used for this and the following questions.

Table 5-5. Political participation: Comparison of mean index scores (1978 cross-section sample)

Index	Cooperatives (N = 206)	Conventional (N = 131)	F	Significant at 0.05 or less (one-way analysis of variance)
Voting*	4.01	3.87	1.04	n.s.
Campaign activity*	2.61	2.58	0.06	n.s.
Community involvement	4.00	3.61	7.15	Yes
Attend government hearings	2.66	2.24	20.42	Yes

*For formats used, see notes to Table 5-4.

Table 5-6. Political participation: Comparison of mean index scores over time (panel sample)

Index		Cooperatives ($N = 95$)	Conventional ($N = 58$)	Significant at 0.05 or less (one-way analysis of variance)
Voting*	T_1	3.96	4.11	n.s.
	T_2	3.90	4.18	n.s.
Campaign activity*	T_1	2.63	2.33	Yes
	T_2	3.02[†]	2.50	Yes
Community involvement	T_1	4.02	3.65	Yes
	T_2	4.33[†]	3.85	Yes
Attend government hearings	T_1	2.70	2.21	Yes
	T_2	2.81	2.26	Yes

*For formats used, see notes to Table 5–4.
[†]Significance, at 0.05 level or less, of differences on index scores between T_1 and T_2; matched sample t-test of mean difference scores.

Table 5–7. Relationships between internal and external political involvements of worker-shareholders: Pearson zero-order correlations of index of co-op participation with indexes of external political participation

	Campaign activity	Community involvement	Attend government hearings
1978 cross-section sample	0.33	0.45	0.36
	(N = 182)	(N = 181)	(N = 179)
	p = 0.001	p = 0.001	p = 0.001
T_2 panel sample	0.26	0.29	0.49
	(N = 90)	(N = 89)	(N = 89)
	p = 0.006	p = 0.003	p = 0.001

workers in co-op and conventional enterprises. By and large, the correlations are high and statistically significant.

The powerful role played by active involvement in the decision-making life of the cooperatives is further affirmed by a series of regression equations designed to assess the relative weight of co-op participation, supervisory climate, social networks, and self-selection in explaining politically relevant attitudes and behaviors (again for a discussion and justification of these four domains, see the section on work satisfaction in Chapter 3). A summary of these equations is reported in Table 5–8, which shows that participation in co-op governance remains a powerful variable for explaining outside political participation even after taking into account the effect of other independent variables.[11]

Workplace Democracy, Community, and Public-Spiritedness

For participatory democrats, the beauty of direct democracy is not only that it encourages participation in social organizations and in political life

Table 5–8. The impact of co-op participation on external political participation: Summary results of regression equations with co-op participation as independent variable* (1978 cross-section sample)

Dependent variable	Beta	F	Significance
Attend government hearings	0.33	15.75	0.00
Community involvement	0.40	25.18	0.00
Campaign activity	0.22	6.7	0.01

*In all three equations, the other independent variables measuring supervisory climate, social networks, and self-selection are statistically nonsignificant.

and nurtures a strong sense of political efficacy among individuals but that it does so in a way that enhances the community and the public interest. The experience of direct democracy, especially at the workplace, is said to develop a vision of commonality; an appreciation for the views of others comes to be naturally incorporated into the political calculations of individuals. In this way, private interests and the public interest are reconciled; through the practice of the arts of democracy, public-spirited citizens are created. Rousseau assumed, for instance, that active involvement in the political life of the community compelled the individual to take into account a wide range of views beyond his immediate private self-interest and, by so doing, to become a public citizen. John Stuart Mill believed that only widespread participation in decision making could educate people to be public-spirited in the sense that they would take into account the interests of others and the general good of the community. In the act of participation, he suggested, a person "is called upon . . . to weigh interests not his own, to be guided in the case of conflicting claims by another rule than his private partialities; to apply, at every turn, principles and maxims which have for their reason of existence the general good. . . . He is made to feel himself one of the public, and whatever is their interest to be his interest."[12]

We have seen already in this chapter that workplace democracy in the plywood cooperatives seems to encourage participation in normal democratic politics. The question remains, however, whether this heightened political participation is directed toward a more community and public-oriented perspective, or whether it is simply an instrument of self-interested aggrandizement. Proponents of the benefits of industrial democracy such as Pateman, Mason, and Cole have advocated reforms not only because of the presumed contribution to the expanded political participation of the individual (with all of its attendant benefits to such individuals) but because of the net contribution that it would make to the common weal by educating more public-spirited citizens. What effects do the cooperatives have on citizenship? What is the breadth of these worker-shareholders' political vision and concern?

I approach this question only indirectly and tentatively, although the data are suggestive, by looking at the degree to which worker-shareholders are committed to what might be called classical liberalism, or what others have termed possessive individualism or competitive individualism. The main concern of this world-view is with the advancement of self-interest, the needs of the community being decidedly secondary. In this view, the

Table 5–9. Workers' responses regarding self-interest (in percentages; 1978 cross-section sample)

Question: "Society is best off when each individual looks out for his own well-being and not the well-being of others."

	Cooperatives ($N = 203$)	Conventional ($N = 129$)
Strongly agree	4.9	1.6
Agree	11.8	11.6
Neither agree nor disgree	18.2	13.2
Disagree	53.7	61.2
Strongly disagree	11.3	12.4

$Tau_c = -0.08$, $p = 0.06$

individual is primary, and the pursuit of self-interest represents the motive force as well as the steering mechanism for society. The social good, it is assumed, is a by-product of individuals seeking aggrandizement. Conscious concern for advancing the social good is not only unnecessary for achieving that goal but usually counterproductive. In classical liberalism, each individual is responsible for his or her own fate as each struggles against all others in the marketplace. Success and failure are arrived at justly through the competitive struggle for rewards. Those who fail have no one to blame but themselves because of their lack of talent, perseverance, or pluck. Those who succeed are entitled to see themselves as deserving and need to have no regard for advancing the public interest because it is assumed that such is a natural by-product.

Given this orientation to the question of individual interest and the public interest in classical liberalism, a measure of commitment to classical liberalism will be used as an indirect measure of the public-spiritedness (or lack of same) of the respondents in this sample. The following Likert-style item was used to measure affirmation of classical liberalism: "Society is best off when each individual looks out for his own well-being and not the well-being of others." The results are reported in Tables 5–9 and 5–10. The respondents tended to reject strictly self-interested values. They overwhelmingly refused to affirm that "looking-out-for-No. 1" is the foundation of the good polity. Worker-shareholders, however, were more likely (though very weakly so) than workers in conventional firms to select self-interested values. Most interesting, worker-shareholders showed a tendency to increase their commitment to such values over time; their experience in the cooperatives seems to nurture a narrowing of focus. The

Table 5–10. Workers' responses regarding self-interest (in percentages; panel sample)

Question: "Society is best off when each individual looks out for his own well-being
         and not the well-being of others."

	T_1		T_2	
	Cooperatives (N = 94)	Conventional (N = 57)	Cooperatives (N = 94)	Conventional (N = 58)
Strongly agree	3.2	1.8	9.6	0.0
Agree	16.0	14.0	13.8	13.8
Neither agree nor disgree	22.3	10.5	19.1	10.3
Disagree	48.9	68.4	52.1	65.5
Strongly disagree	9.6	5.3	5.3	10.3

Tau$_c$ = 0.09
p = 0.13

Tau$_c$ = 0.20
p = 0.01

result is a combination of growing political participation over time par-
alleled by a growing self-interestedness. Although the degree of these
parallel changes is small, it is significant in the sense that it is exactly
contrary to theoretical expectations.[13]

Discussion

In one crucial respect, the experience of the producer cooperatives in
plywood provides powerful support for the claims of the theorists of
participatory democracy. Most important, the suggestion that the experience of direct democracy in the workplace encourages participation in
democratic political life outside of the workplace is strongly supported by
the evidence reported in these pages. With the exception of voting, about
which no differences were found, worker-shareholders were significantly
more active in all phases of political life than workers in conventional
firms. Furthermore, the gap between workers in cooperative and conventional firms increased over time, suggesting the existence of a political
learning process. Finally, the data suggest that the experience of participation by worker-shareholders in enterprise decision making serves as
the principal educative tool for political participation and increases involvement with various voluntary and community organizations.[14]

The experience of industrial democracy in the cooperatives does not
conform to expectations in its relative failure to produce more public-

spiritedness (at least as it is measured in this study) than other work settings. Why is this so? Why are the expectations of the theorists of industrial democracy not met? Only further studies of a wide-ranging comparative nature can hope to answer this question definitively, but one possible explanation might be that such theorists have generally ignored the fact that experiments in workplace industrial democracy in the United States occur in a largely hostile, incompatible, free-enterprise environment in which private property market mechanisms are preeminent. Why should one expect that collective decision making in enterprises whose survival depends on the accumulation of profits in the marketplace can be based upon or produce anything other than a concern for self interest? Although the referent to self-interest in this case is a collective entity (the worker-shareholders as a whole), the tie of that entity to its own property and its position in the market makes the natural evolution of a wider concern for the public interest unlikely. Theories of industrial democracy, then, must be divorced from the lofty, abstract, and reified environment they now inhabit and made dependent upon their relationships to specific social, economic, and political environments.[15] I shall have much more to say about this issue in the next two chapters.

·6·

Class-Consciousness in the Cooperatives

Writers, scholars, and activists of the democratic Left generally assume that workplace democracy, especially in its most highly developed form in self-management, is a powerful school for socialism, teaching workers the values, commitments, and skills appropriate to both the struggle against capitalism and the construction of a socialist society. They generally assume that experience in a cooperative, egalitarian, and democratic workplace will enhance the development of these values in people lucky enough to labor in such work settings and will stimulate in them an impatience with a society that denies or blocks the attainment of such values. Workplace democracy is considered an essential instrumentality by which a "class-in-itself" is transformed into a "class-for-itself," an instrumentality by which the working class becomes, in Lukacs's words, "the sense become conscious of the historic role of the class."

Workplace democracy is in particular favor among those who believe that socialism cannot be imposed from above, that only the activity of the working class can achieve a society characterized by democracy, equality, and fraternity. Most especially, in this view, it is important, if future socialist societies in the West are to avoid the tyranny of presently existing state socialism, that socialism be "prefigured" in the political struggle against capitalism and for socialism. If socialism is to be characterized by democracy, equality, and fraternity, these values must be the foundation of the political movement. Self-governing socialism, in this view, cannot be achieved by the conspiratorial activities of a vanguard party separate from and superior to the working class. Thus, workplace democracy and the principles and ways of life it embodies are seen to represent both a vision of the good society and a tool for its attainment. In the words of several prominent spokesmen for this position, "workers' control suggests both an ultimate goal . . . and a strategy for reaching that goal" (Hunnius, Garson, and Case, 1973:ix).

Although this perspective has many roots, stretching from Marx to the anarchists, contemporary interest in the linkage between workplace democracy and class-consciousness, I believe, can be traced to the rediscovery and popularization of the work of the great Italian Marxist theorist Antonio Gramsci, who, more than any other theorist of the Left, viewed organization and struggles at the point of production as the energizing forces for breaking capitalist domination and catalyzing the process of revolutionary social change.[1] Perceiving the transition to socialism as a very long-term process dependent upon the readiness of the working class for its historic task, Gramsci placed the struggle for democracy at the workplace on center stage as the great classroom for the self-education of the working class.

Gramsci's great theoretical contribution was to grapple with the question of why socialist revolutions had not occurred in the developed capitalist countries that presumably contained all of the objective material conditions for them. He suggested that the continuation of capitalist domination might be explained by the existence of both coercive power, situated in the institutions of the state, and the hegemony of civil society, or domination of capital through the instruments of ideology, legitimation, and false consciousness. In the Western nations, where the state is merely the outer "ramparts," it is hegemony (defined as the spontaneous loyalty that dominant groups gain by virtue of their social and intellectual prestige and their leadership of productive and political life, and conversely, the resignation and confusion that arises out of the experience of being dominated [Williams, 1960]) that must be opposed by a working-class counterhegemony as a prerequisite to social transformation.

In his earliest works, in particular, Gramsci placed great reliance on workers' councils as the seed of a new working-class counterhegemony. Impressed by the ubiquity of soviets in all revolutionary struggles and particularly with their role in the October Revolution, Gramsci conceived of workers' councils as natural proletarian institutions in which workers might enter into socialist relationships and incorporate socialist values and activities. He argued that organizing at the workplace, taking over production from management, and producing cooperatively would educated workers to socialism and give them the capacity to rule society. In these

---

(1)
Direct governance of the production process by workers

↓   will lead to

(2)
Transformation of individual orientations and behaviors appropriate to socialism
and the struggle against capitalism,

↓   which in turn, will foster the

(3)
Development, as workplace democracy spreads throughout society, of a class
with revolutionary consciousness

↓   leading to

(4)
Conscious class struggles for the institution of democratic socialism.

Figure 6–1. The educative effects of workplace democracy

institutions of self-education, workers would acquire skills, capacities, responsibilities, and confidence in their abilities as a class. These councils provided the tools for enabling the formerly subordinate class to gain a belief in itself as a ruling class.[2]

Despite the differences between Gramsci's position on self-management and class-consciousness and those of modern proponents such as Case (1973), Coates (1966), Espinosa and Zimbalist (1978), and Pateman (1970), especially with respect to the role of the revolutionary vanguard party, all stress that in the midst of a larger capitalist society, workers' councils and other forms of cooperative, collective organization at the point of production represent powerful schools for the self-education of the working class and that such institutions provide a setting in which values and behavior appropriate only to wage labor under capitalism can be dissolved and those more appropriate to socialism be given birth. These theoretical claims may be presented in a schematic representation (see Figure 6–1).

Does workplace democracy, in fact serve as an incubator for a "class-for-itself"? Does it nurture values, commitments, and behavior appropriate to democratic socialism and, at the same time, encourage the formation of orientations unfriendly to contemporary capitalism? Does workplace democracy help mold volitions and behaviors that might help construct a movement for democratic, self-governing socialism? Although many advocates of workplace democracy believe that it does, the careful scholar must be impressed with the relative absence of empirical data or other hard evidence that would enable any reasonable judgment to be made about the link between cooperative, democratic, and egalitarian relationships at work and the development of class-consciousness. In this chapter, using data generated from workers in cooperative and conventional plywood firms, and fully recognizing that the plywood co-ops are but one of a variety of possible workplace democratic forms, I hope to address this deficiency in the research literature.

My limited purpose in this chapter is to examine the linkages between boxes (1) and (2) in Figure 6–1, to determine whether employment in a democratic work setting, as compared to a typical hierarchical one, shapes individual attitudes and behaviors in the hypothesized direction. I cannot, of course, examine either the linkage between (2) and (3) or the linkage between (3) and (4), which require an entirely different form of scholarly investigation.[3] Should no relationship be found to exist between workplace democracy and the transformation of values and behavior in the cooperatives (linkage 1→2), the case for workplace democracy as a tool for radical social change must be seriously questioned.

The Effects of Workplace Democracy

We have seen in previous chapters that the cooperatives tend to attract blue-collar workers with entrepreneurial instincts and positive orientations toward the business system. One would presume that this group of people would be a very poor medium for the growth of working-class consciousness. Nevertheless, whatever the reason these workers initially chose to join a producer cooperative, shared cooperative social relations at work might have unanticipated consequences. Almost all of the theorists of workplace democracy believe that the intentions of involved individuals are irrelevant; rather, for the development of particular attitudes among workers (whether they favor greater democratic participation or greater support for cooperative social relations) the actual experience of cooperative and egalitarian labor is vital.

Evidence presented in earlier chapters suggested that such unintended consequences do result from working in the producer cooperatives. Share-holders are more likely than workers in conventional companies to enter into informal cooperative arrangements in activities ranging from inter-acting in general shareholder meetings to mutually working out production problems that invariably arise during the course of building plywood panels. I have also discussed the impressive degree to which a tone of mutuality and group responsibility pervades these unique enterprises. Equal hourly wage rates within the cooperatives and the very strong, almost universal support for this form of compensation among shareholders are also important. The overwhelming impression from the data that fol-low, however, is that the experience of self-management within enterprises oriented to sales in a competitive marketplace largely fails to counteract the original orientations of worker-shareholders. Indeed, in many cases, their experience seems to enhance and nurture their small-property/petit-bourgeois orientations.[4] The cooperative social relations that do exist seem to be entered into and maintained for the pursuit of small-property ends. In this respect, those theorists of industrial democracy who see self-man-agement as an important school for the development of orientations fa-vorable to socialism would seem to be very wide of the mark.

Working-Class Identification

It may be argued that for workers to develop class-consciousness they must understand that they belong to a social class whose interests stand in opposition to those of an economically superior social class. Such an understanding was not evident among the worker-shareholders in this sample. When asked to place themselves in a social class category,[5] worker-shareholders were consistently more likely than workers in con-ventional firms to designate themselves middle class rather than working class. Although the differences are small and statistically nonsignificant (52.4 percent of worker-shareholders thought of themselves as working class and 47.6 percent as middle class at T_1 compared to 62.7 percent of conventional workers who thought of themselves as working class and only 37.7 percent as middle class; the figures at T_2, respectively, are 57.0 percent and 43.0 percent for worker-shareholders and 64.8 percent and 35.2 percent for conventional workers), they are exactly the opposite of theoretical expectations. Co-op workers tended to increase their working-class identification slightly over time, but the change is statistically non-significant and hardly suggestive of a movement toward class-consciousness. This result should not be surprising because co-op workers, though trapped in an alienating production process like other blue-collar workers, are propertyholders engaged in market competition.

Co-op workers were more likely than workers in conventional firms to identify themselves as Republicans. Whereas the vast majority of respondents in the sample identified themselves either as Democrats or Independents, worker-shareholders held an 11.5 to 5.8 percent lead a T_1 (statistically nonsignificant) in Republican identification and and increased that lead at T_2 to 15.7 to 5.6 percent ($\chi^2 p = .01$).[6] Although American parties are not class-oriented in the European sense, an extensive research literature suggests that the parties have clearly identifiable images, with the Republicans traditionally seen as the party of business and of small business ideology and the Democrats as the party of organized labor and the welfare state.[7] The differences in party identification among respondents in this study were not great, but they were consistent with findings about class identification reported above and inconsistent with theories that posit a leftward movement among workers in democratic work settings.[8]

The finding that workplace democracy in the American plywood cooperatives fails to solidify class identification and perspectives is given further support by two test items designed to assess respondents' confidence in the abilities of the working class in general. Table 6–1 shows responses to a question that asks for an assessment of the general managerial capabilities of other working people. The results are sobering. Even though worker-shareholders (who are no better trained or more skilled than other working people) have been competently, skillfully, and profitably running their own industrial enterprises, this experience does not seem to increase their confidence, relative to people in conventional companies, in the abilities of other working people to be equally successful in managing their own firms. In fact, over time, worker-shareholders became slightly less confident in the abilities of other workers outside of their firm. They do not generalize their own experience to the blue-collar class in its entirety.

Responses to a question about confidence in the ability of working people to run not merely the technical, production side of enterprises but also the business affairs, activities even more distant from the direct experience of most working people, affirmed the above findings (see Table 6–2). Not surprisingly, of course, most respondents tended to discount the abilities of their fellows. The extent to which co-op workers, who

Table 6–1. Workers' confidence in the abilities of other working people (in percentages, panel sample)

Question: "Even without the help of managerial personnel, working people have
enough skill and intelligence to run everyday production in their plants."

	T_1		T_2	
	Cooperatives ($N = 95$)	Conventional ($N = 57$)	Cooperatives ($N = 94$)	Conventional ($N = 57$)
Strongly agree	8.4	12.3	6.4	3.5
Agree	37.9	36.8	33.0	36.8
Neither agree nor disagree	8.4	12.3	12.8	24.6
Disagree	30.5	29.8	38.3	31.6
Strongly disagree	14.7	8.8	9.6	3.5

gamma = −0.11,
Tau$_C$ = −0.07,
$p = 0.18$

gamma = −0.12,
Tau$_C$ = −0.08,
$p = 0.17$

Table 6–2. Workers' confidence in the ability of working people to run business affairs (in percentages, panel sample)

Question: "Even without the help of managerial personnel, working people have
enough skill and intelligence to run the business and financial affairs of their
plants."

	T_1		T_2	
	Cooperatives ($N = 95$)	Conventional ($N = 57$)	Cooperatives ($N = 94$)	Conventional ($N = 57$)
Strongly agree	3.2	5.3	3.2	0.0
Agree	9.5	12.3	7.4	7.0
Neither agree nor disagree	5.3	19.3	7.4	21.1
Disagree	52.6	45.6	45.7	57.9
Strongly disagree	29.5	17.5	36.2	14.0

gamma = −0.32,
Tau$_C$ = −0.20,
$p = 0.01$

gamma = −0.34,
Tau$_C$ = −0.21,
$p = 0.01$

actively participate in the business affairs of their own successful enter-prises, are consistently less confident in other members of the working class than are conventional workers is surprising, however.

Finally, the relative absence of working-class identification by worker-shareholders in the cooperatives is further established by their lack of enthusiasm for labor unions. The following observation is typical of worker-shareholders' views on American labor unions:

> I think unions have altogether too much power. They were OK at first but they've outgrown their usefulness . . . the logical thing to do is to dispose of them.

More than a few worker-shareholders mentioned that one of the reasons they joined a cooperative was to get away from labor unions:

> [I left——] because they had a union problem and I wasn't in favor of the union's way of thinking. At that time they was organizing this co-op, and it was naturally nonunion. That's why I went with it, because I was fed up with the union.

Workers in the conventional mill had an altogether different perspective. The following observation was typical:

> If it wasn't for the union we wouldn't have a damn thing. Without unions we'd be working for peanuts.

These impressions from the interviews are powerfully confirmed by the data reported in Table 6–3. Labor unions are hardly the vanguard organ-ization of a socialist political movement in the United States,[9] but they remain the principal workplace defense organization of the American working class and the closest approximation to a mass-based progressive political organization in the United States.[10] The lukewarm attitude worker-shareholders toward the traditional role of labor unions when compared to conventional workers speaks volumes to their orientation toward social classes and their overall sense of identification.

Political and Economic Alienation

Another important component of almost every conceptualization of class-consciousness in the literature is a sense among workers that the

Table 6–3. Workers' opinions about labor unions (panel sample, T_2 only)

Question: "Labor unions are no longer necessary to protect working people in the
United States."

	Cooperatives ($N = 92$)	Conventional ($N = 56$)
Strongly disagree	17.4	46.4
Disagree	22.8	44.6
Neither agree nor disgree	30.4	7.1
Agree	19.6	1.8
Strongly agree	9.8	0.0

Gamma $= -0.70$; Tau$_c = -.52$; $p = 0.00$

prevailing capitalist economic and political order is unfair and illegitimate
to the extent that both serve the interests of the more powerful and privileged in society. For workers to join a movement to overthrow the old
order and create a new one, they must first develop a deep sense that the
politics, governance, and economic arrangements of the old order are
fundamentally unjust or flawed. For class-consciousness to exist, in the
view of both the Marxist and non-Marxist Left, workers must feel alienated
from the old order.

There is no evidence in this study that democratic and egalitarian work
settings, environments that contrast sharply to the organization of economy
and governance outside of the walls of the firm, encourage discontent with
prevailing political and economic arrangements. We can see this in response patterns to a long string of questions about U.S. government,
politics, and economy reported in Table 6–4. No significant differences
appeared between co-op and conventional workers in their affective orientations and judgments. In those few cases on which significant differences did exist, moreover, worker-shareholders were less alienated than
conventional workers. These differences are worth some additional attention. First, though worker-shareholders did not change between 1978 and
1983 regarding their sense of fairness of the American economy (the last
two questions), workers in the conventional firm became slightly less
contented. Membership in a plywood cooperative seems to have insulated
worker-shareholders from some of the harsh effects of the disruptions
caused by the decline of the American economy in general and the wood
products industry in particular between 1970 and 1982. Second, and perhaps in response to that situation, workers in the conventional firm by
1983 were more willing than their compatriots in the cooperatives to

Table 6–4. Evaluations of government, politics, and economics in the United States: Comparison of co-op and conventional workers (summary table)

Questions (Likert-type)	Significant differences between co-op and conventional workers at either T_1 and T_2	Significant change among worker-shareholders between T_1 and T_2
In our political system, people without money don't have much chance to get elected to public office	No	No
It seems that government has lost touch with the people	No	No
Local government officials around here really listen to people's problems	No	No
Elections in this country do a good job of giving the people a real say in what their government does	No	No
Our major parties are so much alike that voters do not really get much choice when they vote	No	No
This country needs a new political party to represent the interests of working people	Yes, at T_2 (Tau$_c$ = 0.15, p = 0.04, gamma = 0.20)*	No
"Trust in government" index[†]	No	No
"A ruling class exists" index[‡]	No	No
Our current economic system does a good job in allowing each American to get his fair share of goods and services	Yes, at T_2 (Tau$_c$ = 0.18, p = 0.02, gamma = 0.25)*	No
"Fairness of economy" Index[§]	Yes, at T_2 (p = 0.05)*	No

*Conventional workers are more discontented.

[†]The "trust in government" index is a simple additive index (after recoding so that high scores equal high trust) ranging from 4 to 20, consisting of the following four Likert-type agree-disagree questions: (1) Most of our political leaders can be trusted. (2) There is almost no way people like me can have an influence on the government. (3) There's not much connection between what I want and what my congressmen and senators do. (4) Once the election is over most public officials stop caring about what people want. Index reliabilities, using Cronbach's alpha, are 0.73 at T_1 and 0.68 at T_2.

Table 6–4. (cont.)

---

‡"A ruling class exists" index is a simple additive index, ranging from 2 to 10, consisting of the following two Likert-type, agree-disagree items: (1) Whether you get a fair trial in this country usually depends on who you are and how much money you have. (2) This country is really run by a small number of men at the top who only speak for a few special groups. Index reliabilities, using Cronbach's alpha, are 0.62 at T_1 and 0.94 at T_2. Although no significant differences existed between worker-shareholders and conventional workers on this index, both scored toward the upper end (mean score = 6.8); that is, both groups tended to believe in the existence of a powerful, distant, and privileged group or class in the United States. Their typical views are captured in the following two observations: "There's about 5 families that form the nucleus of this country. They control about 90 percent of the money. That's your Rockefellers, your DuPonts, Carnegies, the Kennedys, the Mellons. They'll give everybody so much leeway so let them think they're doing something, but as soon as they cross certain bounds, then they slap them back a little bit" [worker-shareholder]. "Well, I can go to court, but I know I'm going to get convicted as soon as I get down there. If you've got money, you can appeal, if they find you guilty, a poor man like me, the judge says, you're guilty. You're guilty. That's all there is to it; you have no recourse unless you got money. And if you got money, you've got recourse."

§The "fairness of economy" index is a simple additive index, ranging from 2 to 10, consisting of the following two Likert-type, agree-disagree items: (1) Our economic system takes advantage of working people. (2) Our current economic system gives almost everyone a fair chance to get what they need to live a decent life. Index reliabilities, using Cronbach's alpha, are 0.80 at T_1 and 0.62 at T_2.

consider the need for a new political party with a greater commitment to working people.

I do not want to imply here that conventional workers in this study are protorevolutionary, only that worker-shareholders show no evidence of growing alienation relative to them. In fact, both groups are highly patriotic and contented with the American system. Perhaps most important, most of the respondents in the poll conducted in 1983 showed strong support for the verities of contemporary conservatism as articulated by Ronald Reagan and others. Thus, 75 percent of both groups believed that government deficits are the main cause of inflation and over 90 percent agreed that government has grown too big and expensive.[11]

Basic Values

Advocates of workplace democracy believe that the main revolutionary effect of participatory and egalitarian workplaces is to cause a basic shift in values among workers such that values most appropriate to market-capitalist society are eroded and those most appropriate to democratic, self-governing socialism are nurtured. This dual transformation, it is suggested, must take place among workers if a decent humane socialism is

Table 6–5. Support for classical liberal values (percentage agreed; panel sample)

	T_1		T_2	
	Cooperatives (N = 95)	Conventional (N = 57)	Cooperatives (N = 94)	Conventional (N = 57)
Many people are poor today because they are really not willing to work.	74.4	62.1	63.5	47.3*
A person should basically depend on himself and not ask or expect the help of others.	80.6	82.5	85.3	77.6*
Society is best off when each individual looks out for his own well-being and not the well-being of others.	19.2	15.8	23.4	13.8*

*Differences between co-op and conventional workers significant at 0.05 level or better using Tau_c statistic. Although only the percent agreed is reported, significance test is for the entire table for each item.

to be "prefigured" in the political movement to overthrow the old order and create a new and better one. Once again, evidence from this study does not support these expectations.

I start with consideration of a series of questions designed to tap support for values consistent with the classical liberal ideas of Adam Smith, John Locke, and others which arose simultaneously with and, I would argue, out of the appearance of market society. These values, labeled "possessive individualism" by political philosopher C. B. MacPherson (1964), entail the familiar notions that each individual is responsible for his or her own fate in a perpetual competition for rewards against others in society, that success in the competition for rewards is justly arrived at through the marketplace, and that those who succeed owe nothing to those who fail in this competition, especially through the intervention of government. The results are reported in Table 6–5.

The table shows, first, that workers both in co-ops and in the conventional firm strongly affirm classical liberal values, suggesting that support for competitive individualism may be so pervasive in American life that it is espoused by the great mass of the blue-collar working class. This finding tends to confirm those of a number of scholars (Lane, 1962; Sennett and Cobb, 1973; Terkel, 1974; Wills, 1970) and suggests the distance that must be traveled by those who perceive of the possibility of a political movement of the Left in the United States in the near future. Second, and more important for our discussion of class-consciousness, worker-share-holders in the cooperatives tend to affirm classical liberal values more strongly than their counterparts in conventional firms. Third, and speaking to the dynamic process involved, the gap between co-op and conventional workers increased significantly over time. Over the course of this study, the commitment of worker-shareholders to possessive individualism strengthened relative to conventional workers. The experience of work-place democracy in the plywood cooperatives does not, whether taken in isolation or compared to work in conventional enterprises, serve to un-dermine or diminish the commitment to classical liberal values, as most theorists of workplace democracy have speculated. The persistence of the belief in a world characterized by self-interested struggles for survival in a group experiencing shared-cooperative productive relations must cer-tainly give us pause for it is exactly the opposite of all theoretical expectations.

The perspectives of worker-shareholders are captured in the following observations about the poor in America and government efforts to assist them:

> I'd say most of them just don't want to work. Honestly, I know a few myself. And they just love to sit home and get that free check.

> I think that people make their own fates. They're poor because they won't get off their butts.

> I think everyone gets their just desserts.

> I think you get what you work for. If you work hard you end up with a little better job than you do if you just don't get in and do it. I feel they're there because they don't want to work.

> I go over here to the grocery store, and I see somebody buy their stuff and use food coupons and go out and get in a brand new car, and drive off. It makes you wonder.

> Yeah, the government will help you if you don't try. If you can sit on your butt and let them hand everything to you, but for the guy who is out there making that buck and paying those taxes, they don't do a damn thing for him except take his money and say keep making it because we want more.

Table 6–6. Support for egalitarianism in cooperative and conventional workplaces (percentage agreed, panel sample)

	T_1		T_2	
	Cooperatives	Conventional	Cooperatives	Conventional
A group of equals will work a lot better than a group with a strong boss.	41.9	48.3	45.3	43.9
Each person ought to get what he needs . . . the things we produce as a society belong to all of us.	34.1	53.4*	35.1	54.5*
Do you agree or disagree that wages and salaries throughout American industry be made as equal as possible?	33.0	45.6*	26.6	39.7*

*Differences between co-op and conventional workers significant at 0.05 level or better using Tau$_C$ statistic. Although only percent agreed is reported, the statistic is for the entire table for each item.

Worker-shareholders' strong and growing commitment to possessive individualism is mirrored in a set of questions designed to determine whether experience in the cooperative nurtures egalitarian values more appropriate to democratic, self-governing socialism than possessive individualist ones. For most theorists of workplace democracy, one of the principal processes by which societal transformation is encouraged is through the generalization of beliefs in human equality gained through the cooperative-egalitarian setting of the self-managed enterprise to other spheres of life. The disappointing results are reported in Table 6–6. We see that workers in conventional plants organized in traditional hierarchical ways are more likely to affirm general egalitarian values than are shareholders in the plywood cooperatives where work is carried out under general conditions of equality. Nor is there any indication that the commitment by worker-shareholders to egalitarian values increases over time. The experience of egalitarian relationships in the cooperatives, then, is not generalized by shareholders so as to incorporate the world beyond the walls of the enterprise. This is especially striking in regard to the question about the desirability of more equal wages and salaries in American industry. Shareholders are paid in an egalitarian fashion, and for them to affirm this question would in some ways represent a simple generalization of their own experience, which has proved successful. Surprisingly, workers in the conventional firm proved more likely at both T_1 and T_2 to affirm the more egalitarian position on wages than were worker-shareholders.

The Welfare State and Beyond

Another essential element of class-consciousness, in my view, is a commitment to the idea that the economy be removed from the realm of the anarchistic mechanisms of the marketplace and placed under public control and that the state redistribute the highly inegalitarian structure of life chances among the population. Class-consciousness, in the prerevolutionary period, must in some sense prefigure commitments to a society and economy that would emerge during some socialist future. Although it is next to impossible to detect such a commitment in the contemporary Western working class, we might perhaps catch a glimmer of such a vision by measuring the level of support among our respondents for various programs of a fully developed welfare state. That is, we might measure support for government policies that might serve as tools for egalitarian redistribution, for public control of the economy, and for the improvement of the health and welfare of the citizenry. When we do so, as I report in this section of the chapter, we find that membership in a producer cooperative either fails to undermine the initial conservative, anti-welfare state orientations of worker-shareholders or makes their conservative commitments even stronger.

I start with two questions about the role of government in guaranteeing health care and jobs for American citizens (see Table 6–7). Obviously, working in a cooperative, egalitarian setting does not enhance commitment to programs of the welfare state outside the walls of the firm. Rather, worker-shareholders in 1978 were much more hostile to these aspects of the welfare state than workers in the conventional firm and either maintained this difference or increased its magnitude over time.

In Table 6–8 I consider worker support for various measures that have been advanced over the years for public control of the economy. These respondents showed virtually no support for the public ownership option. Whether their view is owing to the perceived incompetencies of the federal government, to European experiences with public ownership, or to a

Table 6–7. Workers' support for a government role in medical care and jobs (percentage agreed; panel sample)

	T_1		T_2	
	Cooperatives	Conventional	Cooperatives	Conventional
Do you agree or disagree that the federal government should pay for medical and hospital bills?	44.1	63.8*	44.7	63.6*
Do you agree or disagree that the federal government should guarantee jobs to everyone willing to work?	43.0	63.8*	37.6	69.7*

*Differences between cooperative and conventional workers significant at 0.05 level or better using Tau$_C$ statistic. Although only percent agreed is reported, the statistic is for the entire table for each item.

Table 6–8. Workers' support for public control of the economy (percentage agreed; panel sample)

	T_1		T_2	
	Cooperatives	Conventional	Cooperatives	Conventional
The federal government should control how much profit a company can make in any one year.	6.5	32.8*	7.6	29.1*
The federal government should control the prices set by large corporations.	36.5	59.7*	27.7	60.0*
The federal government should own and operate key industries.	4.4	5.2	2.2	7.0

*Differences between co-op and conventional workers significant at 0.05 level or better using Tau$_C$ statistic. Although only percentage agreed is reported, the statistic is for the entire table for each item.

presumed resemblance to socialism and communism is impossible to say. If these respondents are at all typical of the American working class, then no base exists in the United States for one of the traditional demands of the Social Democratic Left as practiced in several of the European nations. Second, and mirroring the findings on the other welfare state items, worker-shareholders were distinctly more conservative than their peers in the conventional firm; they were significantly less supportive of measures that would impose public purposes and public controls upon important economic enterprises.[12]

The strong anti-welfare state perspectives of the worker-shareholders are captured in the following observations:

> I think that government has just about got its finger far enough into the pie right now.

> The government has grown to a point far beyond what it was intended by our founding fathers. They probe into and delve into every facet of your life and in so doing, they unconsciously assume control of it. Well, the people weren't to be governed by the government. The government was to be governed by the people. And now it's all turned about

> I wish the bureaucrats and politicos would get off our backs.

Conclusion

The expectation held by many theorists of workplace democracy that self-managed work environments might serve to nurture feelings of co-operation, equality, generosity, and self-confidence in one's fellows is, as we have seen in previous chapters, only partly met within the plywood cooperatives. The expectation that such feelings would spill over the walls of the workplace so as to incorporate society, economy, and government is decidedly not met in the cases reviewed here. Indeed, the findings point to the opposite results. With respect to the outside world, the producer cooperatives seem to nurture outlooks characterized not by community, mutuality, equality, and confidence in others, but outlooks more congruent with the tenets of classical liberalism: those of individualism, competition, limited government, equality of opportunity and inequality of condition, and so on. The data indicate that those entering the cooperatives bring with them a small-property/petit-bourgeois experience and outlook and that tenure in the cooperatives serves in some cases to maintain this orientation and in other cases to enhance it.[13] The cooperatives thus seem to attract people with attitudes appropriate to a market economy and further nurture these values. They do not move people to the Left over the years.[14] It would seem, then, at least with respect to the cases reviewed here, that democratic, cooperative enterprises operating within a system of market capitalism seem unlikely settings not only for the practice of socialist relationships but especially for the promulgation of general attitudes appropriate to a more egalitarian/cooperative society outside of the workplace.

The producer cooperatives in plywood are among the oldest, largest, and fully developed democratic enterprises existing in the United States today. As such, they are an important setting in which to observe the effects on workers' political and social outlooks of the experience of workplace democracy in enterprises operating within an overall market system. The findings suggest that the market might be a more powerful educative tool than the cooperative experience itself. Or to put it differently, we may hypothesize that so long as the economic well-being of enterprise members depends upon success in the marketplace, whether it be based on ownership of shares or on profit sharing, bonuses, or other such devices, behavior appropriate to that success will be encouraged even within self-managed enterprises.[15] This is especially true in settings where a political organization devoted to general coordination and socialist education (in the Gramscian sense) does not exist. One gets the strange result, then, of a collective/cooperative/egalitarian spirit that is somewhat encouraged within the enterprise walls running up against the harsh rocks and shoals of the marketplace. This should suggest to theorists of the democratic Left that although workplace self-management is surely the model on which a decent and humane society will organize its productive life in the future, the isolated worker-managed workplace may not be an appropriate educative setting in the present context for nurturing a larger political movement for change. I turn my attention to this issue in greater detail in the next two chapters.

· 7 ·

A Comparative Analysis
of Class-Consciousness

In Chapter 6, I asked whether the experience of direct democracy and egalitarian social relations in the workplace helped to mold volitions and behaviors among American workers that might lead them to support a political movement for democratic, self-governing socialism. I asked whether experience with a radically different form of work experience encouraged American workers to develop outlooks more consistent with a direct democratic, participatory, and egalitarian social order and less consonant with an individualistic, competitive, hierarchical, and market-oriented one. I asked, in response to advocates of the "theory of escalation" (see Chapter 1), whether American workers in producer cooperatives gradually yet inexorably came to generalize their own work experience and outlooks to the world beyond the factory walls; to the industry, the economy, and the society as a whole.

I found that virtually none of these expectations of the democratic Left were met. Empirical evidence gathered in the Pacific Northwest plywood cooperatives offers no support for the proposition that workplace democracy fuels the escalation of political class-consciousness. It appears, in fact, that workplace democracy may deescalate the formation of class-consciousness and, therefore, decrease workers' support for the concept of and a political movement for democratic, self-governing socialism. What I found (reported in previous chapters and in Greenberg, 1981a, 1981b, and 1980) are attitudes and behaviors among workers that are directly contrary to what the theory of escalation would lead one to expect: First, compared to workers in the conventional firm, worker-shareholders in the producer cooperatives are more likely to affirm classical liberal

values (individualism, competition, equality of opportunity but not condition, limited government, and the like), to support systems of hierarchical social relations, and to identify themselves as members of the middle
class. Second, workers in the producer cooperatives are less likely than
their counterparts in conventional firms to affirm egalitarian values, to
support welfare state measures, to express confidence in the abilities of
other working people, or to see cooperation as a generally valued form
of social organization. Third, members of the producer cooperatives do
not see themselves as a model for other enterprises to emulate, nor do
they believe that other people could or should organize their enterprises
on a cooperative basis.

I concluded that the effects of workplace democracy within firms located
in market-capitalist societies such as the Untied States do not support the
expectations of the democratic Left. I will further conclude in this chapter
that the effects of such experiments in workplace democracy in the United
States cannot be otherwise. I shall argue that the overly optimistic assessment of the political possibilities of workplace democracy is derived
from the failure of many scholars and practitioners properly to contex-
tualize their understanding of the effects of workplace democracy.

Producer Cooperatives as Special Cases

No necessary relationship was found between attitudes and behaviors
relevant to internal enterprise relations and those relevant to external ones.
The development of a socialist commonwealth within producer cooperatives (equality, democracy, cooperation, mutual respect, and the like) does
not necessarily guarantee the development of similar orientations to the
world outside the walls of the enterprise.

Such an outcome has long been recognized in the classic Marxist literature. Marx made several observations about producer cooperatives in
general and the mid-nineteenth-century cooperative movement in England
in particular, some positive, some negative. At their best, he argued,
cooperatives were suggestive of the possibility of socialism, evidence that
production and invention could go forward without the capitalist and that
productive relations could be cooperative rather than hierarchical and
coercive. Cooperatives were possible inspirational counterexamples to
capitalism, evidence that "within the old form are the first sprouts of the

new" (1967:440). He also pointed out that their effects were bound to be stillborn in societies in which the working class had not yet taken power and imposed cooperative principles. Marx recognized that cooperatives were deeply embedded in capitalist social relations and assumptions and could serve only to reinforce them. As capitalist institutions, they could not transcend the terrain that gave them birth and form (since "right can never be higher than the economic structure and the cultural development of the society conditioned by it") (1961:556). Most important, as he pointed out in his polemic against Proudhon, socialists who advocated cooperatives as instruments of transformation were disregarding the very essence of this issue: the necessary struggle for state power.[1]

Lenin, of course, like most writers in the Marxist tradition, understood cooperatives to be capitalist institutions. When the Copenhagen Congress of the Second International (1910) passed a resolution that strongly advocated the formation of cooperatives, Lenin introduced a motion (which failed) "declaring that the socializing and democratizing role of cooperatives will become effective only after the expropriation of capitalists" (Horvat, 1975:21). To Nikolai Bukharin, populist and Marxist advocates of agrarian cooperatives (in a prerevolutionary context) were "purveyors of a 'miserable reformist utopia' because they imagined a socialist evolution of cooperatives within the capitalist system . . . cooperatives 'inescapably fall under the influence of capitalist economics' . . . and 'are transformed into capitalist enterprises' " (Cohen, 1980:198). The pro-capitalist effects of cooperatives had been so long recognized, in fact, that they have been advocated at various times by conservatives as an instrument "to strengthen free-enterprise by educating working class entrepreneurs" (Horvat, 1975:21).

Some would surely argue that producer cooperatives are special forms of enterprise and that the attitudinal and behavioral tendencies found within them would not necessarily hold in other worker-managed enterprises in the United States. What makes them special, of course, is that workers *own* these enterprises and do not simply control or manage them. They are therefore not consistent with the organizational forms proposed in the theoretical literature of workers' councils and in the theory of escalation. In producer cooperatives, democratic participation is joined to actual ownership of the enterprise so that shareholders are, at one and the same time, workers and capitalists. As such, they represent unambiguous examples of people who occupy contradictory locations in the class structure as formulated by Eric Olin Wright (1978). Thus, it could be argued, people in producer cooperatives cannot be expected to act like workers because they are not, in fact, located in working-class positions.

The contradictory class situation of people in producer cooperatives is undeniable and suggests that the findings of my research are not generalizable, that producer cooperatives are unique organizations. But it is not entirely obvious that producer cooperatives can be distinguished from any other form of worker self-management that exists or that one might imagine in the United States. For one thing, ownership is easily overemphasized as a factor in the producer cooperatives in the Northwest plywood industry. I would venture that within the cooperatives, the significance of ownership in inculcating values and shaping behavior is not very great. Ownership of a share in the company is generally understood by the worker-shareholders not as participation in capital but as a guarantee to steady employment among a group of people most of whom have experienced long periods without work and of participation in enterprise decisionmaking relevant to one's paycheck. Furthermore, annual division of the enterprise surplus is based on hours of labor performed, not on number of shares owned. Ownership is relevant only to the extent that it serves as an entree to participation in this system of production and remuneration.

Furthermore, it does not seem to me that one could imagine any form of worker participation, control, or self-management in America today that could escape the powerful market logic that determines much of what takes place in the producer cooperatives even if workers did not share in ownership. Except where workers are already caught up in a radical mass movement or located within a fully socialized economy, situations obviously irrelevant to the United States at this time, they would invariably find themselves involved in a workplace participatory situation in which their own livelihoods would depend upon the economic success of the enterprise measured in conventional market terms, very much like any entrepreneur-owned, worker-owned, or managerial firm. Share or non-share in formal ownership, I would argue, is not what is decisive . . . workers involved in making decisions in a context that gives them a powerful stake in market-based profitability will be influenced by market logic and all that that logic entails. Even full self-management would simply represent collective control of the enterprise for the long-run maximization of profits. Thus, I would suggest that any system of workplace democratization situated in the United States would place workers in the same contradictory class location dilemma as found among shareholders in the cooperatives. The issue of ownership of shares is largely irrelevant. What is most relevant is the nature of the incentive system and the most rational forms of behavior encouraged by that incentive system.[2]

The Contextual Factor

Should advocates of democratic socialism reject worker self-management and workplace democracy? Do all forms of worker self-management or workplace democratization, at all times and in all places, have effects similar to those I found in the U.S. cooperatives? Does self-management consistently encourage attitudes and behaviors that hinder the development of a movement for economic democracy, or is it possible to locate cases and situations in which workplace organization serves as an incubator of democratic, egalitarian, and communitarian values and behaviors? It is my view that no grand claims about the effects of self-management are supportable and that self-management will have radically different effects depending upon the particular context in which it is located. In one setting, this organizational form will have negative consequences for democratic self-governing socialism, whereas in another, the same form will have the opposite result. In the remainder of this chapter, I will attempt to delineate a range of contrasting political-economic contexts and speculate about the effects of workplace democracy within each. The discussion is necessarily tentative because of the paucity of empirical evidence. Although there is a veritable gold mine of empirical work related to workplace democracy and self-management, very little of it is directly concerned with their political effects outside the walls of the enterprise or sensitive to context. Most of the literature is either descriptive or concerned with such matters as economic efficiency, forms and rates of participation, the nature of supervision, the effects on alienation, work satisfaction, enterprise loyalty, and the like. All of these matters are of great interest, but they have little bearing on the political effects of workplace democracy on workers as individuals and as members of a class. I will attempt to extrapolate, then, from the theoretical literature and the limited pool of empirical research.

I will address the question of when workplace democracy is likely to be transformative, prefiguring a future democratic, self-governing society, and when it is likely to be integrative and co-optive, strengthening the status quo. I have tentatively identified four contrasting contexts for the consideration of this question: stable market-capitalist societies devoid of class-based politics or ideology (which I call "unmediated"); stable market-capitalist societies with manifest class-based politics or ideology (which I call "mediated"); societies undergoing revolutionary transformation; and postrevolutionary socialist societies.[3]

Unmediated Market-Capitalist Society

As I have suggested above, institutions of worker self-management (whether worker-owned or not) in a stable market-capitalist society devoid of countervailing factors to capitalist economic, political, social, and cultural domination are likely to have objectively reactionary effects. They will not only fail to escalate sympathies for economic democracy but will act as a retardant. A situation in which short-run self-interest is tied to the economic well-being of the enterprise based on market performance and the powerful influence of the market mechanism is not counterbalanced by that of an outside agency (be it a movement, party, or ideology) whose mission or effect is to expand sympathies and to transcend "enterprise egoism," encourages people to act as collective capitalists. Without countervailing tendencies, the disciplines of the market are irresistible. In a decidedly nonsupportive, even hostile environment, the potential emancipatory effects of workplace democracy must be stillborn.

The United States, of course, stands virtually alone as the prototypical case. The United States is unique among the Western industrialized nations for the virtual absence of class-based politics and ideology. I am here making the conventional yet unavoidable case for what has been called "American exceptionalism." The litany is familiar (Greenberg, 1986). The United States is characterized, for instance, by an unusually fragmented working class, divided by ethnicity, race, religion, skill, and career ladders (Aronowitz, 1973; Crispo, 1978; David, 1980; Kolko, 1976; Korpi, 1978; Montgomery, 1979; Wright, 1977); extremely low rates of union membership; the inability to mobilize a labor vote; the absence of powerful labor-oriented political parties (Alford, 1969; Greenstone, 1969; Miliband, 1969) or direct labor representation in government; and the dominance of classical liberal, capitalistic-oriented ideas in the culture (Hartz, 1955; Sennett and Cobb, 1973; Slater, 1970; Tocqueville, 1845; Wills, 1970). The American working class thus finds itself uniquely impotent and divided, organizationally, politically, and ideologically.

Without organizational, political, or ideological linkages between them and with no resources to resist the logic of the market and the power of the capitalist state, democratic enterprises must move inevitably toward enterprise egoism and profit orientation. This is the case with the entire range of examples of workplace democratization in the United States whether one considers the plywood cooperatives, worker takeovers of declining capitalist firms (Diamant, 1982:13), or small countercultural collectives.[4] Without a compatible environment, without a rough symmetry between the micro and macro levels of society, cooperatives and other worker-controlled enterprises show no ability to generate *by themselves* a dynamic supportive of democratic, self-governing socialism. That is not to say, of course, that such enterprises are not better places to work than others (for they clearly are so), or that they do not foster cooperative and egalitarian relations among their members (which they clearly do). It is to say, however, that the political spillover effects are either nonexistent or contrary to the construction of a movement for democratic socialism in the United States.[5]

Mediated Market-Capitalist Societies

It is entirely possible that democratized and self-managed workplaces situated in market-capitalist societies with a strong working-class movement, party, ideology, or culture may have different and more positive political spillover effects than is evident in the United States. In such contexts, factors may be introduced into democratized enterprises which serve to tame the worse effects of the market mechanism, inculcate a set of democratic, communitarian, and egalitarian values, and/or alter the nature of enterprise calculations with respect to the world outside the enterprise walls. I am referring primarily to cases in Western Europe and in Israel, ranging from the Mondragon cooperatives to the kibbutzim. David Jenkins has suggested that democratized enterprises might behave differently and have demonstrably different effects in Europe than in the United States and has linked the possibility to the contextual factor. In this book *Industrial Democracy in Europe* (1974), he shows how in Europe, as contrasted to the United States, workplace democratization initiatives are generally understood in a broad political context, integrated into the programs of labor unions and political parties; how the humanization of work is rarely considered apart from the issue of authority in the plant; how work reform is conventionally linked to broader ideas of social justice; how the enhancement of the in-plant work environment is frequently linked to the provision of social services outside of the plant; and finally, how union and party activists often make the explicit linkage between small-scale work reorganization and the movement for a better society (however defined).[6]

A number of factors seem particularly important in the formation of a countervailing force to the market mechanism and the creation of a more conducive environment for democratized workplaces. First is the existence of strong working-class parties and/or working-class control of or influence over government. In the case of the famous Lipp takeover in France, for instance, workers saw themselves as part of a larger labor movement, received assistance from national political organizations, and were treated sympathetically by government (Carnoy and Shearer, 1980). At Meriden Triumph in Great Britain, the experiment in worker control was supported legislatively and financially by a Labour-controlled government (Carnoy and Shearer, 1980). In the Scandinavian countries, Social Democratic parties, labor unions, and central governments actively support a wide range of work democratizations ranging from work humanization, to co-determination, to worker ownership (Carnoy and Shearer, 1980; Crispo, 1978; Diamant, 1982; Furniss and Tilton, 1977; Garson, 1977; Jenkins, 1974; Korpi, 1978). Second, it has been suggested that an appropriate ideological and cultural climate may serve as a barrier against the powerful logic of the market and reorient the behavior of worker-controlled enterprises. It is often pointed out, for instance, how important Basque culture is to the success of the remarkable Mondragon cooperatives, particularly the high regard in the culture for values like association and cooperation, equality, industrialism, and mutual trust (Gutierrez-Johnson and Whyte, 1977; Oakeshott, 1973, 1978; Stephen, 1982; Thomas and Logan, 1982). The same case is often made for the Israeli kibbutzim, embedded as they are in a kibbutz culture and movement that has been explicitly socialist, cooperative, and egalitarian (Blasi, 1978; Fine, 1973; Palgi and Rosner, 1983; Rosner, 1976, 1982, 1984; Rosenstein, 1977; Stephen, 1982; Whyte and Blasi n.d.) from the beginning. Ain Haas reports (1980) that Swedish workers, as compared to American workers, tend to value self-management because of their belief in equality and democracy and their confidence in fellow workers. Americans support it for profit-sharing reasons. Finally, cooperatives and other democratized work enterprises seem to be more stable, economically successful, and committed to general, extraenterprise goals when surrounded by a network of supporting institutions. One is reminded of the national cooperative associations of the Scandinavian nations, the kibbutz federations in Israel, and the elaborate financial and technical infrastructure of Mondragon.

The empirical evidence gets skimpy, however, when one turns to the issue of the political effects of workplace democracy in such settings. To be sure, there is an enormous literature on work satisfaction, participation, commitment, efficiency, and the like, but few authors have even asked let alone answered empirically whether such institutions contribute to or retard a movement for a new democratic and egalitarian society. There is some evidence that Lipp workers became more community and politically oriented during their takeover. There is much discussion of and even some supporting empirical evidence for the progressive political role of kibbutz members in Israeli society and of their role in articulating and disseminating socialist values (Elon, 1981; Blasi, 1978; Rosner, 1976, 1982; Palgi and Rosner, 1983). The strongest empirical evidence for a transcendence of enterprise egoism is reported by Thomas and Logan in their book on Mondragon (1982). The Mondragon cooperatives apparently attempt to maximize employment in the region (and not simply for their current members), restrain member earnings in the interests of egalitarianism in the community at large, make appropriations out of enterprise earnings for public goods, provide widespread technical and general education in the region, encourage Basque language and culture, and guide research and development in the cooperatives toward social and communitarian goals. Wajcman, on the other hand, found no evidence that women in a British co-op changed their values about politics (1983).

The Thomas and Logan study of Mondragon is impressive in demonstrating some long-term political effects, but it is, unfortunately, virtually the only one that does so. Very little empirical research supports the overall generalization that workplace democratization molds attitudes and behaviors supportive of a self-governing, egalitarian way of life in what I have chosen to call mediated market-capitalist societies. Rather, there is reason to believe that a continuous tension exists in such societies between party, culture, and ideology on the one hand and the larger market-capitalist structure on the other, and there is no reason to assume that the former inevitably wins out.[7] Considering the literature on these cases, there is no reason to reject out of hand the conclusion reached by one set of authors about workplace democracy in "mediated" societies: "that workplace democracy does not in any direct way challenge structural features of capitalist institutions'' (Baumgartner, Burns, and DeVille, 1979:211). It is entirely possible, however, that future empirical research on the political effects of workplace democracy will support the more optimistic view.

The Revolutionary Setting

Self-management that arises in the midst of revolutionary upheaval is generally animated by the same forces that sustain the revolutionary struggle itself. In these circumstances worker control at the point of production is not created as a form of business enterprise whose purpose is to produce and sell commodities, gain market stability, and provide a long-term income for its owners, but as a location of social struggle, a component of the entire revolutionary process whose goal is nothing less than the remaking of society. In this sense, self-management in the form of the soviet or the workers' council has been an important component of every modern revolution whether failed or successful. Spontaneous expressions of worker self-management appeared in the Paris Commune of 1871, the Russian revolutions of 1905 and 1917, the failed 1918–19 revolutions in Hungary, Germany, and northern Italy, in Catalonia during the Spanish Civil War, in the Portuguese revolution in 1974, and in Allende's experiment in Chile. Workers' councils were also prominent features of (ironically?) the anti-Soviet uprisings in Poland in 1956, in Czechoslovakia in 1968, and in Poland again in 1981. As Horvat puts it, "Historically speaking, socialist [revolution] and self-government appear to be synonymous" (1975:39).[8] They are synonymous because, as Hannah Arendt has argued, the essence of modern revolutions is the rush of the vast majority into the public arena to share in the formation and execution of the public business, with the result being the transformation of the people from passive objects to active citizens. Revolutions are struggles for public freedom and a blow against tyranny understood in a special sense:

Tyranny, as the revolutions came to understand it, was a form of government in which the ruler, even though he ruled according to the laws of the realm, had monopolized for himself the right of action, banished the citizens from the public realm into the privacy of their households, and demanded of them that they mind their own, private business. Tyranny, in other words, deprived of public happiness, though not necessarily of private well-being, while a republic granted to every citizen the right to become 'a participator in the government of affairs', the right to be seen in action. [Arendt, 1965:127]

If we conceptualize revolutions in the sense described by Arendt as a flowering of participatory democracy on a national scale, the formation of institutions of direct democracy at points of production is an obvious correlate of the overall phenomenon. Such institutions are necessarily the product of the revolutionary process and not the catalyst and incubator for it (Horvat, 1982:135–37). It is also obvious that in such a setting, though the outward form may be the same, self-management is of an entirely different character than when it is situated in a stable market-capitalist society. There the overriding goal is the economic viability of the enterprise, not the transformation of society; the mode of participation is cool and economically calculating rather than intense and risk-oriented; contact with the world outside the enterprise is through the objective register of the market mechanism, not through a community of shared commitment characteristic of revolutions.

This conception of the self-managed workplace as the incubator of a new society warmed by the revolutionary process is, as I suggested in Chapter 6, associated most intimately with Antonio Gramsci.[9] Gramsci perceived workers' councils to be the seeds of a new workers' hegemony and the basis of a new socialist society. He also placed workers' councils within a broader revolutionary context; he was not naive enough to believe that they could play their great historical role in isolation. They could do so only when they were embedded in settings of revolutionary upheaval. Without a revolutionary movement, and a revolutionary party, the councils were seeds without water or nutrients, doomed to permanent dormancy. Only revolution would bring them to flower and make them into instruments of further social change. Councils were thus both spontaneous organizations created in the midst of struggle and educative devices that carried the struggle to greater heights. Arising directly out of the process of production, councils "were transformed by revolution into the structure of a new proletarian state" (Williams, 1975:102).[10]

It seems highly likely that soviets and other institutions of direct democracy play the role assigned to them in theory, but very little evidence meeting modern historiographic or sociological standards exists. To be sure, numerous histories of the 1905 and 1917 Russian revolutions lend support to the revolutionary role of soviets (Sirianni 1982, 1985), as well as the contribution made by soviet-style institutions in the Algerian revolution, the Catalonian experiment during the Spanish Civil War, and others.[11] From this literature, most of it based on anecdotal and memoir material, we may draw the tentative conclusion that such institutions serve as classrooms for rapid social change. One would hope, however, that future research will better specify the particular processes at work, weigh their import, and delineate their interactions.

Three studies exist, however, that give greater credence to the revolutionary role of democratized workplaces. Ben Ross Schneider found significant attitudinal changes among workers in self-managed enterprises in Peru, where a quasi-revolution was imposed from the top in 1968 by the military based on the slogan "a social democracy of full participation" (1979). Workers in such enterprises, as compared to those in privately owned firms, demonstrated impressive shifts to the left in their political attitudes. In summarizing his data, Schneider points out that self-managed workers are more radical, that they have become more so in the last two or three years, and that the experience of the self-managed firm was one of the most important contributing factors (1979:26). Schneider also demonstrated that workers in self-managed enterprises tended to have the strongest identification with the working class and the poor (which is diametrically opposite of my own findings in the U.S. cooperatives). Evelyn Stephens (1980) also reports the existence of a leftward political movement in self-managed enterprises during this period in Peru as the working class in general pushed the reform process toward socialist transformation. That capitalists in the end rallied the state to their side and halted the reform process does not detract from the political educative effects of direct democratic institutions in Peru. Espinosa and Zimbalist, in a major investigation of Chile during the Allende years, discovered profound political changes among workers in the social-property sector in the predicted direction (1978). After demonstrating how these enterprises were created and energized by the organization, ideology, and struggles of the revolutionary process, they empirically demonstrated the attitudinal and behavioral changes among workers in them. In summarizing their findings, the authors observed:

> One of the most important considerations which can be extracted from the Chilean experience lies in the radical overhaul of purpose and objectives in participatory enterprises. From the unidimensional focus on profit maximization in private firms, social area enterprises were transformed into social communities that pursued the personal and collective development of their members. In addition to concern for efficient and socially useful production, these enterprises sought to stimulate growth in the fields of education, health, and culture and generally radiated these benefits to the surrounding community. [1978:187]

One might object, of course, that neither Peru nor Chile is a truly revolutionary case because in each a revolution was aborted. The objection is well taken. Nevertheless, these studies remain the closest approximation in the literature to empirical, data-based studies of attitude change among workers in self-managed enterprises during periods of rapid social transformation. They are a tantalizing hint of studies yet to come.

Self-Management in Postrevolutionary Settings

Direct democracy at the workplace has always been at the center of the socialist vision of postcapitalist society. It is a conception of a society run on cooperative and egalitarian principles whose main grass-roots institutions are work organizations of freely associated producers. The main differences in this postcapitalist vision concern the role to be played by central planning as opposed to the market mechanism, with Marxist socialists leaning toward the former and non-Marxist socialists leaning toward the latter, though the division is not as neat and precise as one might suspect. Since the vision of direct democracy in the workplace is at least implicit in the work of nearly every socialist thinker, it would serve no real purpose to review each of their ruminations. Of far greater interest is the actual operation of cooperatives and other self-managing institutions in societies that have experienced successful anticapitalist revolutions. These democratic experiences fall into two general categories: planning-centered and market-centered.

In the planning-centered workplace democratizations, the general purpose of the cooperative and other democratized workplaces is to educate and socialize people imbued with attitudes derived from and appropriate to the prerevolutionary society into modes of thinking and acting more appropriate to socialism. As Lenin put the matter in his main statement on the issue, "On Cooperation": "Since political power is in the hands of the working class, . . . the only task that remains for us is to organize the population into cooperative societies . . . [for it is an instrument that is] the simplest, easiest and most acceptable to the peasant. . . . Our task is educational work among the peasants. . . . If the whole of the peasantry had been organized in cooperatives, we would now have been standing with both feet on the soil of socialism" (1975:707).

To Lenin, cooperatives were not free to do as they pleased; they were, rather, instrumentalities of party and class education. On this ground he rejected the proposals of the Worker's Opposition that "the organization of the management of the national economy is the function of an All-Russian Congress of Producers organized in industrial unions which shall elect a central body to run the whole of the national economy of the Republic." To that claim Lenin counterposed the following: "Only the political party of the working class . . . is capable of uniting, training, and organizing a vanguard of the proletariat and of the whole mass of the working people" (1975:497). Worker control and peasant cooperation could be instituted, he argued, only under the guiding hand of the Communist party.

The tradition of using cooperative and democratic work forms under central direction as a noncoercive means for the creation of a new socialist human being was carried on in the Soviet Union by Nikolai Bukharin.[12] To Bukharin, whose ideas and life were eventually erased by Stalin, the peasant cooperatives were the main vehicles for the transition to truly socialist society, the cells that would eventually grow into the sturdy infrastructure of an egalitarian, noncoercive, and cooperative social order. He rejected the notion of his critics that cooperatives were intrinsically capitalist institutions since, he argued, the seizure of state power by the proletariat had changed the environment in which they operated and would give them a totally different character. Cooperation in the Soviet context, he suggested, where these institutions found themselves irretrievably linked to socialist industry and banks, would cause them, "independent of their will, to grow into socialism . . . the cooperatives will grow into the system of *our* institutions, just as in capitalist society they grew into the system of capitalist relations."[13] All of this would happen, however, under the leadership of the party. The masses were not free to choose their destiny but were to be drawn into the construction of socialism.[14]

The danger to democratic socialism in such a system of centralized direction of cooperatives, soviets, and other democratized work settings is too obvious to rehearse. Suffice it to say that when soviets and similar institutions arose in the midst of and were an important element in a successful anticapitalist revolution and the postrevolutionary society came under the direction of a Marxist-Leninist party committed to central direction and planning, units of worker self-management sooner or later were eliminated (though they later reappeared in Yugoslavia). These regimes, however, have not been able totally to erase the idea of self-management or to guarantee that manifestations of the intense desire for it may not reappear in their midst (Horvat, 1982).

The other great tendency in socialist theory and practice is the proposal to organize society, after the conquest of political power and the eradication of capitalism, around both associations of direct producers and the market mechanism. This form is generally termed "market socialism" and is most closely associated with the theory and practice of Yugoslav communism.[15] It is based on the doctrine that the transition to socialism is possible only when society is organized around a system of freely associated direct producers and not state ownership, which inevitably gravitates to state capitalism, bureaucracy, and tyranny. Yugoslav communist thinkers, seeking an ideological and organizational alternative to the Russian communist model after Tito's break with Stalin and the Comintern, found in such classics as Marx's analysis of the Paris Commune and Lenin's *State and Revolution* the inspiration for a new approach to the "withering away of the state": the soviet and institutions of direct democracy. Yugoslav thinkers moved beyond the classics, however, when they came to the realization that institutions of self-management would be a mere charade of direct democracy unless they enjoyed considerable autonomy from central direction. Thus self-management was joined to the market. They were quick to point out, however, that the use of the market device did not necessarily imply a return to capitalism. In the absence of capitalist class relations, and with private property turned into social property (Horvat, 1982:190), the market would be merely an allocative device, a guarantor of economic efficiency no longer hampered by the conditions of exploitation (e.g., capitalist class relations). As one scholar has put the matter, "the market is an allocative device [and] can be put to work against the backdrop of dissimilar institutional forms; its operation is a function of the specific class structure of its social environment" (Di-Quattro, 1978:31).

In the theory of market socialism, the normal anarchy of the market along with its attendant irrationalities and injustices are counterbalanced by the actions of the state (which may be democratic in theory but is not so in the practice of Yugoslav communism), which, based on a national plan, designs investment strategies and taxing and spending policies so as to reduce income inequality, ameliorate externalities, and rectify uneven regional development. National and socialist objectives are also advanced in market socialism by the educative efforts of the vanguard party acting as the conscience of the new society. Such a party, as described by Gramsci, would be based on "analysis rather than ruling, of persuasion and leadership rather than coercion" (Comisso, 1979:15). It would serve not to rule but to help create the conditions for self-rule by the direct producers.[16]

Institutions of direct democracy at the workplace in the theory of market socialism are the bedrock of the system, the principal economic actors and the center of decisions about production. They respond to market signals to maximize economic efficiency. Acting in concert with their fellows in a fully developed deliberative system, workers learn to cooperate and gain confidence in their abilities as subjects rather than objects of history. Being situated in an environment based on socialist principles, with education to socialist conceptions of justice carried out by the schools, the media, and the party, workers come to tame their selfish instincts and tendencies toward enterprise particularism.[17]

Whether all of this is in fact the case in *actual* market socialism remains to be seen. The evidence from Yugoslavia is mixed in this regard. There is abundant evidence, for instance, that worker participation and deliberations in enterprise councils is biased toward skilled and white-collar workers (Obradovic and Dunn, 1978); that enterprise managers retain great power in decision making (many sources); that worker discontent has not disappeared and is often expressed in strikes (Shabad, 1978; Woodward, 1977); that many traditional and "etatist" attitudes are retained by unskilled and semiskilled workers (Horvat, 1982:400); that regional income disparities and wage inequalities have not disappeared (Wachtel, 1973); that enterprise egoism may be becoming a potential barrier to collective social goals (Comisso, 1979; Woodward, 1977) and that many nonsocialist values connected to materialism and consumerism are being propagated (Baumgartner, Burns, and Sekulic, 1979). But even though the Yugoslav economy has generally performed extremely well over the years, there is evidence that participation in enterprise and local government decision making is remarkably widespread; that the support for and the attitudes and skills relevant to self-management are deeply entrenched in the citizenry; that support for equality and the decentralization of power is high; and that workers generally believe in and think they have materially benefited from the system (Denitch, 1976; Horvat, 1982). Although the outlook is mixed in Yugoslavia, I am cautiously optimistic about the role of self-management in the liberation of the human species.

Conclusion: Context and Variation

The objective of this chapter had been to explore the possible relationships between worker self-management and the democratic control of the economy. My overall argument has involved a plea for a greater sensitivity to contextuality; that is, a sensitivity to the historically specific character of self-management and its effects. I have suggested that no single claim is possible with regard to the radicalizing effects of workplace democracy and worker self-management, that the analyst is obligated to specify the general setting within which these institutions operate. The analyst must be sensitive, as well, to the wide range of effects that are possible even within a single general setting. By way of review, let me briefly indicate the range of variation that is apparent in theory and practice.

Within the market-capitalist setting, self-management may have a number of possible effects. Scientific studies, journalistic reports, and personal statements by workers testify that self-managed and other democratic places of work are better places to expend one's labor and exercise one's skills than are conventional, hierarchical, and largely authoritarian ones. Furthermore, whatever the positive physical and pyschological benefits of workplace democracy, no visible expansionary dynamic seems evident in "unmediated" market-capitalist societies like the United States. Neither workers within such enterprises nor those in other enterprises see such democratic workplaces as models to be emulated. There is also considerable evidence that workplace democracy in such settings may actually retard political radicalization. Since the normal tendency of the market to encourage the pursuit of enterprise and individual self-interest is not countered by the educative role of movement, ideology, or party, it appears that self-management in such settings is likely to be objectively reactionary and antidemocratic in the broad sense. There is some evidence, however, that "mediated" market-capitalist societies as in Israel and Western Europe may well escape this dynamic and prove more hospitable to self-management as a tool of a larger democratization.

Self-management may take on an entirely different character in a setting of anticapitalist revolutionary upheaval. To the extent that the ubiquitous soviets and workers' councils are not just epiphenomena of revolution, simple outward indicators of societies in rapid transition, self-management *may* serve as a primary locus of revolutionary agitation, organization, and education. At their best, such institutions of worker democracy may represent the seed of a more democratic, just, and humane society. To play that role, of course, they must be strong enough to resist the powerful tendencies toward centralization evident in postrevolutionary regimes. So far, none have managed to do so, though the theoretical possibility remains attractive.

In postrevolutionary settings, worker self-management can have a variety of contrasting qualities. At worst, the enterprise autonomy that must be a part of true self-management may encourage the restoration of capitalist relations, a point made by several Marxist critics of Yugoslav socialism (Paul Sweezy in particular). Or, equally bad, self-management might simply be a charade in postrevolutionary settings, a form imposed by the party leadership as a tool of administration, surveillance, or indoctrination. It is possible, however, to take the case of Yugoslavia, that worker self-management might be the locus for nurturing a new set of social relations and values consistent with a society organized on broadly cooperative and egalitarian lines. It remains to be seen whether this promise is met over the long run in Yugoslavia.

All of this suggests that confident claims about the existence of a general relationship between workplace democracy and democratic, self-governing socialism are not possible. Clearly, however, without powerful countervailing forces to the market mechanism, democratic, self-managed enterprises drift inexorably toward enterprise egoism and membership behavior as collective capitalists. Without a working-class party, a cooperative or egalitarian culture, a socialist ideology, a revolutionary movement, or a government committed to economic democracy, the logic of the market is determinative and blocks the larger promise of self-management. Without these attributes, workplace democracy tends to be integrative and co-optive rather than prefigurative and transformative.[18] Without a conducive context, self-managed enterprises might well survive and prosper, but they are not likely to play a significant role within a movement for social change. Being without any of these countervailing forces in the United States, being devoid of such a conducive environment, I would venture the opinion that workplace democratization in the United States, even admitting its many intrinsic benefits, does not seem to be a very promising road to take in the general struggle to create a fully democratic society. Indeed, it seems to me to be a political deadend.

· 8 ·

The Political Effects
of Workplace Democracy

Summary of Findings

I opened this book by asking whether democratic Left enthusiasm for workplace democracy, especially in its most fully developed version, self-management, is warranted. The findings of the study reported in these pages must surely disappoint the hopes and expectations of democratic Left advocates of workplace democracy in the United States. The experience of democracy, equality, and self-management in the plywood co-operatives of the Pacific Northwest does not, in general, form attitudes and behaviors that are consistent with democratic, self-governing socialism or inconsistent with the prevailing social, political, and economic climate in the United States. Although theoretical expectations are met occasionally in the analysis, what is most notable is the degree to which workplace democracy in the plywood cooperatives seems to have had either no appreciable effects or effects exactly the opposite of expectations.

The linkage between workplace democracy and the process of dealienation, for example, is tenuous at best in that workplace democracy does not seem automatically to improve the deadening aspects of the technical division of labor, the sense of solidarity and community among workers, or their mental health. Moreover, workplace democracy in the plywood cooperatives not only fails to operate as a "school for socialism," fostering values and commitments appropriate to the struggle against capitalism and for the construction of a democratic, self-governing socialist society, but actually encourages values and commitments inimical to and destructive of these goals. American plywood workers in co-ops, for instance, iden-

169

tified less with the working class over time; failed to develop a critical stance toward prevailing economic, social, and political arrangements; became more committed to basic values associated with market capitalism; and grew less willing to support mass democratic control of the economic life of the nation. These findings cannot be heartening for the democratic Left.

The comparative analyses reported in Chapters 4 and 7 showed, however, that these outcomes are not necessarily inherent in worker self-management. I advanced the argument that the persistence and nurturance of volitions and behaviors antithetical to democratic, self-governing socialism seem to be particularly characteristic of the United States, where market capitalism and its supporting culture and politics are not countervailed by a movement, party, or ideology committed to equality, economic democracy, and nonhierarchical social relations. Thus, though the hopes and expectations of advocates of workplace democracy are severely disappointed in the United States, there is no reason to despair about the effects of workplace democracy in a more hospitable environment.

Democratic Left advocates of workplace democracy, even in the United States, need not wallow in pessimism, moreover, for there is much about the plywood cooperatives that is admirable and perhaps reproducible by other workers in other enterprises. For instance, the plywood cooperatives prove conclusively that ordinary working people are capable of managing the business and production aspects of complex, modern industrial enterprises and in a way that has resulted in stability and prosperity in an industry characterized by instability and hard times. Complex, modern institutions can be successfully operated on the basis of democratic, egalitarian, and nonhierarchical principles even in an environment that is hostile to such principles in the workplace such as in the United States. The plywood cooperatives demonstrate that, given the proper incentive system and social environment, workers can do quite well without a great deal of supervision, invent imaginative solutions to production problems, develop a sense of responsibility toward the work group and the enterprise, gain detailed knowledge about and interest in a broad range of business (marketing, purchasing, financing) and production affairs affecting their enterprise, and learn to keep their leaders responsible and responsive to their needs and interests. The experience of the plywood cooperatives demonstrates, moreover, that important aspects of alienation thought to be inherent in the industrial process can be overcome through institutions of workplace democracy, most particularly those aspects of the alienation of labor having to do with estrangement from product and the decision-making process.

Most heartening is the degree to which the experience of the plywood cooperatives supports many of the expectations of such participatory democratic theorists as J. S. Mill, G. D. H. Cole, and Carole Pateman. This study showed that self-governance at the workplace is educative both by encouraging people to participate actively in the political life of the community outside the enterprise and by training them in the skills necessary to do so. For those interested in the revitalization and enrichment of a pallid American democratic system, where political involvement, interest, and commitment by the citizenry remains seriously deficient, the experience of these unique enterprises must be encouraging.

Taken as a whole, these achievements of the plywood cooperatives are admirable. They represent no small achievement in a society that generally regards ordinary people as untrustworthy in the workplace and apathetic and incompetent in the political life of the nation. If the plywood cooperatives do not live up to the expectations of the democratic Left, they nevertheless are virtually the only enterprises in the United States that give ordinary working people the opportunity to practice the arts of self-direction, equality, and democracy. This is no small achievement even if they do not have the political effects that many have hoped for over the years. Nourished by a supportive political, cultural, and ideological environment, these seeds of a decent and humane society might yet flower. They cannot do so, however, in isolation, in an inhospitable, alien environment. The lesson learned from the comparative examination of worker self-management in Mondragon, Yugoslavia, Peru, Israel, Eastern Europe, and Scandinavia (Chapters 4 and 7) is that the bright promise of workplace democracy and self-management can be achieved only if it is part of a larger struggle for popular democracy and equality in the United States.

The Plywood Cooperatives as Cases

Before speculating on the dimensions of such a movement in the United States, it is appropriate to ask whether the broad conclusions drawn above can be based on a cases as specific as that of the American plywood cooperatives. Are these co-ops not unique institutions with their own idiosyncrasies from which it is dangerous to generalize? Might it not be objected that heavy reliance on hired labor makes these institutions some-thing other than democratic enterprises? Is it relevant that the cooperatives grew out of a cooperative Swedish culture located in the Pacific Northwest? Because this culture is very different from the American norm, are the plywood cooperatives not poor raw material for formulating generaliza-tions for the system as a whole? Since the worker-shareholders in the cooperatives are owners as well as workers, is a study of them a study of the effects of ownership and not of the effects of democratic participation? Finally, it is undeniable that the period of this study, 1978 to 1983, was characterized by rapid change in the political climate of the nation and in the economic conditions of the wood-products industry in the United States. Might it not be reasonable to support that this state of flux makes it virtually impossible to reach stable and lasting conclusions about the effects of workplace democracy?

1. The matter of hired labor

It is true that the plywood co-ops hire labor to do work that worker-shareholders are either unwilling or unable to do themselves. Some are hired to "lay core," a demanding and extremely fast-paced job most appropriate for young people and not the slowly aging population of the co-ops. Electricians, carpenters, and mechanics are hired to do specialized tasks that are beyond the training or competence of the worker-share-holders. Accountants and marketing specialists are hired to run the business affairs of the enterprise. Finally, many hired workers are ordinary pro-duction workers who may be and are often laid off during bad economic times. Nevertheless, these hired workers are a distinct minority in the plywood cooperatives, and they are not universally exploited because most of them have specialized knowledge that makes them indispensable in plywood production and sales. They are a minority that, though not a part of the process of enterprise democracy, is listened to on a continuous basis. Still, the existence of this group of workers makes the cooperatives something other than models of workers' self-management. Even if they come closer to the model than other enterprises in the United States, they fall short to the extent that some workers are left out of the self-governing process.

Despite this shortcoming, the plywood cooperatives remain useful re-search sites for the investigations carried out in these pages because I have focused my attention in them almost exclusively on those workers most intimately involved in the democratic process and not the others. In making claims about the effects of participation in decision making at the workplace, I have confined my attention to those who are involved in the democratic process on the job and asked how such activities have affected them and *only them* over a period of years. Such questions can be raised even when the enterprises themselves are not perfect democracies. The claims made in this book thus are generally about the effects of the experience of democracy at the workplace on individuals directly and intimately involved in such processes and not about the enterprises themselves.

Another more general question is whether, if worker-shareholders must hire various experts to carry out essential functions, it is impossible to create genuinely democratic work organizations? Are the demands of modern industrial production so complicated that ordinary working people cannot run their own enterprises? I think not. First, democracy does not preclude the possibility of hiring experts so long as such experts carry out their specialized tasks under the general control of the work community. Democracy involves procedures by which a community defines its own goals and objectives as well as a general path along which it intends to travel to meet such goals and objectives. Specialists may be required to help in the specifics of these processes, but so long as they remain under the control of the community and work to fulfill its mandate, democracy is not threatened.[1] Second, it is not self-evident that expertise on a broad front is beyond the competence of ordinary working people, as the cases of Mondragon and the kibbutz vividly demonstrate. What seems to be required is a commitment in self-managed enterprises to the continuous training and skill upgrading of the membership. Thus both the Mondragon community and the kibbutz federations provide an elaborate mix of educational institutions to train their members in technical and business areas. Neither of these democratic communities feels it necessary to go outside of its membership on a regular basis to secure specialized assistance.

2. The matter of an atypical culture in the Pacific Northwest
There is no denying that the plywood cooperatives have grown out of and been nurtured in a culture that is somewhat more cooperative and egalitarian than that which is most characteristic of the United States.[2] Rather than creating a problem for the conclusions reached in these pages, however, it powerfully affirms them. Had we discovered that workers in the cooperatives were more prone to express cooperative and egalitarian values than were workers in conventional mills, it would be entirely

appropriate to object that such findings might be more attributable to the early socialization of co-op workers than to the effects of the democratic experience. The exact opposite was found, however: workers in the co-ops were less prone to hold orientations congruent with a cooperative and egalitarian culture than were other workers. Apparently the experience in the cooperatives trains people to take an individualistic and competitive view of the world. It would be reasonable to suspect that these individualistic and competitive educational tendencies would be even more pronounced in democratic work settings where the dominant culture is not entirely friendly to cooperation and equality. If workplace democracy does not nurture the attitudes and behaviors expected by the democratic Left among the worker-shareholders in this study, then where in the United States might it be expected to do so?

3. The matter of ownership

The producer cooperatives in plywood are not only democratic enterprises; they are also worker-owned enterprises. The findings of this study might be attributed to the ownership factor, and had we examined the effects of workplace democracy in enterprises whose workers participated in decision making but held no ownership shares the results might have been more encouraging. As I pointed out in Chapters 6 and 7, however, it is clear that without the comfort, encouragement, and support of egalitarian, cooperative, and democratic culture, mass movements, political parties, or public policies, democratically run enterprises whose financial remuneration depends entirely on success in the marketplace are likely to encourage outlooks and behaviors appropriate to success. The most likely outcome of workplace democracy in what I have called unmediated market-capitalist societies (as in the United States) is the nurturance of both enterprise egoism and possessive individualism. Formal ownership, I have argued, is far less important in attitude formation than the constraints placed on enterprise behavior by the rigors of market logic.

4. The matter of ''changing times''

This study was conducted during a period of significant change in the wood-products industry and in the nation. The years 1978 to 1983 were ones of near depression in the industry because high interest rates and excess capacity contributed to a serious slump in commercial and residential building. Many of the plywood cooperatives barely survived, and the worker-shareholders in nearly all of them were forced to take cuts in their annual compensation. In the nation, the last years of the Carter presidency and the first years of the Reagan era were characterized by a significant shift to the political Right as Americans increasing lost confidence in the ability of government to solve significant social and economic problems. But such transformations do not seriously affect the conclusions of this study because panel studies with suitable comparison groups are designed to take such change into account. Had I simply tracked changing attitudes and behaviors among worker-shareholders over time and attributed such changes to their life in democratic enterprises, I would have been vulnerable to the charge of not considering changes in the larger environment. Such a strategy has not, of course, been followed in this study. The attitudes and behaviors of worker-shareholders have not been tracked by reference to any set standard. Rather, attitude and behavior change has been measured in comparison to attitude and behavior change among workers in conventional mills who were subject to the same influences of these changing times. A panel design with comparison groups automatically controls for the possible impact of exogenous and environmental factors. In such a design, statements of the form "worker-shareholders in comparison to workers in conventional firms come to believe x, y, and z" are defensible and appropriate. In this study, more general conclusions are drawn from a range of such comparisons.

Fulfilling the Promise of Workplace Democracy

Now that I have addressed the question of the suitability of the plywood cooperatives as the basis for the general claims made in this study, let me return to the question of the future of workplace democracy in the United States in the context of the decidedly mixed and often disappointing results I have reported in this study. In one sense, this has been a cautionary tale in which I propose that the democratic Left stop applauding every time workers buy out an enterprise, form a cooperative, or become involved in a democratic experiment in the workplace. Is it necessary to go to the other extreme? Must the democratic Left abandon workplace democracy entirely both as ideal and strategy? I think not. I am prepared to argue that workplace democracy is necessary in a future social order that is decent and humane and in the political movement that might help to bring it to reality. Indeed, a mutually reinforcing relationship may be relevant here, for not only is workplace democracy an essential part of such a future society and the movement to bring it to fruition, but it is only within these nurturing environments that the bright promise of workplace democracy may be realized: the end of alienating labor; the creation of an educated, engaged, and empathetic citizenry; and the encouragement of a self-confident working class. Workplace democracy can realize its bright expectations only in environments characterized by democracy, equality, and fraternity. Such environments may be found, in my view, in two locations: in a postcapitalist, postsocialist[3] society that I shall describe below, and in the popular political struggle that is necessary to create such a society.

Self-Governing or Democratic Socialism

I suggest that workplace democracy is most likely to flower when its central values are affirmed, nurtured, and protected by the society in which it is embedded. The central values of workplace democracy are equality, democracy, and cooperation. I would call a society in which such values define the shape of social, political, and economic relations a self-governing or democratic socialism. Speculation about such a society has already been admirably done by Branko Horvat in his landmark book *The Political Economy of Socialism* (1982), so I will not offer an elaborate discussion concerning the details of its form and operations here.[4] My understanding of its general parameters and defining characteristics, however, is in order.

1. Equality

One bedrock condition of democratic or self-governing socialism is equality, the organization of society in a manner that ensures that the resources produced by society are distributed so as to meet the common needs of its members. Exact mathematical equality is neither possible nor necessary, but all members of society must share in the enjoyment of those goods and services produced by society which are requisite to a life of decency, fulfillment, and self-respect. Recognizing that production is the outcome of the shared contribution of the skills, intelligence, and labor of the man, democratic socialism insists that the distribution of the fruits of production take a majoritarian form as well and not be hoarded in the hands of the few. Material equality is also a bedrock principle of social organization in self-governing socialism because of the understanding that people are free to cultivate their talents and interests only when basic needs for food, shelter, and security are met. The development of meaningful individualism for the vast majority becomes possible only when people have access to the resources that enable them to broaden their horizons and cultivate their abilities.

The principle of equality of condition is significantly more than and superior to notions of equality that are confined simply to the enjoyment of legal and political rights. Striking inequalities of condition make a mockery of rights, for material inequalities give some members of society greater access and ability to use and enjoy them. As R. H. Tawney has put it, "economic realities make short work of legal abstractions" (quoted in Terrill, 1973:122). Equality of condition must also be distinguished from equality of opportunity, which is surely inoperative in any society (including the United States) characterized by wide disparities in material conditions. The notion of equality of opportunity in a setting of extreme inequality of condition is such a contradiction that it has the appearance of being, again in Tawney's words, a bit like "the impertinent courtesy of an invitation offered to unwelcome guests in the certainty that circumstances will prevent them from accepting it" (quoted in Terrill, 1973:122).

2. Dispersal of power

Intimately connected to and logically derived from the concept of equality of condition is the concept of the dispersal of decision-making power into the hands of the many. If the service of human needs, interests, and capacities requires an environment of rough equality of condition, it follows that the distribution of power, the ability to shape the directions of group life, must also be distributed in some roughly proportional fashion. To organize society in any other manner would be to introduce significant inequality into the social order and largely to negate the advances made through the equalization of material conditions. The reintroduction of inequality in decision-making power would not only undermine the common humanity and fellowship implicit in material equality but would act, as well, to block the development of the human capacity for self-direction, autonomy, and self-determination. To be a passive receiver of orders, to leave the direction of one's life to others, is to be stunted in one's growth and to be less than human.

In a self-governing socialist society, the principle of broad dispersal of power must obtain whenever decisions are made that affect others. In this view, decisions that have social implications and consequences must be arrived at socially. The dispersal of power, the widespread involvement of the many in the making of decisions, thus significantly broadens the concept of the political and makes it relevant to a diverse range of institutions in society, economy, and polity, including the workplace. Workplace democracy, in such an environment, is not an odd curiosity as it is in present market-capitalist societies but an essential institution congruent with the prevailing value structure of society.

3. Democratic planning

In a self-governing socialist society, even admitting of the need for the existence of a modified market mechanism, the overall directions of economic life and material production are defined by a democratic planning process in which a politically active and informed people are deeply involved. Production, being social, must come under the direction of society, but it must do so in a way that does not locate planning power in a bureaucratic, political, or party elite no matter how decent their intentions. To place production under the direction of the few is to reintroduce inequality, social distinctions, and passive citizenship and thereby to destroy the most central values of self-governing socialism. The existence of autonomous centers of power in decentralized democratic institutions like the workplace and the enterprise help ensure against the centralizing tendencies in the planning system.

Democratic, self-governing socialism does not, of course, exist anywhere on the planet though it exists in germinal form in such places as the Israeli kibbutz. It is a utopian vision but one that is not entirely beyond imagining given the proper circumstances. Of its eventual occurrence in human society, one cannot be certain. That workplace democracy is consistent with, or more accurately, necessary to the proper functioning of such a society is beyond doubt.

The Movement for Self-Governing Socialism

True self-governing socialism is surely a part of a very distant and only dimly and imprecisely imagined future. Much closer to home and to everyday possibilities is to imagine workplace democracy as part of a popular political movement to create a more egalitarian, democratic, and cooperative society. To understand the political role of workplace democracy in such a fashion is to take much of the undue burden off of it and to place it in its proper political context. To recognize that it is but a small part of a diverse movement for social change can reaffirm its importance and help guard against inflated and unrealizable expectations.

Any movement aimed at the creation of democratic, self-governing socialism, if it is to have any chance of meeting its goal, must operate, I believe, from two inescapable, bedrock assumptions: first, that the traditional strategies of the Left are inappropriate to the United States; and second, that the movement for change must prefigure self-governing socialism in its own structures and practices.

The Poverty of Traditional Strategies

The Left in the West has typically depended upon two basic strategies for the creation of a socialist society: frontal assault on capitalism by a party of professional revolutionaries (the Marxist-Leninist strategy) and entrance into the arena of electoral politics (the Social Democratic strategy). Both are highly problematic.

The Marxist-Leninist strategy suffers from at least two fatal flaws. First, there is no evidence that such an approach to change, even if it were desirable (which it is not), is possible in the West. It is not possible because the advanced industrial capitalist state, unlike prerevolutionary Russia, China, and Vietnam, enjoys a monopoly of coercive power which is in no danger of collapse. It is not possible, furthermore, because even if its monopoly of coercive power were to unravel, modern capitalism is buttressed by more than naked military and police power. Most important, modern capitalism enjoys widespread legitimacy among its population and stable social institutions. As Antonio Gramsci understood better than anyone else (1973, 1975), the durability of modern capitalism is located in a complex of social institutions and practices that legitimate capitalism, provide its justifications, and teach appropriate values and behavior. If this is true, then a strategy of direct assault on the state, with coercive power directed against coercive power, is doomed to impotence either before the power of the state or the impressive array of social structures and practices that stand behind it. The state in modern capitalism, as Gramsci graphically put it, is but the outer ramparts behind which stand the sturdy structures of civil society.

Second, and perhaps more important in the long run for the creation of self-governing socialism, the outcome of the Marxist-Leninist cure is more to be deplored than the disease itself. We have learned by bitter experience in this century that revolutionary vanguard parties are loath to give up power once they have successfully carried out a revolutionary struggle. A hierarchical revolutionary party tends to remain a hierarchical governing party, one that is inconsistent with self-governing socialism. As the dissident "Il Manifesto" group of the Italian Communist party once put it, "the goal of an eventual end to hierarchy cannot be met by a strategy that permits hierarchy" (Adams 1971:459). A democratic society is unlikely to emerge out of a nondemocratic or antidemocratic movement.

Yet parties calling themselves socialist have not been notably successful in hastening the transition from capitalism to socialism.[5] Indeed, it may be argued that the main effect of Social Democratic parties in Western Europe has been to stabilize modern capitalism to the extent that it has instituted those reforms necessary to the smooth functioning of the system (macroeconomic countercyclical policies, collective bargaining, unemployment insurance, government provision of infrastructural services, and so forth) yet generally distasteful to the political Right. This behavior on the part of Social Democratic parties is partially derived from their strategy of building the welfare state out of the economic surplus created by capitalism, a strategy that requires a healthy and productive capitalism. The nonrevolutionary behavior of Social Democracy has also been a product of the constraints of the electoral system, which, because of the need to build winning coalitions in societies where blue-collar workers represent but a minority of the population, causes socialist parties over time to move to the center of the political spectrum (Przeworski, 1985).

Perhaps even more important, the Social Democratic strategy, concentrating as it does on elections, encourages a politics of occasional or intermittent involvement among the people. It asks its adherents to read its literature, to attend meetings and rallies, and to cast votes. It does not ask that they create and run their own institutions in their neighborhoods and workplaces. It does not ask people to become self-governing citizens but to be followers, responding to the signals of well-meaning but distant and powerful institutions. In so doing, the Social Democratic approach ignores strategies that might help mobilize the great majority for its own liberation.

A Strategy for Change

Any strategy for change that is to be both successful and consistent with the societal form outlined above must develop the consciousness and capacity of the working class,[6] demonstrate that it is both necessary and possible to transcend presently existing capitalism and socialism, and offer a vision of a society that is worth the struggle. I can offer no positive blueprints to achieve these objectives, but I can sketch the very broad outlines of the many areas of activity that must be involved.

1. Struggle on the ideological/cultural front

Much of the endurance of existing societies can be traced to the power of the prevailing ideology and culture to teach, encourage, and solidify ways of thinking and behaving that are functional to their survival and domination. The prevailing ideology and culture in any stable society, including capitalist ones, helps determine for most people the "evaluation of the possible and the impossible, the future and the past, the useful and the useless, the rational and the irrational, the good and the bad" (Gorz, 1973:169). The thorough dissemination of capitalist ideology and culture throughout American society means that the working class is largely without the language, concepts, skills, or perspectives that would enable it fully to understand its situation, generate alternatives to current reality, or feel confident in its ability to manage society in a self-governing manner were it to be successful in its political struggle. One of the great roles of a movement committed to the creation of democratic, self-governing socialism would be, therefore, that of educator with a mandate not only to subject presently existing capitalism and socialism to criticism and offer a clearly articulated vision of a better society but also to help generate from within the working class the skills, capacities, and intelligence necessary for the task of creating a new social order. Gramsci, among others, understood that this complex task would require winning over elements of the intelligentsia to the movement for change; identifying, encouraging, and training a stratum of technical, scientific, and literary personnel from within the working class (which he called "organic intellectuals"); and creating counterinstitutions in the midst of existing society that would train people for a new way of life. It is with respect to the last that institutions of workplace democracy have an important role to play.

2. Creating institutions of self-governing socialism

One of the great goals of a movement for change must be to create institutions within society that challenge the prevailing order and anticipate the new. People within such institutions must learn ways of thinking and acting that distance them from behaviors appropriate to presently existing systems and train them in ways more appropriate to self-governing socialism. These institutions must encourage equality, democracy, and co-operation. One might imagine a wide range of such institutions fitting these requirements in areas as diverse as education, health care, community services, leisure, and productive work. Workplace democratic institutions (whether cooperatives or other forms of worker control) have a role to play in this respect, but only within the context of a much wider educational effort directed at the transformation of ideology and culture and the cre-ation of a broad range of counterinstitutions beyond the workplace. In the absence of this supportive environment, workplace democracy cannot transcend the walls of the enterprise and is doomed to enterprise egoism and the inculcation of the outlooks of possessive individualism. All such counterinstitutions must be not only alternative but oppositional organi-zations (that is, their members desire not so much to be left alone as to change the society around them), a possibility that can exist only to the extent that they are embedded in a broad-scale political movement.[7]

3. The long march through the institutions

The effort to transform ideology and culture and to create counterin-stitutions does not preclude the possibility or the necessity for people committed to self-governing socialism to work for change within the normal institutions of society. But because their goal is transformation and not reform, they must do so openly at all times as democratic socialists. Not to do so would be seriously to undermine the power of democratic socialism's critique of presently existing society and its vision of a better way of life and to rob it of its educative function. The goal of any movement for democratic, self-governing socialism must be to encourage the involvement of socialists openly so that its views and understandings might become an integral part of the ongoing deliberations within all important institutions whether they be elections, schools, work, scholar-ship, or mass communications. Again, if the struggle to democratize work takes place in the context of this broader political movement, it can po-tentially play an important educative and institution-building role.

Workplace Democracy and Self-Governing Socialism

I opened this chapter with a review of the findings from a close empirical examination of the plywood cooperatives and concluded that most of the expectations of the democratic Left about the benefits of workplace democracy are not supported even though there is much in these work institutions that is to be admired. Starting from these rather pessimistic findings, I then asked whether the democratic Left ought to abandon workplace democracy as an integral part of a utopian vision of a better society or as part of a strategy for the creation of such a society. I have spent the greater part of this chapter arguing that advocates of workplace democracy and self-governing, democratic socialism need not take such a drastic step in their thinking. Workplace democracy remains an essential element of such a political program, but it must be understood in all of its complexity. To do otherwise is to rob it of its potentially great transformative power and to doom it to ineffectual isolation.

METHODOLOGICAL APPENDIXES

Appendix I

Data Collection and Sample Characteristics

Data for this study were collected in four stages:

1. Initial information about cooperative and conventional plywood firms was gathered through interviews with enterprise managers, union officers (in conventional firms), officers and members of enterprise boards of directors (in the co-ops), and members of the technical and legal staffs of the American Plywood Association. Interviews lasting, on average, fifty to sixty minutes, were held with sixteen such individuals. The purpose of these initial interviews was to gain an understanding of the legal, technical, and economic environment of the plywood cooperatives as well as a general picture of their internal operations in comparison to conventional companies. The interviews were also used to develop a list of potential candidates for the second stage of interviews described below. Sessions were not tape-recorded though notes were taken. My research assistant and I also spent considerable time in the plants watching, asking questions, and finally learning how plywood is produced both technically and in a social organizational sense.

2. In the second stage, depth interviews using a common format were held with twenty worker-shareholders and three hired workers from the cooperatives and twelve workers from a conventionally organized, un-ionized plywood firm. Respondents were selected by means of a snowball technique in which individuals identified as suitable candidates by our interviewees from the first stage described above or encountered by us during our stay in the plants suggested additional candidates. The interviewees had a wide range of characteristics so that virtually all skill levels, ages, work experiences, and backgrounds were included in our pool. The

interviews varied in length from forty-five minutes to almost four hours, averaging about ninety minutes. All sessions were tape-recorded and transcribed. The interviews were designed to generate a wide range of information about the operations of the plywood plants and about the respondents themselves: personal and family backgrounds; work histories; experiences in the plant; observations and judgments about the technology and social organization of work in the plants; general attitudes concerning society, economy, and polity; and the forms and frequency of participation in voluntary organizations and community affairs. My objective was to try to gain not only a deeper and more subtle understanding of the work and extrawork lives of these people than would have been possible by use of other social science data-collection techniques, but to generate the necessary raw materials for the formulation of the test items used in the questionnaire in stage 3. The interviews in stages 1 and 2 were conducted over a period of four months.

3. In stage 3, questionnaires were mailed in 1978 to workers in four producer cooperatives and one conventional plywood firm in the Puget Sound region of the state of Washington. The questionnaire was pretested on a group of plywood workers not involved in the main study and on a small group of undergraduate students at the University of Washington. Target plants were selected on the basis of the companies' willingness to cooperate in the study. Names and addresses of respondents were provided by the companies after assurances were made about confidentiality and the voluntary nature of the individual participation. Each respondent was paid $10 to complete a questionnaire requiring, on average, forty-five minutes. A total of 875 questionnaires were mailed; 551 usable questionnaires were returned. This 63 percent return rate is within the general range of acceptability for mail questionnaires using a working-class sample. A random telephone survey of the 37 percent who did not respond revealed no significant systematic differences between the two groups. Because one of the cooperatives was no longer in operation in 1983 at the time the second questionnaire was mailed, and since it was necessary for the panel analysis that the two sampling frames be identical, respondents from this firm were dropped from the analysis, thereby reducing the sample size. Moreover, because their numbers were so few as to make statistical analysis impossible, female and nonwhite respondents were also dropped from the sample (there were a total of 8 female and 13 nonwhite worker-shareholders and 13 female and 11 nonwhite conventional workers). With these deletions, the final analytic sample for the 1978 survey included 206 worker-shareholders, 131 conventional workers, and 97 hired workers in the co-ops, all of whom were white males.

female and 11 nonwhite conventional workers). With these deletions, the final analytic sample for the 1978 survey included 206 worker-shareholders, 131 conventional workers, and 97 hired workers in the co-ops, all of whom were white males.

Worker-shareholders in this sample were slightly younger on average than conventional workers (forty-two years as compared to forty-four), though the differences are not statistically significant. The latter had been on the job for a considerably longer time than the former (70 percent of conventional workers had worked in their present firm for more than ten years compared to only 33.7 percent of worker-shareholders). Worker-shareholders made considerably more money than conventional workers, with 50 percent of the former making over $19,000 but only 18.4 percent of the latter doing so. Worker-shareholders were also considerably better educated than conventional workers; 28.6 of them had at least some college education compared to only 18.1 percent. Because of these sample characteristics, controls for age, education, job tenure, and income are introduced into the statistical analysis throughout the book; controls are not introduced for sex and race because the final sample is sexually and racially homogeneous.

4. The final stage of data collection was directed at creating a sample for a longitudinal panel analysis. After eliminating those who were no longer working for the same firm five years after the initial survey, questionnaires were mailed in 1983 to all of the remaining respondents in the 1978 sample. The questionnaire was virtually identical to the one mailed earlier though a few items were dropped (having mainly to do with redundant demographic and family information) and a few were added (having mainly to do with the safety issue and the rightward drift of American politics in the intervening years). Of the 383 receiving these questionnaires, 153 returned usable ones, for a response rate of 40 percent. Because of the relatively low response rate, it was important to determine whether these respondents were representative of the overall original sample or whether they were, in some sense, an unusual self-selected group. To make this determination, a "goodness-of-fit" analysis was conducted comparing the respondents in the panel sample to the remainder of the respondents in the 1978 sample. Thus worker-shareholders in the panel sample were compared to the remainder of worker-shareholders in the 1978 sample. The same was done with conventional workers and hired workers in the co-ops. Comparisons were run on all demographic items

and a random sample of twenty-five attitude questions and scales. The results were striking; not a single statistically significant difference was discovered between the panel and cross-section samples. Data analysis was conducted using the panel sample, therefore, with great confidence in its representativeness as a fair reflection of the original sample.

Appendix II

Data-Analysis Strategy

As described above, two data bases are used in this study. The first is a cross-section sample of 434 respondents from three plywood cooperatives and one conventional plywood firm tested in 1978. Throughout the discussion, this is referred to as the 1978 cross-section sample. The second is a panel sample with 95 worker-shareholders and 88 conventional workers. Testing of this sample took place at two points in time: in 1978 (termed the T_1 sample throughout the book) and in 1983 (termed the T_2 sample).

Analytic Question 1: Are co-op workers different from conventional workers on variables related to alienation, participation in politics, and political class-consciousness? To answer this question, both the 1978 cross-section and the panel sample are used. Appropriate statistical tests are used to determine the significance of differences between the two groups.

Analytic Question 2: Do co-op and conventional workers change over time in their response patterns to items related to alienation, political participation, and political class-consciousness? For this analysis, the panel sample is used with appropriate statistical tests to determine the significance of any observed changes.

Analytic Question 3: If the differences between co-op and conventional workers are statistically significant on either question 1 or 2, do the differences hold when statistical controls are introduced for age, income, education, and time on the job? That is, are observed differences better explained by background factors or by the differences between a democratic and nondemocratic workplace?

Analytic Question 4: If differences are found to exist between co-op and conventional workers on alienation, political participation, and/or political class-consciousness, and if these differences survive the introduction of control variables, what is it about the organization and operation of the co-ops that makes them different? In this section of the analysis, attention is paid to factors like the forms and styles of supervision, patterns of social interaction, participation in the governance of the enterprise, and possible self-selection into the co-ops on the part of people with atypical characteristics (atypical, that is, of working-class people). Multiple regression is the principal form of analysis used in this part of the discussion. Most of the variables in this study are ordinal in nature. When regression analysis is used with ordinal data, estimation of regression equations can provide information only about the relative weights of the multiple independent variables (which is precisely my purpose in this study). For that reason, beta weights rather than regression coefficients are reported. Furthermore, since the objective at this stage is not to develop models to provide a full explanation of alienation, political participation, and political class-consciousness but to examine the relative causal weight of various background, work-related, and social interaction factors, adjusted R-square values are not reported.

Index Construction

by Lorraine Blank, American University*

This appendix discusses the development of the indexes used in this study. Because the dissertation builds upon previously reported research by Greenberg (1981a, 1981b), a note on the methodology used in the original analysis of the questionnaire data is necessary. The original pool of items thought to measure a given construct was subjected to exploratory factor analysis (EFA) techniques. The decision criterion as reported by Greenberg was as follows: "Items were selected for each index by subjecting pools of potential items having surface similarity to factor analysis procedures (principal factor with iteration, varimax rotation). An index item was selected only if its loadings on a factor exceeded .40 and if it did not load significantly on any other factor. Once these items falling along a unidimensional scale were identified, indices were constructed by summing the responses to each item" (1981a:976).

Except for the use of additive indexes in lieu of factor scores, the above represents the standard approach to exploratory factor analysis. Although factor loadings are typically used in scale construction, panel data present special problems in the use of factor scores because of the lack of a clear-cut decision criterion for selection of first-wave versus second-wave factor scores for the creation of the scales. Additive indexes are used to circumvent this problem.

In the present research, the measures previously reported in Greenberg were reanalyzed by subjecting the original items used to create the additive

---

*Lorraine Blank used the data from this research for her doctoral dissertation at American University. The indexes she created for the dissertation are used in this volume.

indexes to confirmatory factor analysis (CFA). When appropriate, the scales have been redefined to reflect the results of this CFA. The data analysis presented here uses the Linear Structural Relations Program (LISREL).

A brief explanation of the differences between confirmatory and exploratory factor analysis will serve to orient the reader to the differences in measurement techniques used in the previously reported works by Greenberg and in the present dissertation research.

The general measurement model for both confirmatory and exploratory factor analysis is as follows:

$$X = \lambda \xi + \delta$$

where:

X = observed variables

λ = factor loadings, i.e., the expected change in the observed variables for a one-unit change in the latent variable

ξ = latent variables

δ = random errors of measurement for the observed variables

The primary difference between these two factor analysis techniques is that CFA allows the researcher to impose theoretically substantive constraints on a data set. A confirmatory factor analysis allows the researcher to specify a measurement model and to test this model against the observed data. In CFA the researcher specifies the number of factors and the items hypothesized to demonstrate significant factor loadings on a given construct. Loadings for items that are not hypothesized to measure a given construct are constrained to equal zero. EFA does not allow the researcher to constrain any of the factor loadings to zero. In a standard EFA, the number of factors is typically determined by relying on fairly arbitrary guidelines. For example, the most commonly accepted rule is to use factors with eigenvalues greater than one. Using an arbitrary rule such as this does not necessarily imply that substantively meaningful factors will emerge. A further difference between EFA and CFA is that if two or more factors exist, EFA requires all factors to be either orthogonal (uncorrelated) or oblique (correlated). CFA allows a mixture of orthogonal and oblique factors. Finally, EFA does not permit correlated errors of measurement.

CFA allows correlated errors of measurement to be incorporated into a measurement model (Long, 1983a).

The LISREL program provides information on the following: (1) factor loadings and their respective scores; (2) reliabilities for the observed indicators; (3) the error variance of the observed indicator and its associated z score; (4) the total coefficient of determination for the observed variables; (5) the adjusted goodness-of-fit index for the measurement model; and (6) a chi-square statistic and its associated probability level.

The use of the chi-square test statistic is different when applied to a CFA measurement model than in a traditional chi-square hypothesis tests. The null hypothesis in a CFA is that a given measurement model provides an acceptable fit for a set of observed indicators. As Long describes the testing procedure, "Values of the chi-square larger than the critical value result in the rejection of the null hypothesis and the conclusion that the proposed model did not generate the observed data; values smaller than the critical value result in the acceptance of the null hypothesis and the conclusion that the proposed model did generate the observed data" (Long, 1983b:64).

Since the assumptions necessary to apply the chi-square test are rarely met, the general procedure in CFA is to use the chi-square test as a general indicator of model fit rather than as a formal test of a measurement model. Large chi-square values indicate poor model fit; small values indicate good model fit. The chi-square test is used in this manner rather than as a formal hypothesis test of a measurement model.

The procedure for the assessment of each of the scales used in the original research was as follows. The original scales were subjected to a CFA. Specification of each measurement model was based on the scales originally reported by Greenberg (1981a, 1981b). Overall summary fit measures, including the chi-square, adjusted goodness-of-fit and coefficient of determination measures, were evaluated to determine the overall fit of the measurement model. Indicators of a misspecified model are high chi-square values, low coefficients of determination, and low adjusted goodness-of-fit measures. Individual items were also examined to determine if and how respecification should occur. At the individual item level, indicators of poor model fit are negative error variances, low indicator reliabilities, and nonsignificant factor loadings. Reliability measures below .200 were generally considered to be too low to justify retention of the indicator.

Respecification proceeded in two stages. Items demonstrating negative factor loadings were eliminated because it was felt that our knowledge of these constructs is too rudimentary to support consideration of bipolar factors. If adequate model fit was not obtained through elimination of these items, items with the nonsignificant factor loadings and/or low reliability estimates were then eliminated and latent constructs as specified by Greenberg (1981a, 1981b) were maintained. Respecification in this stage progressed until adequate model fit, as indicated by the summary fit measures, was obtained. If acceptable model fit was not obtained through elimination of single indicators, respecification proceeded through the elimination or reformulation of the latent constructs themselves.

Because of the high intercorrelations between questionnaire items measured at T_1 and T_2, mathematical manipulation of the data proved impossible. Because of this difficulty in applying LISREL techniques to this data set, it was decided to use the LISREL program as a guide in the selection of observed indicators. Additive indexes were then created from the indicators suggested by the confirmatory factor analysis. It is these additive indexes that are used in this study. To evaluate the additive indexes, Cronbach's alpha, a measure of scale reliability, was estimated for each index and is reported in the body of the test. Because this research uses additive indexes, the measures of scale reliability were also examined in the respecification procedure described above to ensure that reliability estimated for the indexes would not be significantly increased by elimination of any of the items in the index.

Questionnaires

Questionnaire #1: 1978 Survey, Worker-Shareholders

PART I

We would like to begin with some questions about your background. Remember, all answers will be kept strictly confidential. Again, except where otherwise noted, all questions can be answered by placing a check next to the most appropriate response. (Please ignore numbers in far left column. They are for computer use only.)

Are you

_____ 1. Male

_____ 2. Female

How old are you?

_____ (write in age)

Are you now or have you ever been a member of a *labor union*?

_____ 1. *Presently* a member

_____ 2. *Previously*, but not now a member

_____ 3. *Never* a member

If you answered (1) or (2), how many years *were you* or *have you been* a member?

_____ (write in number of years)

Do you own or rent the place where you live?

_____ 1. Own

_____ 2. Rent

_____ 3. Other

Other than owning a share or piece of stock in a company, have you ever *owned a business* of your own?

____ 1. Previously owned a business, but not now

____ 2. *Now* own a business

____ 3. *Never* owned a business

What was the last grade you completed in school?

____ 1. 0–8th grade

____ 2. Some high school

____ 3. High school graduate

____ 4. Some technical or trade school

____ 5. Technical or trade school graduate

____ 6. Some college

____ 7. College graduate

____ 8. Other

Taken as a whole, what is your family's approximate yearly income?

____ 1. Under $10,000

____ 2. $10,000–$12,900

____ 3. $13,000–$15,999

____ 4. $16,000–$18,999

____ 5. $19,000 and over

What is your ethnic group?

____ 1. White

____ 2. Asian-American or Oriental

____ 3. Mexican-American or Chicano

____ 4. Afro-American or Black

____ 5. Native-American or Indian

____ 6. Other

Have you ever been a member of the armed forces?

____ 1. Yes

____ 2. No

If yes,

In what year did you leave the service? (write in) ____

How many years were you in the service? (write in) ____

At what rank did you leave the service? (write in) ____

Do you regularly attend the meetings of any of the following kinds of groups or organizations? (You may check more than one category. You may also place more than one check on a line if you are active in more than one group or organization in any category.)

____ 1. Labor union

____ 2. Political party club (like Young Democrats, Young Republicans, etc.)

____ 3. Fraternal organization or lodge (like Moose, Elk, etc.)

____ 4. Business or civic group (like Kiwanis or Lions)

____ 5. Farm group (like the Farm Bureau or the Grange)

____ 6. Church or church connected group

_____ 7. Other (write in) _____

_____ 8. None

In how many of these groups do you hold office or otherwise play an active leadership role? (Write in number) _____

What is your marital status?

_____ 1. Married

_____ 2. Single, never married

_____ 3. Separated

_____ 4. Divorced

_____ 5. Widowed

_____ 6. Other

If you are now married, does your wife work outside of the home?

_____ 1. Yes, full-time

_____ 2. Yes, part-time

_____ 3. No

If you are married, what role does your spouse play in making important family decisions (like major expenditures)?

_____ 1. You make most family decisions

_____ 2. You and your spouse make most family decisions

_____ 3. Your spouse makes most family decisions

Do you have any children?

_____ 1. Yes

_____ 2. No

If yes, how many children do you have?   _____ (write in)

If yes, how many of your children live with you at the present time?   _____ (write in)

If your children live with you at the present time, do they help make any of the following family decisions? (Please *circle* the number of the most appropriate response.)

	Often	Occasionally	Never
About TV programs	1	2	3
About family vacations	1	2	3
About meals	1	2	3
About family entertainment	1	2	3

Do you talk very often to members of your immediate family (wife, child, parent, brother, sister) about what is going on at the plant or on the job?

_____ 1. Once a week or more

_____ 2. Several times a month

_____ 3. About once a month

_____ 4. Once every few months

_____ 5. Once a year

_____ 6. Never

_____ 7. Don't have an immediate family to talk to

Do you feel that your immediate family understands what it is like for you on your job?

_____ 1. Yes, a great deal
_____ 2. Yes, a little
_____ 3. No, not much
_____ 4. No, not at all
_____ 5. Don't have an immediate family

Other than the period when you were looking for your first job after school or the service, have you ever been *unemployed for more than a few days*?

_____ 1. Yes
_____ 2. No

If yes,

What is the longest period you have been unemployed?

(Write in)_____/_____

(months/weeks)

When was that? _____ (write in year).

Some people say there are social classes in America. Do you agree or disagree that there are social classes?

_____ 1. Strongly agree
_____ 2. Agree
_____ 3. Neither agree nor disagree
_____ 4. Disagree
_____ 5. Strongly disagree

If you agree that there are social classes in America, do you generally think of yourself as

_____ 1. Working class
_____ 2. Middle class
_____ 3. Upper class

Next, we are interested in learning a little about how you spend your time when you are not working.

How do you usually spend whatever "free time" you have during the week?

How do you usually spend whatever "free time" you have on the weekend?

Stop and think for a moment about how much TV you generally watch in a week. How many *hours a week* would you say you spend watching the following kinds of programs *on the average*?

No. of Hours/Week

1. Entertainment (comedies, variety shows, sports, cartoons, westerns, adventures, dramas)   _____

2. Information (news, panel discussions, educational programming) _____

	Very important	Pretty important	Not too important	Not important at all
How important a contribution would you say TV makes to your *understanding of what's going on in the world*? (Circle one.)	VI	PI	NTI	NIAA
How important a contribution does TV make to your personal *entertainment and recreation*?	VI	PI	NTI	NIAA

Do you regularly attend religious services?

_____ 1. Yes

_____ 2. No

If yes, on the *average*, how many times a *month* do you attend religious services? _____ (write in)

Please indicate how important the following activities are in your life?

	Not Important	Slightly Important	Important	Very Important
Joining and participating in religious programs and activities	NI	SI	I	VI
Relying on religious counsel or teachings when you have a problem	NI	SI	I	VI
Believing in God	NI	SI	I	VI
Turning to prayer when you're facing a personal problem	NI	SI	I	VI

Next, we turn to some items that ask you to describe certain aspects of your job, your feelings about your job, and your reactions to the people you work with.

How long have you been employed at this plant? (write in) _____

What is the name of your current job in the plant? (write in) _____

How many different jobs in the plant have you worked on?
(write in number) _____

How many different jobs in the plant do you feel you are able to do without additional training?
_____ 1. Most of the jobs
_____ 2. More than half of the jobs
_____ 3. About half of the jobs
_____ 4. Less than half of the jobs
_____ 5. Only my present job

On the average, how long does it take you to get to work (one way) each day?
_____ (write in)

When you eat your lunch at work, do you *generally*,
_____ 1. Eat alone
_____ 2. Eat with one or a few close friends
_____ 3. Eat with a large group of co-workers
_____ 4. Other

If you think of the people you spend time socializing with outside of working hours, about how many of them are people from this plant?
_____ 1. Nearly all
_____ 2. Great many
_____ 3. Only a few
_____ 4. None

Do you have any relatives working in this plant?
_____ 1. Yes
_____ 2. No

If you answered *yes*, how many? (Write in) _____

Does your supervisor or foreman take into account your opinions and suggestions when you make them?
_____ 1. Never
_____ 2. Occasionally
_____ 3. Often
_____ 4. Always
_____ 5. I never offer opinions and suggestions

Do you feel that your supervisor or foreman treats you with respect?
_____ 1. Never
_____ 2. Occasionally
_____ 3. Often
_____ 4. Always

Does your foreman act more as a coordinator or more as a boss?
_____ 1. More as a coordinator
_____ 2. More as a boss
_____ 3. Neither

_____ 4. Not sure

Thinking about supervisors and foremen in this plant, do you think that

_____ 1. There should be *more* of them

_____ 2. There are about the *right* number

_____ 3. There should be *fewer* of them

Here are some statements other people have made about work. do you agree or disagree with them? (Circle the most appropriate response)

	Strongly agree	Agree	Neither agree nor disagree	Disagree	Strongly disagree
If I had it to do over again, I'd probably go to work here again.	SA	A	NA/ND	D	SD
When I start off for work in the morning, I'm generally enthusiastic about going.	SA	A	NA/ND	D	SD
This plant is *not* as good a place to work as most other plants around here.	SA	A	NA/ND	D	SD
I get a great feeling of satisfaction from the work I am doing.	SA	A	NA/ND	D	SD

Which of the following best describes your attitude about working here?

_____ 1. I do as little as possible.

_____ 2. I do an average day's work.

_____ 3. I do the *best* work I can for the time I'm paid.

_____ 4. I not only do the best work I can, but I do whatever extra needs to be done.

To what extent do you feel responsible for the success of: (circle one)

	Hardly at all	Somewhat	Very much
Your own work group or production line	1	2	3
The whole plant	1	2	3

Next, we turn to a set of items that ask about your experiences as a shareholder in a cooperative.

Do you

_____ 1. Attend almost all shareholder meetings

_____ 2. Attend only an occasional shareholder meeting

_____ 3. Never attend shareholder meetings

Do you participate in discussions at the shareholder meetings?

_____ 1. Always

_____ 2. Very often

_____ 3. From time to time

_____ 4. Seldom

_____ 5. Never

Do you talk about decisions of the Board of Directors with other shareholders in the plant?

_____ 1. Always

_____ 2. Very often

_____ 3. From time to time

_____ 4. Seldom

_____ 5. Never

Have you ever run for the Board of Directors?

_____ 1. Yes

_____ 2. No

If *yes*, how many times have you run? (Write in) _____

Have you ever served on the Board of Directors?

_____ 1. Yes

_____ 2. No

If *yes*, in what years did you serve? (Write in years) _____

Among the people you know well in the plant, is there much discussion of company policies that have to do with in-plant *production* policies and *working conditions*?

_____ 1. Almost every day

_____ 2. Very often

_____ 3. From time to time

_____ 4. Seldom

_____ 5. Never

Among the people you know well in the plant, is there much discussion of company policies that have to do with *finances*, *sales*, and *investment* policies?

_____ 1. Almost every day

_____ 2. Very often

_____ 3. From time to time

_____ 4. Seldom

_____ 5. Never

Which of the following comes closest to how you feel?

_____ 1. Shareholders should take a more active role in running this company.

_____ 2. Shareholders do about the right amount now in running this company.

_____ 3. Shareholders should do less in running this company.

Please complete the following sentence:

If I were to leave this company today,

_____ 1. I would definitely look for another cooperative to work in.

_____ 2. Finding another cooperative would be *one* of the most important considerations in choosing where to work.

_____ 3. It wouldn't make much difference to me whether or not a place was a cooperative in choosing where to work.

_____ 4. I would definitely *not* look for another cooperative to work in.

As a shareholder in a cooperative (where you are both an owner and a worker), do you feel more like an owner or more like a worker?

_____ 1. More like an *owner*

_____ 2. More like a *worker*

_____ 3. About half and half

What is it that is most attractive to you about being a member of a cooperative? (Write in)

Here are some comments other people have made about what is important to them in a cooperative. How important are each of the following reasons why you remain a member of this cooperative? (Please circle the most appropriate response.)

	Very important	Somewhat important	Not too important	Not important at all
The workers in the plant get along well with each other	VI	SI	NTI	NIAA
The supervisors and workers get along well with each other	VI	SI	NTI	NIAA
I have a financial investment in the company	VI	SI	NTI	NIAA
I have a guaranteed job for when times get hard	VI	SI	NTI	NIAA
It's hard to get fired when you are a shareholder	VI	SI	NTI	NIAA
The wages are good	VI	SI	NTI	NIAA
There are no other jobs available	VI	SI	NTI	NIAA
It's too inconvenient and difficult to find another job	VI	SI	NTI	NIAA
I like to work with lumber	VI	SI	NTI	NIAA

What were the main reasons why you decided to first become a member of this cooperative? (Write in)

Here are some reasons that other people have given. How important were each of the following in your decision to *first* become a shareholder in this cooperative?

	Very important	Somewhat important	Not too important	Not important at all
Heard that workers in the plant got along well with each other	VI	SI	NTI	NIAA
Heard that supervisors and workers got along well	VI	SI	NTI	NIAA
Thought it would be a good financial investment	VI	SI	NTI	NIAA
Wanted an opportunity to help run a company	VI	SI	NTI	NIAA
Wanted a guaranteed job in case times got hard	VI	SI	NTI	NIAA
Heard it was hard to get fired once you were a shareholder	VI	SI	NTI	NIAA
The wages were good	VI	SI	NTI	NIAA
There were no other jobs available at the time	VI	SI	NTI	NIAA
I wanted to work with lumber	VI	SI	NTI	NIAA

Thinking about the *hired workers* in this plant, do you believe that they
_____ 1. should form a union to have their interests represented.
_____ 2. should participate in making company decisions, but without a union.
_____ 3. should have their interests taken into account by the shareholders but should not participate in decisions.
_____ 4. have no right to have their interests taken into account.
About what number of the *shareholders* in this plant are capable of the following activities? (Please circle the number of the most appropriate response.)

	Almost all of them	More than half	About half	Less than half	Almost none
Capable of doing a good day's work	1	2	3	4	5
Capable of working *without* close supervision	1	2	3	4	5
Capable of being a foreman	1	2	3	4	5
Capable of making a positive contribution at the shareholders' meeting	1	2	3	4	5
Capable of performing as a member of the Board of Directors	1	2	3	4	5
Capable of managing the plant	1	2	3	4	5

In this section of the questionnaire, we shift focus and ask you about your views and opinions about politics, government, and some of the major social issues of the day. We begin by raising a set of questions about the extent of your political participation. It may be of interest to know that very few Americans are active participants in the areas we will be asking about.

Did you vote in the 1976 presidential election? (the Ford/Carter election)

_____ 1. Yes

_____ 2. No

_____ 3. Don't remember

Did you vote in the 1974 congressional election?

_____ 1. Yes

_____ 2. No

_____ 3. Don't remember

Did you vote in the most recent local *school board* election?

_____ 1. Yes

_____ 2. No

_____ 3. Don't remember

Generally speaking, do you usually think of yourself as a Republican, a Democrat, or an Independent?

_____ 1. Republican

_____ 2. Democrat

_____ 3. Independent

_____ 4. Other (write in) _____

_____ 5. Unsure

If you chose Independent do you consider yourself as closer to the Republican or Democratic party?

_____ 1. Closer to the Republican party

_____ 2. Closer to the Democratic party

_____ 3. Not closer to either party

Here are some other types of political activities. Have you been active in any of them?

Have you:	No, never	Yes, once or twice	Yes, often	Don't remember
a. Attended meetings of your city or town council?	1	2	3	4
b. Attended a public hearing of some government agency, such as a school board?	1	2	3	4
c. Contacted a public official about some public issue?	1	2	3	4
d. Written a letter to the editor of a newspaper or magazine about some public issue?	1	2	3	4
e. Worked with others in your community to try to solve some community problem?	1	2	3	4
f. Tried to get your friends or neighbors to vote for the candidate you support?	1	2	3	4
g. Been a volunteer worker during a political campaign?	1	2	3	4

Next, we are interested in what you think about government and politics in the United States. Here are a number of statements that people often make about government and politics. Please indicate whether you *agree* or *disagree* with them.

	Strongly agree	Agree	Neither agree nor disagree	Disagree	Strongly disagree
(1) In our political system, people without money don't have much chance to get elected to public office.	SA	A	NA/ND	D	SD
(2) It seems that government has lost touch with the people.	SA	A	NA/ND	D	SD

(3) There is almost
no way people
like me can have
an influence on
the government.   SA   A   NA/ND   D   SD

(4) Local govern-
ment officials
around here
really listen to
people's
problems.   SA   A   NA/ND   D   SD

(5) In general I'm
pleased with the
way our govern-
ment handles
most things.   SA   A   NA/ND   D   SD

(6) Most of our po-
litical leaders can
be trusted.   SA   A   NA/ND   D   SD

(7) When you look
at the results of
most government
programs, they
seem to have
done more harm
than good.   SA   A   NA/ND   D   SD

(8) Elections in this
country do a
good job of giv-
ing the people a
real say in what
their government
does.   SA   A   NA/ND   D   SD

(9) There's not much
connection be-
tween what I
want and what
my congressmen
and senators do.   SA   A   NA/ND   D   SD

(10) Our major parties
are so much alike
that voters do not
really get much

choice when they vote.	SA	A	NA/ND	D	SD
(11) Once the election is over most public officials stop caring about what people want.	SA	A	NA/ND	D	SD
(12) This country needs a new political party to represent the interests of working people.	SA	A	NA/ND	D	SD
(13) Whether you get a fair trial in this country usually depends on who you are and how much money you have.	SA	A	NA/ND	D	SD
(14) This country is really run by a small number of men at the top who only speak for a few special groups.	SA	A	NA/ND	D	SD

Could you describe any specific changes you would like to see made in American society, or do you think things are pretty much o.k. the way they are?

Some people have suggested that the Federal government should do the following things. Do you agree or disagree? (Circle the most appropriate answer)

	Strongly agree	Agree	Neither agree nor disagree	Disagree	Strongly disagree
Own and operate key industries	SA	A	NA/ND	D	SD
Control how much profit a company can make in any one year	SA	A	NA/ND	D	SD
Pay for medical					

and hospital bills	SA	A	NA/ND	D	SD
Guarantee jobs to everyone willing to work	SA	A	NA/ND	D	SD
Control the prices set by large corporations	SA	A	NA/ND	D	SD

Here are some things people have said about American corporations. Do you agree or disagree?

	Strongly agree	Agree	Neither agree nor disagree	Disagree	Strongly disagree
There is too much power concentrated in the hands of a few large companies for the good of the American people	SA	A	NA/ND	D	SD
The profits of the large companies help make things better for everyone who buys their products or services	SA	A	NA/ND	D	SD
Large companies are essential for the nation's growth and expansion	SA	A	NA/ND	D	SD
Big corporations have too much influence in the government in Washington, D.C.	SA	A	NA/ND	D	SD
There's no such thing as a company making too much profit	SA	A	NA/ND	D	SD

The government
  ought to control
  big corporations
  so they would
  better serve the
  public interest   SA   A   NA/ND   D   SD

Which of the following statements comes closest to your way of thinking?
____ 1. Big business controls government.
____ 2. Government controls big business.
____ 3. Government and big business work closely together to advance their own interests.
____ 4. Government and big business work closely together to advance the interests of the American people.
____ 5. Government and big business have very little to do with each other.
____ 6. Unsure/no opinion.

Do you agree or disagree with the following statements about the operation of the American economy? (Circle the most appropriate answer)

	Strongly agree	Agree	Neither agree nor disagree	Disagree	Strongly disagree
Our current economic system does a good job in allowing each American to get his fair share of goods and services.	SA	A	NA/ND	D	SD
Our economic system takes advantage of working people.	SA	A	NA/ND	D	SD
Our current economic system gives almost everyone a fair chance to get what they need to live a decent life.	SA	A	NA/ND	D	SD

Do you believe that working people in the United States have made economic gains since the end of World War II?

_____ 1. Yes, substantial gains
_____ 2. Yes, minor gains
_____ 3. No, things have stayed about the same
_____ 4. No, they are slightly worse off today
_____ 5. No, they are substantially worse off
_____ 6. Unsure

If you answered YES (1 or 2)

How important do you believe each of the following have been in *causing* these gains? (Circle the most appropriate response)

	Very important	Somewhat important	Not too important	Not important at all
Unions strong enough to force business and government to listen to them	VI	SI	NTI	NIAA
The natural growth of the economy	VI	SI	NTI	NIAA
The concern of national political leaders for the welfare of working people	VI	SI	NTI	NIAA
The willingness of working people to work hard as individuals	VI	SI	NTI	NIAA
The concern of national business leaders for the welfare of working people	VI	SI	NTI	NIAA

if you answered NO (3, 4, or 5), go to *NEXT* page

↓

If you answered NO (3, 4, or 5)

How important do you believe the following have been in *preventing* gains? (Circle the most appropriate response)

	Very important	Somewhat important	Not too important	Not important at all
Unions unable to force business and government to listen to them	VI	SI	NTI	NIAA

The lack of growth in the economy	VI	SI	NTI	NIAA
The lack of concern by national political leaders for the welfare of working people	VI	SI	NTI	NIAA
The lack of concern by national business leaders for the welfare of working people	VI	SI	NTI	NIAA
The unwillingness of working people to work hard as individuals	VI	SI	NTI	NIAA

When you hear the word *socialism*, what does it mean to you?

Do you agree or disagree with the following statements about American working people?

Even without the help of managerial personnel, working people have enough skill and intelligence to run everyday production in their plants.

_____ 1. Strongly agree

_____ 2. Agree

_____ 3. Neither agree nor disagree

_____ 4. Disagree

_____ 5. Strongly disagree

Even without the help of managerial personnel, working people have enough skill and intelligence to run the business and financial affairs of their plants.

_____ 1. Strongly agree

_____ 2. Agree

_____ 3. Neither agree nor disagree

_____ 4. Disagree

_____ 5. Strongly disagree

Except for issues like wages and benefits, workers in conventional, privately owned plants should have *little* to say about running their plants. Those who own companies should run them.

_____ 1. Strongly agree

_____ 2. Agree

_____ 3. Neither agree nor disagree

_____ 4. Disagree

_____ 5. Strongly disagree

People often make the following statements about their basic values and beliefs. Do you agree or disagree with them?

	Strongly agree	Agree	Neither agree nor disagree	Disagree	Strongly disagree
People in positions of authority are owed our highest respect.	SA	A	NA/ND	D	SD
Patriotism and loyalty are the most important requirements of a good citizen.	SA	A	NA/ND	D	SD
People should maintain their respect for the police even when the police are clearly in the wrong.	SA	A	NA/ND	D	SD
People have no obligation to obey a law that goes against their moral beliefs.	SA	A	NA/ND	D	SD
A group of equals will work a lot better than a group with a strong boss.	SA	A	NA/ND	D	SD
Each person should get what he needs . . . the things we produce as a society belong to all of us.	SA	A	NA/ND	D	SD
For society to run better the really talented people should be rewarded more than others.	SA	A	NA/ND	D	SD

	Strongly agree	Agree	Neither agree nor disagree	Disagree	Strongly disagree
When a person is *unable* to work, society has a responsibility to support that person.	SA	A	NA/ND	D	SD

Here are some more statements about personal values and beliefs. Do you agree or disagree with them?

	Strongly agree	Agree	Neither agree nor disagree	Disagree	Strongly disagree
Many people are poor today because they are really not willing to work	SA	A	NA/ND	D	SD
When people don't succeed financially, it's almost always their fault and not society's	SA	A	NA/ND	D	SD
A person should basically depend on himself and not ask or expect the help of others	SA	A	NA/ND	D	SD
Most people wouldn't work if they didn't need the money for eating and living	SA	A	NA/ND	D	SD
Society is best off when each individual looks out for his own well-being and not the well-being of others	SA	A	NA/ND	D	SD
A person's first duty is to himself and his family	SA	A	NA/ND	D	SD

Some people have suggested that wages and salaries throughout American industry be made as equal as possible. How do you feel about this suggestion? Do you agree or disagree with it?

_____ 1. Strongly agree

_____ 2. Agree

_____ 3. Neither agree nor disagree

_____ 4. Disagree

_____ 5. Strongly disagree

If you Agreed—(answered 1 or 2) with the last question

How important are each of the following as reasons why you believe that wages and salaries should be as equal as possible?

	Very Important	Somewhat Important	Not Too Important	Not Important At All
Because all human beings are inherently equal	VI	SI	NTI	NIAA
Because all people have similar needs	VI	SI	NTI	NIAA
Because all working people are making some contribution to what we produce as a society	VI	SI	NTI	NIAA
Because people would work better if wages and salaries were equal	VI	SI	NTI	NIAA

If you Disagreed (answered 4 or 5) with the last question

How important do you think each of the following *should* be in determining wage and salary differences?

	Very important	Somewhat important	Not too important	Not important at all
The *skill* requirements of the job	VI	SI	NTI	NIAA
Seniority	VI	SI	NTI	NIAA

The *unpleasantness* of the job	VI	SI	NTI	NIAA
The *danger* of the job	VI	SI	NTI	NIAA
How much a person *produces*	VI	SI	NTI	NIAA
The amount of *physical labor* involved in doing a job	VI	SI	NTI	NIAA
How much a person *needs* to support his family	VI	SI	NTI	NIAA

These questions are about how you see yourself as a person—how you feel about yourself and how you evaluate yourself. Please answer the questions in terms of how you see yourself at this point in your life. Circle one response for each question.

1. How well do you handle important decisions in your life?

    Very well   Fairly well   Not too well   Not well at all

2. How competent do you feel you are to do the things you're really interested in doing?

    Not competent at all   Not too competent   Fairly competent   Very competent

3. How much respect do you feel for yourself as a person?

    A great deal   A fair amount   Not too much   Not much at all

4. How confident do you feel about your potential for self-development in the next few years?

    Very confident   Fairly confident   Not too confident   Not confident at all

5. How interesting do you feel you are to other people?

    Not interesting at all   Not too interesting   Fairly interesting   Very interesting

6. On the whole, how satisfied are you with yourself?

    Very satisfied   Fairly satisfied   Not too satisfied   Not satisfied at all

Would you say that you agree or disagree with the following statements? (Circle the most appropriate response)

	Strongly agree	Agree	Neither agree nor disagree	Disagree	Strongly disagree
No one I know cares about what happens to me.	SA	A	NA/ND	D	SD
Most people I know don't					

really care about
what happens to
the next fellow. SA   A   NA/ND   D   SD
I don't know who I
can depend on
for help when I
have a problem. SA   A   NA/ND   D   SD
I often feel left out
of things that
others are doing. SA   A   NA/ND   D   SD

Over the past year, have you been bothered by headaches, indigestion or any of the other common ailments you see in the list below? (You may check more than one)

____ Headaches   ____ Neuralgia

____ Indigestion or stomach trouble   ____ Hemorrhoids or piles

____ Constipation or diarrhea   ____ Nervousness

____ Sleeplessness   ____ Nose, throat or sinus troubles

____ Tiredness without knowing   ____ Many colds or coughs
       why

____ Heartburn

____ Backache

____ High blood pressure

Thank you very much for your cooperation. If you have any further comments you would like to make, please feel free to make them in this space.

Please fold over back cover, seal, and mail. No postage is necessary.

Questionnaire #2: 1978 Survey, Workers in Conventional Firm (This section substitutes for Section III in questionnaire #1)

Next, we turn to a set of items that ask about your experiences working in a unionized company.

Do you consider yourself a strong union member?

____ 1. Yes, very strong

_____ 2. Yes, moderately strong

_____ 3. No

Do you

_____ 1. Attend almost all union meetings

_____ 2. Attend only an occasional union meeting

_____ 3. Never attend union meetings

Have you ever run for union office?

_____ 1. Yes

_____ 2. No

If *yes*, how many times have you run? (Write in) _____

Have you ever served as a union officer?

_____ 1. Yes

_____ 2. No

If *yes*, in what years did you serve? (Write in) _____

Have you ever served as a union shop steward?

_____ 1. Yes

_____ 2. No

If *yes*, in what years did you serve? (Write in) _____

Among people you know well in the plant, is there much discussion about union activities *at contract time*?

_____ 1. Almost every day

_____ 2. Very often

_____ 3. From time to time

_____ 4. Seldom

_____ 5. Never

Among the people you know well in the plant, is there much discussion about union activities when it is *not* contract time?

_____ 1. Almost every day

_____ 2. Very often

_____ 3. From time to time

_____ 4. Seldom

_____ 5. Never

Do you participate in discussions at union meetings?

_____ 1. Always

_____ 2. Very often

_____ 3. From time to time

_____ 4. Seldom

_____ 5. Never

Do you talk about decisions of union officials with other workers in the plant?

_____ 1. Always

_____ 2. Very often

_____ 3. From time to time

_____ 4. Seldom

_____ 5. Never

In general, do you think that union officials

_____ 1. Should be more aggressive with management

_____ 2. Do about all they can do

_____ 3. Should do less

Please complete the following sentence:

If I were to leave this company today,

_____ 1. I'd definitely look for another union plant to work in.

_____ 2. finding another place that was unionized would be one of the most important considerations in choosing where to work.

_____ 3. it wouldn't make much difference to me whether or not a place was unionized in choosing where to work.

_____ 4. I would definitely look for a place to work that was *not* unionized.

About what number of the people you work with in this plant are capable of the following activities?

	Almost all of them	More than half	About half	Less than half	Almost none
Capable of doing a good day's work	1	2	3	4	5
Capable of working *without* close supervision	1	2	3	4	5
Capable of making a positive contribution at union meetings	1	2	3	4	5
Capable of being a union officer	1	2	3	4	5
Capable of being a foreman	1	2	3	4	5
Capable of managing the plant	1	2	3	4	5

Would you agree or disagree with the following statement?

This company would run better if the employees had an active role in deciding how to run it.

_____ 1. Strongly agree

_____ 2. Agree

_____ 3. Neither agree nor disagree

_____ 4. Disagree

_____ 5. Strongly disagree

Questionnaire #3: 1983 Panel Survey, Additional Items Added to 1978 Survey Instrument, Worker-Shareholders and Workers in Conventional Firms

In thinking about your present job in the plant, would you say that it is interesting most of the time, or dull most of the time? Please rate how interesting your job is on a scale of 1 to 5. (circle one)

1	2	3	4	5
Dull				Interesting
most of				most of
the time				the time

Have you witnessed any accidents in this plant during the past five years in which a person has been seriously injured (causing him or her to stay away from work for at least a week)?

_____ 1. Yes

_____ 2. No

If so, how many such accidents have you witnessed? _____

Please rate how safe you think this plant is.

_____ 1. Safer than most plywood plants

_____ 2. About as safe as other plywood plants

_____ 3. More dangerous than most plywood plants

How important in your opinion are each of the following in causing accidents in this plant?

	Very important	Somewhat important	Not too important	Not important at all
Worker carelessness	VI	SI	NTI	NIAA
Poorly designed machines	VI	SI	NTI	NIAA
The pace of work	VI	SI	NTI	NIAA
Fatigue	VI	SI	NTI	NIAA
Lack of management concern	VI	SI	NTI	NIAA

	Strongly agree	Agree	Neither agree nor disagree	Disagree	Strongly disagree
Things would be a lot better in this country if government would stop interfering with the economy and let the free market do its work.	SA	A	NA/ND	D	SD
Deficit spending by government is the main cause of inflation.	SA	A	NA/ND	D	SD

| The government in Washington has grown too big and expensive over the years. | SA | A | NA/ND | D | SD |

The government in
Washington has
grown too big
and expensive
over the years.   SA   A   NA/ND   D   SD
Labor unions are
no longer neces-
sary to protect
working people
in the United
States.   SA   A   NA/ND   D   SD

The best way to cut government deficit spending would be to

_____ 1. Cut the size of social programs

_____ 2. Cut the size of the defense budget

_____ 3. Cut both social spending and defense spending

_____ 4. Raise taxes

_____ 5. None of the above

Do you agree or disagree with the following statements about American working people?

Even without the help of managerial personnel, working people have enough skill and intelligence to run everyday production in their plants.

_____ 1. Strongly agree

_____ 2. Agree

_____ 3. Neither agree nor disagree

_____ 4. Disagree

_____ 5. Strongly disagree

Even without the help of managerial personnel, working people have enough skill and intelligence to run the business and financial affairs of their plants.

_____ 1. Strongly agree

_____ 2. Agree

_____ 3. Neither agree nor disagree

_____ 4. Disagree

_____ 5. Strongly disagree

Questionnaire #4: 1983 Panel Survey, Additional Items Added to 1978 Survey Instrument, Worker-Shareholders Only

Have you ever taken part in a discussion at a shareholders' meeting on possible ways to change the way plywood is made in order to make the work in the plant more interesting?

_____ 1. Yes

_____ 2. No

Have you ever talked with other shareholders about possible ways to change the way plywood is made in order to make the work in the plant more interesting?

_____ 1. Often

_____ 2. Occasionally

_____ 4. Never

Being a shareholder in a cooperative means that you are both an *owner* of the company and (at least indirectly) a decision-making *manager*. If you had to go to another company where you could only play one of these roles, which type would you choose? (check one)

_____ 1. A company where I would own a share but would play no part in decision-making.

_____ 2. A company where I would take part in decision-making but would *not* own a share.

_____ 3. I can't say/I don't know.

Notes

1. The Democratic Left and the Appeals of Workplace Democracy

1. Although there is no general agreement about the definition of "democratic Left," I shall understand it to mean that political position which (1) advocates full democratization of the decision-making process in society, including public control of the economy (e.g., placing decisions about the direction of economic life into the hands of the majority acting through democratic mechanisms; these democratic decision processes would pertain to the full range of micro- and macro-level concerns, including the workplace, the economic sector, the region, and the nation); (2) advocates greater equality in the distribution of material goods; (3) rejects "vanguardism" of the Marxist-Leninist variety as a strategy of change in the developed capitalist states; and (4) dismisses rule by a party or bureaucratic elite in postrevolutionary societies. To put it another way, the democratic Left is defined by its support for what has been called democratic socialism. For the most comprehensive and convincing discussion of these issues, see Branko Horvat's *Political Economy of Socialism* (1982).

2. Many of these cases will be described in detail in later chapters. The relevant literature concerning each case will be cited at the most appropriate point in the discussion.

3. I do not want to overstate the case, however, for in these publications one may occasionally encounter a piece that is highly critical of workplace democratization. See, for example, Fable (1982). The claims generally made on behalf of worker buyouts of marginal companies include the likelihood that such companies will be less concerned with profit maximization than will privately owned ones, that they will be better attuned to the needs of the community, that they will produce less socially wasteful or diseconomic products, and that they will create work organizations more consistent with basic human needs. In this regard, see Bluestone and Harrison (1982a) and Lynd (1982). The evidence supporting such claims is exceedingly skimpy.

4. Because the issue of workplace democracy and workers' self-management is continually on the agenda of the democratic Left does not mean that it is an important

component of the agenda for the larger political system, especially in the United States. Indeed, the issue largely disappeared from sight (except for the Left) during the serious recessions of the late 1970s and early 1980s.

5. Not everybody on the Left, to be sure, sees workplace democracy as an instrument for the creation of a new society. Some see it as ineffectual and co-optive; others see it as morally proper irrespective of its contribution to change.

6. I am certain that many would disagree with my usage, but I suggest that socialism, properly understood, conforms generally to the position of the democratic Left as described in note 1. I also suggest that those societies that presently call themselves socialist do not fit such a description and ought not, perhaps, to be understood as socialist. For discussion of these issues see Bahro (1978) and Horvat (1982).

7. "Self-managed work organizations are . . . those where workers . . . have the right to control the means of production; the resources of the organization in which they work, its organizational structure and processes, and its products" (Baumgartner, Burns, and Sekulic, 1979: 81). Or, as Branko Horvat has succinctly put it, self-management is "the combining of management and work by the same people" (1982: 239). I shall argue later in this chapter and in Chapter 2 that although the plywood cooperatives are not fully worker self-managed enterprises, they come very close to the model. Self-management must be differentiated from simple worker participation, in which management retains the decisive voice in enterprise decision making, and worker ownership, which may or may not involve managerial or control responsibilities, as in Employee Stock Ownership Plan schemes and at places such as Vermont Asbestos. For an illuminating discussion of these issues, see Gunn (1984:chap. 1).

8. Enthusiasm for workplace democracy has not, of course, been confined to the democratic Left. Capitalist managers and owners, for instance, have periodically turned to increased worker participation in workplace decision making as a method to encourage motivation, attentiveness, loyalty, morale, and responsibility when traditional methods of control and management have temporarily failed (Clegg, 1983; Greenberg, 1975; Ramsey, 1983). During the late 1960s and early 1970s, there was evidence of a certain disintegration in the American workplace. A spate of books documented the growing discontent of the American worker expressed in excessive drinking and drug use, psychosomatic illness, alienation, violence, despair, and resignation (Page and O'Brien, 1972; Sennett and Cobb, 1973; Sheppard and Herrick, 1972; Terkel, 1974; U.S. Department of Health, Education and Welfare, 1972). Business leaders during the 1970s were especially concerned about the expression of this discontent in absenteeism, job turnover, shoddy workmanship, sabotage, and the greatest outbreak of wildcat strikes since the 1930s.

Many managers eventually came to realize that advancing job fragmentation and simplification, combined with a much younger and better-educated work force—a work force less willing to work under conditions of rigid hierarchy, close supervision, minute and repetitive tasks, and unfulfilling and uncreative labor—represented a truly explosive mixture. This realization led many business leaders to institute fairly substantial reforms of industrial work, ranging from sensitivity sessions to job enrichment, and finally, to experiments in limited worker participation. Notable participatory schemes were instituted during this period at General Foods, Texas Instruments, Corning Glass, the Bell System, Polaroid, Monsanto, and Bankers Trust of New York, all of which reported significant improvements in economic performance and labor relations (Blumberg, 1969; Sheppard and Herrick, 1972; Zwerdling, 1973). During the 1980s, a period of high unemployment, union retreat, and general worker docility, management generally abandoned its commitment to democratic participation at the workplace, suggesting that management tends to support democratization only when threats exist to its traditional means of control (Baumgartner, Burns, and De Ville, 1979; Berg et al., 1979; Clegg, 1983; Ramsey, 1983).

A prominent branch of organizational psychology has also periodically advocated participatory reforms at the workplace. It has done so because of the felt needs of industrial managers in capitalist firms and because of a general belief among such psychologists that the organization of modern industrial work life tends to stunt the development of healthy human personalities. Organizational psychologists have argued that the present organization of work in industrial society, based upon hierarchy, the minute division of labor, and passive labor power, robs workers of their creative powers, the use of their inherent skills and talents, their autonomy, and, ultimately, their humanity. None of this is understood to be inevitable or irreversible, in this view, for human beings are assumed to be infinitely more capable than they are at present. Organizational psychologists have supported a theory of human development which proposes a vision of what people might become in social settings where work itself is reorganized, so that participation in decision making becomes an integral part of work (Argyris, 1962, 1965; Bay, 1958; Blumberg, 1969; Hampden-Turner, 1970; Horney, 1950; Kornhauser, 1965; Maslow, 1957; Rogers, 1951; Vroom, 1960; Whyte, 1983).

Understanding modern industrial life, particularly the blue-collar factory, as the progenitor of a set of conditions that is not conducive either to the healthy development of human beings or to the economic performance of the organizations of which they are a part, these organizational psychologists have thus posited strong ethical and practical grounds for advocating the alteration of most worklife in industrial societies, with job enrichment and decisional participation at the top of their agenda. These organizational psychologists are more than a little ambiguous about the scope and intensity of their own participatory proposals, however. They seem to be caught in the dilemma of visualizing meaningful participation as requisite to mental health, yet at the same time of being profoundly aware of the limits of feasibility (most of them having worked for business organizations at one time or another.) Lacking any anticapitalist orientation, they see no reason, moreover, to challenge managerial and ownership prerogatives.

9. That such concerns were not confined to socialists may be seen in the following observation made by Adam Smith in *The Wealth of Nations*: "The man whose life is spent in performing a few simple operations . . . has no occasion to exert his understanding or to exercise his invention in finding out expedients for removing difficulties . . . and generally becomes as stupid and ignorant as it is possible for a human creature to become, [and when factory work becomes widespread] all the nobler parts of the human character may be, in great measure, obliterated and extinguished in the great body of people" (1937).

10. Of particular importance in delineating the meaning of the *Manuscripts* for Marxist thought in general are Avineri (1968), Fromm (1961), and Ollman (1971).

11. From *The Economic and Philosophical Manuscripts*, trans. T. B. Bottomore and printed in Fromm (1961).

12. This position is argued forcefully and persuasively in Harrington (1972). That Marx never lost interest in direct and industrial democracy is demonstrated by his favorable treatment of the Paris Commune in his *Civil War in France* (Marx and Engels, 1958).

13. The Yugoslav economist and political theorist Branko Horvat makes the most sophisticated defense in the literature of participatory democracy as the basis of the just society in his monumental work, *The Political Economy of Socialism* (1982).

14. For excellent discussions of these issues, see Bachrach (1967).

15. Horvat (1982) calls this form "etatism" and Bahro (1978) calls it "presently existing socialism."

16. The reasons are brilliantly explored by Przeworski (1980, 1985).

17. "A strategy of workers' control—in which demand builds on demand and the *autonomous* power of the workers slowly increases—can be a critical educatory force which, one day, can help make democratic Socialism a reality" (Case, 1973:449).

18. "The message is clear. When workers begin to participate, their sense of isolation and ignorance begins to break down. A dynamic can be created which first attacks the lower levels of the executive hierarchy and then proceeds upwards . . . [this] suggests an ultimate incompatibility between industrial democracy and private ownership of industry" (Espinosa and Zimbalist, 1978:23–24).

19. These enterprises come very close to the worker self-management model but are flawed by the existence of hired labor. I shall have more to say about this issue in Chapter 2. For a review of the state of worker self-management in the United States see Gunn (1984). I shall review cases of worker self-management outside of the United States throughout the book but especially in Chapters 4 and 7.

20. Implicit in the literature is the assumption that an increase in workplace democracy leads to an increase in the predicted effects. It is mainly for this reason that this book focuses on the plywood cooperatives. If the many claims in the literature are tenable, they should be evident in these cases.

2. The Plywood Cooperatives

This chapter is a substantially revised version of my chapter "Producer Cooperatives and Democratic Theory: The Case of the Plywood Firms," in Jackall and Levin (1984), pp. 171–214.

1. Between 1977 and 1984, the number of plywood cooperatives decreased from fifteen to twelve, including one new cooperative (Anacortes) founded in 1984. The decrease is less than one might have predicated given the near depression in the lumber industry and the experience of conventional firms. The failure rate was so high for conventional firms during this period that the percentage of total softwood plywood production accounted for by the cooperatives increased.

In the time between my two panel sampling points important changes occurred in the plywood industry and in the nation. The period 1978 to 1983 was one of hard times in the wood-products industry and of "rightward" drift in American politics. If this study were to focus solely on workers in the cooperatives, the longitudinal analysis would be contaminated in important ways by these changes. But because cooperative workers will be compared at all points to workers in conventional firms experiencing the same changes, it will be possible at all times to make claims about the effects of workplace democracy. Cooperative and conventional workers, in this analysis, are studied in relationship to each other and not to some fixed external reference point.

2. There is one glaring exception; hired workers who do not participate in decision making. I shall have more to say about them and their relationship to the enterprise later in the chapter.

3. In this study I am not interested in producer cooperatives as such but as useful research sites for the investigation of the effects of workplace democracy on alienation, political participation, and political class-consciousness. The reader interested in the theory, practice, and history of producer cooperatives should consult the following sources: Abell (1983); Coates (1976); Comisso (1979); Gunn (1984); Jackall and Levin (1984); Jones (1979); Jones and Svejnar (1982); Lindenfeld and Rothschild-Whitt (1982); Oakeshott (1978); and Shirom (1972). The reader interested in learning about the history of the plywood cooperatives, as well as their legal, financial, and market characteristics, should consult Bellas (1972), Berman (1967), Bernstein (1974, 1976), and Gunn (1984).

4. Again, I must admit to the glaring exception of hired workers. As we shall see later in this chapter, the differences between these hired workers and those in conventional enterprises are of such a character, I believe, that one may still reasonably designate the plywood cooperatives as near worker self-managed enterprises. On this point I disagree with Gunn (1984).

5. This form is called "unitary democracy" by Jane Mansbridge in her brilliant treatment of the subject (1980). She considers unitary democracy as a form of self-governance characterized by consensus among members on basic values and goals, face-to-face forms of decision making, rough equality, common interests, and fraternity.

6. The Greeks held to a narrowly constricted conception of the eligibility pool. Slaves and women, for instance, were not admitted to citizenship in the Greek polis.

7. The classic treatise on representative government is that of John Stuart Mill (1958).

8. See Mansbridge (1980) for a compelling discussion about the necessary existence within the same organization or institution of both unitary and adversary forms of democracy.

9. This is not the case for the many small handicraft, food, and service cooperatives that blossomed in the late 1960s and early 1970s in several urban areas, particularly on the West Coast. Almost all of these cooperatives, whose business activities range from groceries, to woodworking, to baked goods, to health food outlets, to health clinics, were formed by a few people of upper-middle-class and college-educated background, active in either antiwar, ecology, or countercultural politics, with the explicit purpose of establishing small businesses that would both serve the community

and provide a work environment devoid of the "hassles," hierarchy, and "rat race" of the conventional business world. They were inherently political. For descriptions and analyses see Gunn (1984), and Rothschild-Whitt (1983).

10. This finding may be unique to the United States. A study in Scotland indicates that workers there tend to join co-ops because they want to control their work situation and take part in enterprise decision making. See Oliver (1984).

11. He also reported that production per worker-hour was about the same as before even though the plant had been heavily modernized with the latest technology. This observation lends credence to other evidence about the impressive productivity of the plywood cooperatives.

12. One manager, perhaps in a fit of bravado, reported that he could not remember ever being turned down on an issue he considered to be important.

13. Although worker-shareholders in general like working where they do, their commitment to democratic/cooperative forms remains distinctly limited, as will become more obvious in later chapters. Note the responses of worker-shareholders to a question asking them what kind of company they would look for if they were to leave their present cooperative (panel sample; N = 88):

	T_1	T_2
I would definitely look for another cooperative [or] Finding another cooperative would be *one* important consideration.	36.3	35.2
It wouldn't make much difference if it were a cooperative [or] I would definitely *not* look for another cooperative to work in.	63.6	64.8

14. The manager of one of the cooperatives, pondering why they seemed to move on every two to three months, concluded that "they are generally young men with a lot of money in their pockets and no family responsibilities . . . It also explains why they generally live up to their reputation as the drinkingest, fightingest men in the industry."

15. There are, however, in these plants some regular production workers who can be (and are) laid off in economically depressed times.

16. Joyce Rothschild-Whitt places the plywood cooperatives in the category of existing enterprises with the highest level of workers' control in her very useful typology developed in "Worker Ownership and Control" (1983).

17. Obviously, for worker-shareholders, the plywood cooperatives are completely self-governing enterprises; for them, these enterprises are fully democratic. And it is only among these worker-shareholders that I shall be examining the possible effects of workplace democracy. Obviously also, the plywood cooperatives cannot stand for all cases of workplace democracy whether in the United States or in the world. I shall have more to say about how this inescapable fact affects the generalizability of the empirical results of this study during the course of the discussion.

18. As a result, the cooperatives seem to have overcome most of the problems identified by John Witte as inherent in democratically managed industrial enterprises. See Witte (1980).

3. *Alienation in the Cooperatives*

1. This concept of self-realization should not be understood as a return to some unchanging human essence but, rather, as the fulfillment of historically created human possibilities allowing freedom and creativity. On this point see Bottomore (1983:13).

2. As the Marxist economist Ernest Mandel has so vividly put it: "Our optimism comes from the fact that, after all this analysis of the roots of the alienation of labor and the specific expressions of the alienation of man in bourgeois society is completed, there emerges the inescapable conclusion that a society can be envisaged in which there will be no more alienation of labor and alienation of human beings. This is a historically produced and man-made evil, not an evil rooted in nature or human nature. Like everything else which has been made by man, it can also be unmade by man. . . . Thus the marxist theory of alienation implies and contains a theory of dis-alienation through the creation of conditions for the gradual disappearance and eventual abolition of alienation (1973:29, 30).

3. The Marxian approach pays most attention to social structure and process. Nevertheless, and contrary to conventional interpretations, the Marxian approach does not (or need not) slight psychological states and feelings. The latter plays a significant role in this chapter.

4. Alienation, so understood, might (and most certainly does) exist in noncapitalist or postcapitalist societies. See Mandel (1970).

5. In the following discussion, I avoid many of the issues concerning the Marxian concept of alienation that remain under intensive debate among scholars and philosophers. I do so not because I think these issues unimportant but because their resolution is irrelevant to the empirical analysis that follows. I will, thus, not have much to say about the incidence of alienation in state socialist societies (for this see Horvat, 1982; Israel, 1971; and Mandel, 1973). I will avoid the endless debates concerning an early humanistic and a late scientific Marx. I will leave to others the consideration of reification as well as the possible relationship between alienation and existentialism and will have nothing to say about the philosophical background of Marx's concept of alienation in Hegel and Feurbach (for an introduction to this vast literature see Schacht, 1971; and Walton and Gamble, 1972). My discussion will also bypass the lively debate concerning trends in the division of labor and control of workers in industrial capitalism sparked by the brilliant contributions of Harry Braverman (1974). Also see Burawoy (1979); Clawson (1980); and Edwards (1979).

6. It is in this sense, the control of production and the enjoyment of its fruits, that some analysts have identified Soviet-style states as being characterized by the prevalence of a form of private property.

7. "It is known that human labor is able to produce more than it consumes, and this capacity for surplus labor (which produces surplus value) is sometimes treated as a special and mystical endowment of humanity or of its labor. In reality, it is nothing of the sort, but is merely the prolongation of working time beyond the point where labor has reproduced itself, or in other words brought into being its own means of subsistence or their equivalent" (Braverman, 1974:56).

8. It is important once again to point out that rational, conscious, purposive, and

social do not refer to some fixed, transhistorical standard but to what is possible in any given historical period.

9. Using these standards makes it clear that, although Marx was referring primarily to industrial capitalism, alienating social relations of production are by no means confined to it. As Henri Lefebvre has put it, "Marx never restricted the sphere of alienation to capitalism" (1958:74).

10. For the basis of this discussion, see Schacht (1971:chap. 3).

11. By comparison, participation by workers in the conventional plywood firm in various union activities, the only form of enterprise governance open to them, is low and remains low over time. The tables on p. 233 report participation in a range of union activities; participation is consistently lower, as might be expected, than participation by worker-shareholders.

12. This index is a simple additive one. See Appendix III for discussion of the methodology used for construction of the index.

13. The level of participation in the co-ops remains unaffected by the level of respondents' education. Since education is usually associated with organizational participation, this suggests that being a democratic work setting has an independent effect on participation. Level of participation is also unaffected by whether respondents had owned a business in the past or now own one, suggesting that entrepreneurial self-selection is not at issue here. There is a very slight tendency for worker-shareholders with lower family incomes to participate more, perhaps suggesting a degree of instrumental motivation for participation. There is also a very slight tendency for those who are married and for those who participate in outside organizations (church, fraternal, and the like) to participate at lower levels in the cooperatives, perhaps suggesting the effects of time constraints. On the relationship between time constraints and participation, see Dahl (1970). Participation is significantly related to job tenure suggesting (in conjunction with the fact that educational level and business background are unrelated to participation) that worker-shareholders learn the attitudes and skills relevant to participation on the job. Democracy appears to be educative.

14. The important distinction between objective and subjective alienation should be recalled. Shareholders may feel that their views are not respected and acted upon, whereas in actuality supervisors do respect them and act upon them. The questions used in this survey might be tapping issues of personal style among foremen, issues of supervisory "bedside manner," and not the real set of social relations existing on the production line.

15. One co-op manager told me that any effort to put surplus funds into plant modernization instead of wages always leads to bitter fights and that an effort to do the same in the interests of more meaningful work is not worth trying. Above all else, he claimed, the worker-shareholders want to maximize their take-home pay.

16. Interviews with APA officials and co-op managers convince me that the findings cannot be attributed to differences in reporting and data-collecting procedures. Grunberg, however, strongly disagrees (1985). In his in-depth investigation of the subject of safety in the cooperatives, he discovered evidence of significant differences in reporting practices with the co-ops showing a tendency to underreport accidents and injuries. I would suggest, however, that the data taken together and reported in Tables 3–9, 3–10, and 3–11 tend to support my position. Grunberg could find little evidence

Union Participation (in percentages)

Question: "Do you attend union meetings?"

	$T_1 (N = 50)$	$T_2 (N = 49)$
Almost always	15.7	6.1
Occasionally	74.5	75.5
Never	9.8	18.4

Significance of association between T_1 and T_2 measures: $Tau_B = 0.432$; $p = 0.001$.

Question: "Do you participate in discussions at union meetings?"

	$T_1 (N = 51)$	$T_2 (N = 49)$
Always	2.0	8.2
Very often	9.8	10.2
From time to time	41.2	28.6
Seldom	23.5	34.7
Never	23.5	18.4

Significance of association between T_1 and T_2 measures: $Tau_B = 0.599$, $p = 0.000$.

Question: "Do you talk about decisions of union officials with other workers in the plant?"

	$T_2 (N = 49)$	$T_2 (N = 48)$
Always	6.0	6.3
Very often	16.0	10.4
From time to time	54.0	45.8
Seldom	14.0	20.8
Never	10.0	16.7

Significance of association between T_1 and T_2 measures: $Tau_B = 0.308$, $p = 0.011$.

Participation as a candidate for union office (in percentages)

Question: "Have you run for union office?"

	$T_1 (N = 50)$	$T_2 (N = 49)$
Yes	6.0	10.2
No	94.0	89.8

Significance of association between T_1 and T_2 measures: $Tau_B = 0.612$, $p = 0.000$.

Participation as a union officer (in percentages)

Question: "Have you ever served as a union officer?"

	T_1 ($N = 51$)	T_2 ($N = 49$)
Yes	5.9	12.2
No	94.1	87.8

Significance of association between T_1 and T_2 measures: $\text{Tau}_B = 0.552$, $p = 0.00$.

Question: "Have you ever served as a shop steward?"

	T_1 ($N = 50$)	T_2 ($N = 49$)
Yes	10.0	14.3
No	90.0	85.7

Significance of association between T_1 and T_2 measures: $\text{Tau}_B = 0.439$, $p = 0.001$.

that the cooperatives were very interested in the problem of workplace safety or were doing much to improve it.

17. This result is not an artifact of time on the job. Indeed, as reported in Appendix I, conventional workers have greater average job tenure than co-op workers, so they have had a greater chance to see accidents over the years.

18. Scale reliabilities at t_1 and t_2, measured by Cronbach's alpha, are .87 and .85. The items are from Kalleberg (1977).

19. I use education, income, and age not only because each has been traditionally associated with a wide range of attitudes and behaviors in the social sciences but because virtually all other background and demographic factors have been automatically controlled for in the design of the study. Because this study examines only white males in closely matched factories in the Pacific Northwest, sex, region, and work technology are already accounted for. See Appendixes I and II for more detail.

20. Dummy variables are used in the equation to designate the distinction between cooperative and conventional firms; education is measured on an ordinal scale; job tenure is measured on an interval scale according to the number of years worked in the plant.

21. Time on the job, which is theoretically more interesting than age, remains statistically nonsignificant, even after age is dropped from the equation.

22. Factor analysis confirms the unidimensionality of the two items. Cronbach's alpha reliability on the index is .88.

23. Scale reliabilities at T_1 and T_2, measured by Cronbach's alpha, are .71 and .75.

24. These findings—the relationship of the index of self-esteem with work setting—are unaffected when controls are entered for age, education, income, and tenure on the job.

4. *Alienation: The Comparative Record*

1. One student of the kibbutz, Joseph Blasi, has pointed out that "the kibbutz is probably one of the most studied societies of the world" (1978:ix). For an introduction to this vast literature see Shur et al. (1981). The literature on the Yugoslav system is also extensive. For an introduction see Adizes (1971); Blumberg (1973); Comisso (1979); Horvat (1975); Pateman (1970); and Wachtel (1973).

2. On the Mondragon case see especially Bradley and Gelb (1985a); Johnson and Whyte (1976); Thomas and Logan (1982); and Oakeshott (1973).

3. Yohanan Stryjan claims that the influence of the market has become so powerful that it threatens basic kibbutz values (1983). This claim is strongly rejected by such students of the kibbutz as Menachem Rosner and Joseph Blasi (1984).

4. This fund helps explain why the Mondragon cooperatives enjoy very high rates of capital investment and growth.

5. There is an important exception to this general observation. In Yugoslavia, where the enterprise is "social property," and in the kibbutz, where the enterprise is communal property, the worker-members may not liquidate the firm and take the assets as individual private property.

6. Since the early 1980s, however, the Mondragon cooperatives have taken a series of small steps designed to enhance the weight of the Social Council in the decision-making process. It remains too early to judge how effective these changes will be.

7. Vejnovic reports a penetrating observation by one worker: "You talk about workers' self-management, but during my two years of membership in this body I have noticed that the first rows of this hall are occupied by managers. Then come experts, then clerks, and then us, the workers. The rear left corner of the hall is reserved for us. Evidence is beginning to come in from as yet unpublished [in English] field studies that the Social Council has started to exercise greater powers and that the system of shop floor discussion is alive and well. Wouldn't it be normal that we workers have the first row?"

8. But it is not a perfect fit. For an analysis of the inability of the kibbutz in practice to match its own aspirations see Rosner and Blasi (1984); they demonstrate that the "failures" are serious yet not fatal and that major ameliorative efforts are well under way.

9. Rosner reports that plant managers spend a mean of 3.5 years in office.

10. One crucial shortcoming is that women are underrepresented in important industrial decision-making positions (Palgi, Blasi, Rosner, and Safir, 1983; Rosner, 1981).

11. I know of no studies on the safety issue published in English, so a comparison with the U.S. plywood cooperatives is not possible.

12. I say "seems to be" because here, again, very little hard empirical evidence is available.

13. There is, of course, an extensive literature that links mental health to workplace democracy in the United States and Europe. For an introduction to this literature see Blumberg (1973) and Mason (1982:chap. 5).

14. The use of the word "shepherd" indicates that Sartre was probably not referring to the industrial worker on the kibbutz though I believe the same conclusion is warranted.

15. I am assuming here that crime is a good if indirect indicator of personal disintegration.

16. Drug and alcohol abuse are also striking for their virtual absence. Furthermore, life expectancy is higher on the kibbutz than in the rest of Israeli society, though properly dividing the credit between health care, nutrition, and mental health is impossible to do at this time.

5. *Participation in Normal Politics*

1. Not all theorists of democracy agree that the two terms are synonymous, and for that reason, I shall continue to use the phrase "participatory democracy."

2. For a lengthy and illuminating discussion of the empirical literature that connects participatory democracy with the development of capacities see Mason (1982:chap. 2). See MacPherson (1973) for the best philosophical defense of this position.

3. (Dahl, 1970: chap. 3). In his most recent work, Dahl considerably broadens his call for participatory democracy in society and poses the defense of his position in the following rather Kantian terms: "If democracy is justified in governing the state, then it must be justified in governing economic enterprises; and to say that it is *not* justified in governing economic enterprises is to imply that it is not justified in governing the state. . . . Members of any association for whom the assumptions of the democratic process are valid have a right to govern themselves by means of the democratic process" (1985:111, 135).

4. See Pateman (1970) for the most complete statement of this view and a comprehensive review of theoretical and empirical materials related to it.

5. This felicitous distinction between "pleased" and "empowered" is that of political scientist J. Maxwell Elden (1981:51).

6. Specifically, respondents were asked to reply to the following question:

Do you regularly attend the meetings of any of the following groups or organizations?

1) Labor unions	5) Farm group
2) Political party clubs	6) Church or church-connected
3) Fraternal organizations or lodges	group
4) Business or civic group	7) Other

Respondents were asked to check in which of these organizations they participated and to place more than one check next to a particular category if they regularly attended meetings of more than one organization in that category.

7. Multiple regression analysis, with organization participation as the dependent variable and factory type (co-op or conventional firm), age, education, and income as the independent variables, demonstrates that the distinction between co-op and conventional work settings remains significant (Beta $= .23$, $F = 14.48$, $p = .000$) when the effects of background variables are controlled.

8. Elden admits, however, that his correlations between participation and efficacy, though significant, were fairly weak.

9. Mason suggests that the following thinkers have made the principal contributions to this line of analysis: Chris Argyris, Peter Bachrach, Ernest Barker, C. George Benello, T. B. Bottomore, John Case, Ken Coates, Terrance Cook, Erich Fromm, G. David Garson, Tom Hayden, David Jenkins, Henry Kariel, C. B. MacPherson, C. Wright Mills, Carole Pateman, David Thompson, Tony Tompham, and Graham Wooten.

10. Two multiple regression equations, with community involvement and hearings serving as dependent variables, and factory type, age, education, and income as the independent variables, demonstrate again that the distinction between co-op and conventional work settings is significant for these two areas of political involvement when the effects of other variables are controlled (Beta $= .11$, $F = 3.35$, $p = .07$; Beta $= .22$, $F = 13.1$, $p = .000$).

11. A series of regression equations with T_2 political participation as the dependent variable and T_1 political participation, co-op participation, supervisory climate, social networks, and self-selection as independent variables demonstrate that co-op participation is significantly related to the increase in rate of attendance at government hearings by worker-shareholders but not to increases in community involvement and campaign activity.

12. *Collected Works*, quoted in Mason (1982:39).

13. I must again stress how weak the differences are between workers in co-op and conventional firms. In a regression equation with this item as the dependent variable and factory type, age, education, and income as independent variables, the beta weight for factory type is statistically nonsignificant.

14. The data do not support theoretical claims about the link between workplace democracy and efficacy though this finding may be an artifact of an inadequate measuring instrument.

15. The only scholarly and political tradition that consistently considers producer cooperatives on its contextual ground is the Marxist one. Marx, for one, saw producer cooperatives as, on the one hand, a compelling demonstration that industry could be managed without capitalists, and, on the other, as an institution tied irrevocably to capitalist social relations (Marx, n.d.: vol. 3, chap. 27) and thus, an institution with no possibilities for social change. To Engels, though the various cooperatives proposed by the utopian socialists were pleasing because of the moral commitments of their adherents, they were based on pure fantasy because state power was not yet in the hands of the working class. The hostility of Lenin and Rosa Luxembourg to cooperative schemes also seems to be tied to the contextual factor: e.g., their location in the general social relations of capitalism, an agreement perhaps with the familiar notion advanced by Marx that "right can never be higher than the economic structure and the cultural development of the society conditioned by it" (Marx, 1961:556). In his last testament, for instance, Lenin proposed the widespread development of cooperatives as a way gradually to bring the peasantry to socialism since the problems of state power and the political revolution, in his view, had been solved by the October Revolution ("On Cooperation"). This view that cooperatives are inevitably capitalist institutions when embedded in capitalism but potentially socialist in another setting

was perhaps best expressed by Nikolai Bukharin. As his biographer, Stephen F. Cohen, has pointed out, Bukharin argued that those Populists and Marxists who imagined a socialist evolution of cooperatives within the capitalist system were purveyors of "a miserable reformist utopia" since such cooperatives, tied to capitalist banks, industry, and the bourgeois state, are inevitably "transformed into capitalist enterprises." Soviet cooperatives, however, functioning within the dictatorship of the proletariat, relying on and connected with socialist industry and banks, would "become part and parcel of the proletarian economic body" (Cohen, 1980).

6. Class-Consciousness in the Cooperatives

1. Since the rediscovery and translation of Gramsci's works in recent years, there has been a virtual avalanche of scholarship about Gramsci. Among the best secondary works are Anderson (1976), Boggs (1976), Cammett (1967), Famia (1981), Fiori (1970), Sassoon (1982), and Williams (1975). For primary sources see Gramsci (1954, 1973, 1975).

2. Gramsci's views on workers' councils differ dramatically from those of many other enthusiasts of self-management and workplace democracy, particularly in the United States, in two important respects. First is his position that workers' councils are incapable of completing the revolutionary task by themselves. It is striking that from the earliest days of his euphoria about the prospects of the councils, through the collapse of the Turin Council movement, to the writing of his main theoretical work in Mussolini's prisons, Gramsci always linked the councils to the larger struggle for socialism and to the necessary efforts of a vanguard party as general educator and coordinator. Second, Gramsci conceived of workers' councils as spontaneous organizations that arise out of struggles at the point of production—as natural proletarian institutions which are not only tools of class struggle but also the effect of such struggle. Councils are not, in short, formal organizational divisions created by unions, management, or government. Nor are they producer cooperatives, the organizations that form the basis of the present study. In more contemporary times, similar positions on councils and the larger revolutionary movement have been taken by Gorz (1967) and Mandel (1970, 1973b).

3. This chapter examines the status of individual attitudes and not class-consciousness per se. It is not appropriate simply to aggregate individual attitudes to understand the latter, for class-consciousness is an attribute of a class, not of individuals. More concretely, class-consciousness involves the formation not only of shared attitudes but also of communication networks, distinctive institutions, and political organization among structurally located population groups. The outstanding historical works that sensitively examine the formation of class-consciousness in this sense are Thompson (1968) and Trotsky (1959).

4. In its pure form, the petite bourgeoisie is that class centered in the simple-commodity sector of the economy. In contrast to both the bourgeoisie and the proletariat, it owns property and produces goods and services directly but does not hire and live off the labor of others. Politically it has traditionally been characterized by its support for a free market of small producers and its hostility to both labor unions

and giant corporations. In this book, the term "petite bourgeoisie" is used in this technical sense, not in the frequently encountered pejorative sense.

5. This item was used only after a screening question was used to eliminate from the analysis those who did not believe social classes exist. Interestingly, less than 10 percent of the sample rejected the notion of social class.

6. A regression equation, with party identification as the dependent variable and factory type (co-op vs. conventional), income, education, and age as the independent variables, indicates that the effect of factory type remains significant even when controlling for other variables. In the remainder of this chapter, unless otherwise indicated, statistically significant differences between co-op and conventional workers will be reported only if regression analysis indicates that factory type remains significant after controlling for income, education, and age. Controls for region, work technology, race, and sex are automatically accounted for by virtue of the study design.

7. Both American political parties are parties of business; only their images say otherwise. On this point, see my book *Capitalism and the American Political Ideal* (Armonk, N.Y.: M. E. Sharpe, 1985).

8. Again, I do not mean to exaggerate the leftist qualities of the centrist Democratic party.

9. On the limited political role of organized labor in the United States see Aronowitz (1973 and 1983). For the opposing view, see Greenstone (1969).

10. Labor unions are progressive in that they support programs of the welfare state and the idea of the social wage. Their lack of progressivism in relation to sexual and racial equality or to U.S. foreign policy toward the Third World demonstrates the feeble nature of progressive forces in the United States.

11. The more conservative cast of worker-shareholders is suggested by the 15 percent who would cut defense spending as a way to deal with the deficit as compared to the 35 percent of conventional workers who would do so.

12. All statistically significant differences hold even after controls are entered for a range of background variables.

13. The argument that the outlook of shareholders is best characterized as a small-property/petit-bourgeois orientation is further affirmed by findings that indicate the existence of a strongly anticorporation, anti-big government outlook among worker-shareholders. On an index designed to tap shareholders' attitudes about large corporations, less than 10 percent responded positively and well over 50 percent responded negatively. Other indexes demonstrate strong distaste for government intervention and initiatives in economic and social affairs. The sample almost universally opposed current tax and spending levels. This complex combination of attitudes about individualism, competition, government, and concentrated economic power is the essence of classical liberalism, what we would today call conservatism.

14. It may be objected that the failure of worker-shareholders to move to the political Left may be partially explained by the growth of a conservative political climate in the United States. The effects of such a climate cannot be ignored, but the relevant comparison in this study is to workers in conventional plants who found themselves in the very same climate. This study shows that worker-shareholders failed to move to the political Left relative to other workers and, in some cases, became even more conservative than they.

15. It might be argued that producer cooperatives, because they are enterprises owned by workers, represent a special case and are therefore inappropriate for the examination of the theoretical issues raised here. To be sure, producer cooperatives are by no stretch of the imagination workers' councils in the Gramsci, Mandel, and Gorz sense. Nevertheless, producer cooperatives can help us to understand some of the effects of cooperative labor in a distinctly hostile setting. Indeed, except for cases in which full-scale revolution is in progress, it is difficult to imagine enduring cases of self-management in industry which can in actuality or in theory escape the inherent logic of producer cooperatives, e.g., collective control of enterprise productive apparatus with an eye toward profit making in the marketplace. Attitude development in the producer cooperatives, then, must surely hold to some degree in any self-management arrangement situated in capitalist market societies.

7. A Comparative Analysis of Class-Consciousness

This chapter is a substantially revised version of my article "Context and Cooperation: Systematic Variation in the Political Effects of Workplace Democracy," which first appeared in *Economic and Industrial Democracy* 4 (1983), pp. 191–223.

1. Much the same position was taken by Rosa Luxembourg in her debate on revisionism with Eduard Bernstein. To Engels, also, the various cooperatives proposed by the utopian socialists, though pleasing because of the moral commitments of their adherents, were based on pure fantasy because state power was not yet in the hands of the working class (1935).

2. It should also be obvious that I view the distinction between ownership (private or collective) and social property made by Horvat and others as less than convincing. Devoid of any countervailing force, market logic will tend to prevail when livelihood is tied to enterprise profits.

3. A similar plea for contextual sensitivity is made by Stephens (1980) and Russell (1984). Stephens specifies a range of politico-economic contexts which, though fundamentally different from my own, are provocative and illuminating. Her approach is also noteworthy for its focus on the origins and introduction of workers' participation schemes in contrasting political environments.

4. One student of countercultural cooperatives indicates that, over time, they become characterized by extreme self-exploitation, increasing distance from the community, declining social concern, more profit orientation, and a- or antipolitical orientations (interview with Herbert Stratton, director, New School for Democratic Management, San Francisco, July 1982). Gunn (1984) has found some evidence that one of the small co-ops in his study managed to avoid these developments.

5. Bachrach and Botwinick (1984) argue, however, that workplace democracy might have the expected political effects even in the United States when it is introduced in a context of labor/capital conflict when the spirit of anticorporatism is strong among workers. This proposition is plausible but the authors offer no evidence in support. It is also often suggested that the strong Swedish cultural influence in the Northwest lumber industry, and especially its cooperative traditions, is an important factor in the

success of the plywood co-ops. If so, the growth of individualistic orientations among worker-shareholders is even more impressive.

6. These effects seem especially marked in Sweden, where powerful labor unions, a prevailing socialist ideology, and a ruling Social Democractic party have created a uniquely (with the possible exception of Norway) hospitable environment for workplace democracy. In this regard see Haas (1980) and Gardell (1983).

7. I believe it to be significant that the Mondragon cooperatives were founded during the Franco era, suggesting, at the least, that the revolutionary possibilities of this form of work organization were perceived by those in power to be minimal or nonexistent.

8. Self-government during the process of revolutionary struggle does not guarantee self-government in the postrevolutionary period, the Soviet Union being the most obvious example. I am reminded of Benjamin Franklin's response to the question of a citizen who asked him what form of government had been created by the Constitutional Convention: "A republic, if you can keep it."

9. For a useful annotated bibliography of primary and secondary works see Kaye (1981) as well as the notes on Gramsci in Chapter 6.

10. Self-management in the form of soviets was also understood to be an instrument for the advance of the revolutionary process by Lenin and Trotsky, particularly to the extent that it contributed to the formation of a dual power in society.

11. For a summary and citations of this literature, see Horvat (1982).

12. In China it was done by Mao. The period from 1955 to 1956 was characterized by a massive reorganization of the countryside into cooperatives, at first, organized so that income was distributed on the basis of the amount of land and capital contributed. By the end of the period, most were reorganized so that the income share to each member was based purely on the contribution of labor. It is estimated that more than 60 million peasant households were drawn or forced into such arrangements in this very short period of time. See Schram (1966).

13. Quoted in Cohen (1980:197).

14. To his everlasting credit, Bukharin insisted that the actions of the party be noncoercive, depending solely on persuasion and education, and be based upon explicit legal principles, not administrative arbitrariness or official lawlessness. On the experience of direct democracy at the workplace during and after the Russian Revolution and the missed Bukharinist and Left Communist alternatives to Stalinism, see Sirianni (1982).

15. The literature on market socialism and the Yugoslav system is too vast to list here. For an introduction see Burns, Karlsson, and Rus (1979); Carter (1982); Comisso (1979); Horvat (1982); Milenkovitch (1971); Obradovic and Dunn (1978); Stephen (1982); and Wachtel (1973).

16. Yugoslav workers see the party as one way to enhance their role in enterprise decision making to the extent that the party helps to counteract the influence of the manager, the technical staff, and highly skilled workers. There is also evidence that over the past decade and a half the party has acted formally to increase the relative representation of blue-collar workers in workers' councils. On these issues see Carter (1982).

17. Many critics claim that the main problem of the Yugoslav system of self-

managing socialism is its overreliance on the market and its unwillingness to exercise more central direction in the interests of socialist justice. Many cite evidence of trends toward materialism, enterprise selfishness, and inequality. See, among others, Schweickart (1980), Stojanovic (1973), Wachtel (1973), and various essays in Obradović and Dunn (1978). The influence of the market in Yugoslavia is partially counterbalanced by the role in enterprise decision making of the commune governments, the unions, and party members. Socialist values, national development, and regional equity are partially served, moreover, by the fiscal policies of the central government, bank practices, and recommendations of the Economic Chambers. Most important in counterbalancing the problem of enterprise egoism, however, has been the role since 1972 of a revitalized League of Communists committed to the service of socialist values (equality, participation by the working class, and solidarity) and the fight against managerialism, the anarchy of the uncontrolled market, and regional fragmentation. On these developments see Baumgartner, Burns, and Sekulic (1979) and Carter (1982).

18. On the need and the possibilities for such "linkage" institutions in the United States see Gunn (1984) and Schweikart (1980).

8. *The Political Effects of Workplace Democracy*

1. I thus fundamentally disagree with the point made by Robert Dahl in *After the Revolution* (1970) that democracy is irrelevant to issues involving specialized expertise for which the criterion of competence is most appropriate. He suggests in defense of his position that we would not want a democratic process to be involved in the selection by the passengers of the pilot and destination every time we board a plane. He is correct, of course, but his example is a straw man, for what is at issue in the example he uses is how democratic processes might be involved in the formulation of general policies concerning air service: routes, pricing structure, balance with other means of transportation, and the like. In a democracy, experts can always be hired without threat of damaging the process so long as they are held accountable.

2. I do not want to overstate the degree to which the cultural base of the cooperatives is egalitarian and cooperative. After all, the Swedes who represent a significant proportion of the membership of these enterprises are two or three generations removed from the mother country, and their basic values seem to be only marginally different from those of other Americans.

3. I mean here presently existing socialism (Bahro, 1978) or what Horvat has called "etatism" (1982).

4. Also see the compelling philosophical work on this form of socialism by David Schweickart, *Capitalism or Worker Control?* (1980). Alec Nove (1983) and Irving Howe (1985) also illuminate this subject.

5. On this point, see the brilliant analysis in Przeworski (1985).

6. By working class, I mean more than blue-collar workers. See the pathbreaking conceptualization offered by Eric Olin Wright (1978:chap. 2). He demonstrates convincingly that the great majority of the American people fit within or close to the definition of working class.

7. The distinction between alternative and oppositional organizations is that of economist Christopher Gunn (1984:206–8).

Bibliography

Abell, Peter. 1983. "The Viability of Industrial Producer Co-operation." In Crouch and Heller, 1983.

Adams, Gordon. 1971. "Notes on Il Manifesto." *Politics and Society* 1 (August): 449–62.

Adizes, I. 1971. *Industrial Democracy: Yugoslav Style*. New York: Free.

Alford, Robert. 1969. *Party and Society*. Westport, Conn.: Greenwood.

Alford, Robert A., and Harry M. Scoble. 1968. "Sources of Local Political Involvement." *American Political Science Review* 62:1192–1206.

Almond, Gabriel, and Sidney Verba. 1963. *The Civic Culture*. Princeton: Princeton University Press.

Anderson, Perry. 1976. "The Antinomies of Antonio Gramsci." *New Left Review* 100:5–78.

Andrews, F. M., and S. B. Withey. 1976. *Social Indicators of Well-Being in America*. New York: Plenum.

Arendt, Hannah. 1965. *On Revolution*. New York: Viking.

Argyris, Chris. 1962. *Interpersonal Competence and Organizational Effectiveness*. Homewood, Ill.: Dorsey.

———. 1965. *Organization and Innovation*. Homewood, Ill.: Dorsey.

Aronowitz, Stanley. 1973. *False Promises*. New York: McGraw-Hill.

———. 1983. *Working-Class Hero*. New York: Pilgrim.

Avineri, Shlomo. 1968. *The Social and Political Thought of Karl Marx*. London: Cambridge University Press.

Bachrach, Peter. 1967. *The Theory of Democratic Elitism*. Boston: Little, Brown.

Bachrach, Peter, and Aryeh Botwinick. 1984. "An Objective Concept of Democratic Participation." Paper presented at the American Political Science Association meetings. Washington, D.C.

Bahro, Rudolf. 1978. *The Alternative in Eastern Europe*. London: New Left Books.

Bardo, John W., and Robert H. Ross. 1982. "The Satisfaction of Industrial Workers and Predictors of Production, Turnover, and Absenteeism." *Journal of Social Psychology* 118:29–38.

Baumgartner, Tom; Rom R. Burns; and Philippe DeVille. 1979. "Work, Politics, and Social Structuring under Capitalism: Impact and Limitations of Industrial Democracy Reforms under Capitalist Relations of Production and Social Reproduction." In Burns, Karlsson, and Rus, 1979.

Baumgartner, Tom; Tom R. Burns; and Dusko Sekulic. 1979. "Self-Management, Market, and Political Institutions in Conflict." In Burns, Karlsson, and Rus, 1979.

Bay, Christian. 1958. *The Structure of Freedom*. Stanford: Stanford University Press.

Bellah, Robert N., et al. 1985. *Habits of the Heart: Individualism and Commitment in American Life*. Berkeley: University of California Press.

Bellas, Carl. 1972. *Industrial Democracy and the Worker Owned Firm*. New York: Praeger.

Berelson, Bernard. 1952. "Democratic Theory and Public Opinion." *Public Opinion Quarterly* 16:313–30.

Berg, Ivor, et al., eds. 1979. *Managers and Work Reform: A Limited Engagement*. New York: Free.

Berman, Katrina. 1967. *Worker-Owned Plywood Companies*. Pullman: Washington State University Press.

Bernstein, Paul. 1974. "Run Your Own Business: Worker-Owned Plywood Firms." *Working Papers* 2 (Summer):24–34.

———. 1976. *Workplace Democratization*. Kent: Kent State University Press.

Blasi, Joseph. 1979. *The Communal Future: The Kibbutz and the Utopian Dilemma*. Norwood, Pa.: Norwood Publications.

Blauner, Robert. 1964. *Alienation and Freedom*. Chicago: University of Chicago Press.

Bluestone, Barry, and Bennett Harrison. 1982a. *The Deindustrialization of America*. New York: Basic.

———. 1982b. "Radical Reindustrialization." *Nation*, September 11, pp. 199–204.

Blumberg, Paul. 1969. *Industrial Democracy: The Sociology of Participation*. New York: Schocken.

Boggs, Carl. 1976. *Gramsci's Marxism*. London: Pluto.

Bottomore, Tom. 1983. *A Dictionary of Marxist Thought*. Cambridge: Harvard University Press.

Bowles, Samuel; David M. Gordon; and Thomas E. Weisskopf. 1983. *Beyond the Wasteland*. Garden City, N.Y.: Anchor/Doubleday.

Bradley, Keith, and Alan Gelb. 1985a. *Co-operation at Work: The Mondragon Experience*. London: Heinemann.

———. 1985b. *Worker Capitalism: The New Industrial Relations*. London: Heinemann.

Brannen, Peter. 1983. *Authority and Participation in Industry*. New York: St. Martins.

Braverman, Harry. 1974. *Labor and Monopoly Capitalism*. New York: Monthly Review.

Buber, Martin. 1949. *Paths in Utopia*. Boston: Beacon.

Burawoy, Michael. 1979. *Manufacturing Consent: Changes in the Labor Process under Monopoly Capitalism*. Chicago: University of Chicago Press.

Burns, Tom R.; Lars Erik Karlsson; and Velijko Rus. 1979. *Work and Power: The Liberation of Work and the Control of Political Power.* London: Sage.

Burstein, Paul. 1972. "Social Structure and Individual Political Participation in Five Countries." *American Journal of Sociology* 77 (May):1103–14.

Cammett, John H. 1967. *Antonio Gramsci and the Origins of Italian Communism.* Stanford: Stanford University Press.

Campbell, Angus; Philip E. Converse; and Willard L. Rodgers. 1976. *The Quality of American Life.* New York: Russell Sage Foundation.

Carnoy, Martin, and Derek Shearer. 1980. *Economic Democracy.* White Plains, N.Y.: Sharpe.

Carter, April. 1982. *Democratic Reform in Yugoslavia: The Changing Role of the Party.* Princeton: Princeton University Press.

Case, John. 1973. "Workers' Control." In Hunnius, Garson, and Case, 1973.

Champoux, J. E. 1978. "Perceptions of Work and Nonwork." *Sociology of Work and Occupations* 4:402–22.

Cherns, Albert, ed. 1982. *Quality of Working Life and the Kibbutz Experience.* Proceedings of an International Conference in Israel. Norwood, Pa.: Norwood Publications.

Clawson, Dan. 1980. *Bureaucracy and the Labor Process: The Transformation of U.S. Industry, 1860–1920.* New York: Monthly Review.

Clegg, Stewart. 1983. "Organizational Democracy, Power, and Participation." In Crouch and Heller, 1983.

Coates, John. 1966. "Democracy and Workers' Control." In *Towards Socialism.* London: Collins.

Coates, Ken. 1976. *The New Worker Cooperatives.* Nottingham: Spokesman.

Cohen, Joshua, and Joel Rogers. 1983. *On Democracy.* New York: Penguin.

Cohen, Stephen. 1980. *Bukharin and the Bolshevik Revolution.* Oxford: Oxford University Press.

Cole, G. D. H. 1919. *Self-Government in Industry.* London: Bell.

———. 1920. *Guild Socialism Restated.* London: Parsons.

Comisso, Ellen Turkish. 1979. *Workers' Control under Plan and Market.* New Haven: Yale University Press.

Compa, Lance. 1982. "The Dangers of Work Control." *Nation,* October 2, pp. 299–302.

Crispo, John. 1978. *Industrial Democracy in Western Europe: A North American Perspective.* Toronto: McGraw-Hill.

Crouch, Colin, and Frank A. Heller, eds. 1983. *Organizational Democracy and Political Processes.* New York: Wiley.

Dahl, Robert A. 1956. *Preface to Democratic Theory.* Chicago: University of Chicago Press.

———. 1963. *Modern Political Analysis.* Englewood Cliffs, N.J.: Prentice-Hall.

———. 1970. *After the Revolution?* New Haven: Yale University Press.

———. 1985. *A Preface to Economic Democracy.* Berkeley: University of California Press.

Dahl, Robert A., and Charles E. Lindblom. 1953. *Politics, Economics, and Welfare.* New York: Harper & Row.

Davis, Mike. 1980. "Why the U.S. Working Class Is Different." *New Left Review* 123 (September/October):3–44.

Dean, Dwight. 1960. "Alienation and Political Apathy." *Social Forces* 38:185–89.

Denitch, Bogdan. 1976. *The Legitimation of a Revolution: The Yugoslav Case*. New Haven: Yale University Press.

Dewey, John. 1927. *The Public and Its Problems*. New York: Holt.

Diamant, Alfred. 1982. "Industrial Democracy in Western Europe." Paper presented at the American Political Science Association meetings. Denver, Colo.

DiQuattro, Arthur. 1978. "Alienation and Justice in the Market." *American Political Science Review* 73 (September):871–87.

Dubin, R. 1956. "Industrial Workers' Worlds: A Study of the Central Life Interests of Industrial Workers." *Social Problems* 3:131–42.

———. 1979. "Central Life Interests." *Pacific Sociological Review* 22:405–26.

Duffy, P. J.; S. Shiflett; and R. G. Downey. 1977. "Locus of Control." *Journal of Applied Psychology* 62:214–19.

Dunn, William N., and Josip Obradovic. 1978. "Workers' Self-Management and Organizational Power." In Obradovic and Dunn, 1978.

Eckstein, Harry. 1966. *A Theory of Stable Democracy*. Princeton: Princeton University Press.

Edwards, Richard. 1979. *Contested Terrain: The Transformation of the Workplace in the Twentieth Century*. New York: Basic.

Elden, J. Maxwell. 1981. "Political Efficacy at Work: The Connection between More Autonomous Forms of Workplace Organization and a More Participatory Politics." *American Political Science Review* 75:43–58.

Elon, Amos. 1981. *The Israelis*. New York: Penguin.

Engels, Friedrich. 1935. *Socialism: Utopian and Scientific*. New York: International.

Espinosa, Juan G., and Andrew S. Zimbalist. 1978. *Economic Democracy: Workers' Participation in Chilean Industry*. New York: Academic.

Fable, Mary. 1982. "The Weirton Steel That Was and May Yet Be." *Progressive* 46 (November):30–36.

Famia, Joseph V. 1981. *Gramsci's Political Thought*. Oxford: Clarendon.

Fine, Keithe Sapsin. 1973. "Worker Participation in Israel." In Hunnius, Garson, and Case, 1973.

Fiori, Giuseppe. 1970. *Gramsci: Life of a Revolutionary*. New York: Schocken.

Form, William H. 1973. "The Internal Stratification of the Working Class." *American Sociological Review* 38:697–711.

Foulkes, Fred. 1969. *Creating More Meaningful Work*. New York: American Management Association.

Fromm, Eric. 1961. *Marx's Conception of Man*. New York: Ungar.

Furniss, Norman, and Timothy Tilton. 1977. *The Case for the Welfare State*. Bloomington: Indiana University Press.

Gardell, Bertil. 1976. "Reactions at Work and Their Influence on Non-work Activities." *Human Relations* 19:885–904.

———. 1977. "Autonomy and Participation at Work." *Human Relations* 30:515–33.

———. 1983. "Worker Participation and Autonomy." In Crouch and Heller, 1983.

Garson, G. David, ed. 1977. *Worker Self-Management in Industry*. New York: Praeger.

Goldy, Robert. 1977. "The Kibbutz in Theory and Practice." In Yassour, 1977.

Gorz, André. 1967. *A Strategy for Labor*. Boston: Beacon.

———. 1973. *Socialism and Revolution*. Garden City, N.Y.: Doubleday.

Gramsci, Antonio. 1954. *L'Ordine Nuovo*. Turin: Einaudi.

———. 1973. *Letters from Prison*. New York: Harper & Row.

———. 1975. *The Modern Prince*. London: Lawrence & Wishart.

Greenberg, Edward S. 1975. "The Consequences of Worker Participation and Control: A Clarification of the Theoretical Literature." *Social Science Quarterly* 55 (September) :215–32.

———. 1979. *Understanding Modern Government*. New York: Wiley.

———. 1980. "Participation in Industrial Decision-Making and Work Satisfaction." *Social Science Quarterly* 60(4):551–69.

———. 1981a. "Industrial Democracy and the Democratic Citizen." *Journal of Politics* 43:965–81.

———. 1981b. "Industrial Self-Management and Political Attitudes." *American Political Science Review* 75:29–42.

———. 1986. *The American Political System*. 4th ed. Boston: Little, Brown.

Greenstone, J. David. 1969. *Labor in American Politics*. New York: Knopf.

Grunberg, Leon. 1985. "Safety, Productivity, and Social Relations in Production: An Empirical Study of Worker Cooperatives." Paper presented at the American Sociological Association meetings. Washington, D.C. Mimeo.

Gunn, Christopher Eaton. 1984. *Workers' Self-Management in the United States*. Ithaca: Cornell University Press.

Gutierrez-Johnson, A., and W. Foote Whyte. 1977. "The Mondragon System of Worker Producer Cooperatives." *Industrial and Labor Relations Review* 31 (October):18–30.

Haas, Ain. 1980. "Worker Views on Self-Management." In *Classes, Class Conflict and the State*, ed. Maurice Zeitlin. Cambridge, Mass.: Winthrop.

Hampden-Turner, Charles. 1970. *Radical Man*. Cambridge, Mass.: Schenkman.

Harrington, Michael. 1972. *Socialism*. New York: Bantam.

Hartz, Louis. 1955. *The Liberal Tradition in America*. New York: Harcourt, Brace & World.

Horney, Karen. 1950. *Neurosis and Human Growth*. New York: Norton.

Horvat, Branko. 1976. *The Yugoslav Economic System*. White Plains, N.Y.: Sharpe.

———. 1982. *The Political Economy of Socialism: A Marxist Social Theory*. Armonk, N.Y.: Sharpe.

Horvat, Branko; M. H. Markovic; and Rudi Supek, eds., 1975. *Self-Governing Socialism*. White Plains, N.Y.: International Arts & Sciences.

Howe, Irving. 1985. *Socialism and America*. New York: Harcourt Brace Jovanovich.

Hunnius, Gerry; G. David Garson; and John Case. 1973. *Workers' Control: A Reader on Labor and Social Change*. New York: Vintage.

Hyman, Herbert. 1959. *Political Socialization*. New York: Free.

Israel, Joachim. 1971. *Alienation: From Marx to Modern Sociology*. Boston: Allyn & Bacon.

Jackall, Robert, and Henry M. Levin, eds. 1984. *Worker Cooperatives in America*. Berkeley: University of California Press.

Jenkins, David. 1974. *Industrial Democracy in Europe: The Challenge and Management Responses*. Geneva: Business International.

Johnson, Ana Gutierrez, and William Foote Whyte. 1976. "The Mondragon System of Worker Production Cooperatives." In Lindenfeld and Rothschild-Whitt, 1982.

Jones, Derek. 1977. "The Economics and Industrial Relations of Producer Cooperatives in the U.S., 1791–1939." *Economic Analysis and Workers' Management* 11 (3–4):295–317.

———. 1979. "U.S. Producer Cooperatives: The Record to Date." *Industrial Relations* 18:342–57.

Jones, Derek C., and Jan Svejnar, eds. 1982. *Participatory and Self-Managed Firms: Evaluating Economic Performance*. Lexington, Mass.: Lexington Books.

Jovanov, Neca. 1973. "Strikes and Self-Management." In Obradovic and Dunn, 1978.

Kalleberg, Arne. 1977. "Work Values and Job Rewards: A Theory of Job Satisfaction." *American Sociological Review* 40:124–43.

Kalleberg, Arne, and Karyn A. Loscocco. 1983. "Aging, Values, and Rewards: Explaining Age Differences in Job Satisfaction." *American Sociological Review* 48:78–90.

Karasek, Robert. 1976. "The Impact of the Work Environment on Life outside the Job." Ph.D diss., Massachusetts Institute of Technology.

Kaye, Harvey J. 1981. "Antonio Gramsci." *Politics and Society* 10 (Fall):334–53.

Kemper, Theodore, and Melvin Reichler. 1976. "Work Integration, Mental Satisfaction and Conjugal Power." *Human Relations* 29:929–44.

Keynes, Milton. 1982. *Mondragon Cooperatives: Myth or Model*. London: Co-operatives Research Unit, Open University.

Kohn, Melvin. 1969. *Class and Conformity*. Homewood, Ill.: Dorsey.

Kolko, Gabriel. 1976. *Main Currents in Modern American History*. New York: Harper & Row.

Kornhauser, Arthur. 1965. *The Mental Health of the Industrial Worker*. New York: Wiley.

Korpi, Walter. 1978. *The Working Class in Welfare Capitalism*. London: Routledge & Kegan Paul.

Krausz, Ernest. 1983. *The Sociology of the Kibbutz*. New Brunswick, N.J.: Transaction.

Lacy, William B.; James G. Hougland, Jr.; and Jon M. Shepard. 1982. "Relationship between Work and Non-Work Satisfaction: Is It Changing and Does Occupational Prestige Make a Difference?" *Sociological Spectrum* 1:157–71.

Lane, Robert. 1962. *Political Ideology*. New York: Free.

Lawler, E. D. 1973. *Motivation in Work Organization*. Monterey: Brooks/Cole.

Lefebvre, Henri. 1958. *Critique de la vie quotidienne*. Paris: L'Arche.

Leman, Gudrun. 1975. "Economic Units in Yugoslav Enterprises." In Horvat, Markovic, and Supek, 1975.

Lenin, V. I. 1975. "On Cooperation." In Robert C. Tucker, ed., *The Lenin Anthology*. New York: Norton.

Leviatan, Uri, and Menachem Rosner. 1982. *Work and Organization in Kibbutz Industry*. Darby, Pa.: Norwood.

Lindenfeld, Frank, and Joyce Rothschild-Whitt, eds. 1982. *Workplace Democracy and Social Change* Boston: Porter Sargent.

Lipset, Seymour Martin. 1962. *Political Man*. New York: Doubleday.

Lipset, Seymour M.; Martin A. Trow; and James S. Coleman. 1956. *Union Democracy*. Glencoe, Ill.: Free.

Lipsitz, Lewis. 1964. "Work Life and Political Attitudes: A Study of Manual Workers." *American Political Science Review* 58:951–61.

Locke, E. 1970. "Job Satisfaction and Performance," *Organizational Behavior and Human Performance* 5:484–500.

Long, J. Scott. 1983a. *Covariance Structure Models: An Introduction to LISREL*. Beverly Hills: Sage.

———. 1983b. *Confirmatory Factor Analysis*. Beverly Hills: Sage.

Lukes, Steven. 1975. "Socialism and Equality." *Dissent* (Spring):154–68.

Lynd, Staughton. 1982. "The Lesson of Republic Rubber." *Nation*, October 23, pp. 395–96.

MacPherson, C. B. 1964. *The Political Theory of Possessive Individualism*. Oxford: Clarendon.

———. 1973. *Democratic Theory: Essays in Retrieval*. Oxford: Clarendon.

Mandel, Ernest. 1970. "The Leninist Theory of Revolution." *International Socialist Review* 31:10–25.

———. 1973a. "The Causes of Alienation." In *The Marxist Theory of Alienation*, ed. Mandel and George Novack. New York: Pathfinder.

———. 1973b. "The Debate on Workers' Control." In Hunnius, Garson, and Case, 1973.

Mansbridge, Jane. 1980. *Beyond Adversary Democracy*. New York: Basic.

Marglin, Stephen. 1974. "What Do Bosses Do?" *Review of Radical Political Economics* 6 (Summer):60–112.

Marrow, Alfred J.; David G. Bowers; and Stanley E. Seashore. 1967. *Management by Participation*. New York: Harper & Row.

Marx, Karl. 1961. *Political Theory: Philosophy, Ideology, Science*. New York: Macmillan.

———. 1967. *Capital*. Moscow: Foreign Language Publishing House.

———. n.d. *Economic and Philosophical Manuscripts*. Moscow: Foreign Language Publishing House.

Marx, Karl, and Friedrich Engels. 1958. *Selected Works*. Moscow: Foreign Language Publishing House.

Maslow, Abraham. 1943. "A Theory of Human Motivation." *Psychological Research* 50:370–396.

———. 1957. *Motivation and Personality*. New York: Harper & Row.

Mason, Ronald M. 1982. *Participatory and Workplace Democracy*. Carbondale: Southern Illinois University Press.

Meissner, M. 1971. "The Long Arm of the Job: A Study of Work and Leisure." *Industrial Relations* 10:239–60.

Miliband, Ralph. 1969. *The State in Capitalist Society*. New York: Basic.

Mill, John Stuart. 1958. *Considerations on Representative Government* (1861), ed. Currin U. Shields. Indianapolis: Bobbs-Merrill.

Mitchell, T. R. 1974. "Expectancy Models of Job Satisfaction." *Psychological Bulletin* 81:1053–77.

Montgomery, David. 1979. *Workers' Control In America: Studies in the History of Work, Technology and Labor Struggles.* Cambridge: Cambridge University Press.

Morse, Nancy, and E. Reimer. 1956. "The Experiental Change of a Major Organizational Variable." *Journal of Abnormal Social Psychology* 52:120–29.

Novack, George 1970. "Introduction." In *The Marxist Theory of Alienation*, ed. Ernest Mandel and George Novack. New York: Pathfinder.

Nove, Alec. 1977. *The Soviet Economic System.* London: Allen & Unwin.

———. 1983. *The Economics of Feasible Socialism.* London: Allen & Unwin.

Oakeshott, Robert. 1973. "Mondragon, Spain's Oasis of Democracy." *Observer* (London), January 21.

———. 1978. *The Case for Workers' Co-ops.* Boston: Routledge & Kegan Paul.

Obradovic, Josip. 1970. "Participation and Work Attitudes in Yugoslavia." *Industrial Relations* 9:161–69.

———. 1978. "Participation in Enterprise Decision-Making." In Obradovic and Dunn, 1978.

Obradovic, Josip, and William N. Dunn, eds. 1978. *Workers' Self-Management and Organizational Power in Yugoslavia.* Pittsburgh: University Center for International Studies.

Oliver, Nick. 1984. "An Examination of Organizational Commitment in Six Workers' Cooperatives in Scotland." *Human Relations* 37:29–45.

Ollman, Bertell. 1971. *Alienation: Marx's Conception of Man in Capitalist Society.* New York: Cambridge University Press.

Oppenheimer, Martin. 1971. "The Limitations of Socialism." In *The Case for Participatory Democracy*, ed. George C. Benello and Dimitrios Roussopoulos. New York: Grossman.

Page, Joseph A., and M. W. O'Brien. 1972. *Bitter Wages: Nader Study Group Report on Disease and Injury on the Job.* New York: Grossman.

Palgi, Michal, and Menachem Rosner. 1983. *Industrial Democracy in Israel.* Haifa: Center for the Study of Industrial Democracy and Self-Management.

Palgi, Michal; Joseph Blasi; Menachem Rosner; and Marylin Safir. 1983. *Sexual Equality.* Norwood, Pa.: Norwood Editions.

Palmore, Erdman. 1969. "Predicting Longevity." *Gerontology* 9:247–50.

Pateman, Carole. 1970. *Participation and Democratic Theory.* London: Cambridge University Press.

Przeworski, Adam. 1980. "Social Democracy as a Historical Phenomenon." *New Left Review* 122:27–58.

———. 1985. *Capitalism and Social Democracy.* New York: Cambridge University Press.

Ramsey, Harvie. 1983. "Evolution or Cycle? Worker Participation in the 1970s and 1980s." In Crouch and Heller, 1983.

Rogers, Carl. 1951. *Client-Centered Therapy.* Boston: Houghton Mifflin.

Rosenstein, Eliezer. 1977. "Worker Participation in Israel: Experience and Lessons." *Annals* (May):113–22.

Rosner, Menachem. 1965. "Principal Types and Problems of Direct Democracy in the Kibbutz." Givat Haviva, Israel: Social Research Center on the Kibbutz.

———. 1976. *The Kibbutz as a Way of Life in Modern Society*. Cambridge, Mass.: Institute for Cooperative Community.

———. 1981. *Participatory Political and Organizational Democracy and the Experiences of the Israeli Kibbutz*. Haifa: Institute for Study and Research of the Kibbutz and the Cooperative Idea.

———. 1982. "The Quality of Working Life in the Kibbutz." In Cherns, 1982.

———. 1984. "A Search for Coping Strategies or Forecasts of Cooperative Degeneration." *Economic and Industrial Democracy* 5:391–400.

Rosner, Menachem, and Joseph R. Blasi. 1984. "Theories of Participatory Democracy and the Kibbutz." In *Festschrift Volume for S. N. Eisenstadt*, ed. Erik Cohen. Boulder, Colo.: Westview.

Rothschild-Whitt, Joyce. 1983. "Worker Ownership and Control: A Typology of Reform." In Crouch and Heller, 1983.

Rus, Veljko. 1975. "Problems of Participatory Democracy." In Horvat, Markovic, and Supek, 1975.

———. 1978. "Enterprise Power Structure." In Obradovic and Dunn, 1978.

Russell, Raymond. 1984. "Using Ownership to Control: Making Workers Owners in the Contemporary United States." *Politics and Society* 13:253–94.

Sartori, Giovanni. 1962. *Democratic Theory*. Detroit: Wayne State University Press.

Sassoon, Anne Showstock, ed. 1982. *Approaches to Gramsci*. London: Writers & Readers.

Schacht, Richard. 1971. *Alienation*. Garden City, N.Y.: Doubleday/Anchor.

Schneider, Ben Rose. 1979. "The Politics of Worker Self-Management: The Case of Peru." Columbia University, unpublished.

Schram, Stuart. 1966. *Mao Tse-Tung*. Harmondsworth: Penguin.

Schumpeter, Joseph. 1943. *Capitalism, Socialism and Democracy*. London: Allen & Unwin.

Schweickart, David. 1980. *Capitalism or Worker Control?* New York: Praeger.

Seeman, Marvin. 1961. "On the Meaning of Alienation." *American Sociological Review* 26:753–58.

———. 1967. "On the Personal Consequences of Alienation in Work." *American Sociological Review* 32:273–85.

———. 1972. "Alienation and Engagement". In *The Human Meaning of Social Change*, ed. Angus Cambpell and Philip E. Converse. New York: Russell Sage.

Sennett, Richard, and Jonathan Cobb. 1973. *The Hidden Injuries of Class*. New York: Vintage.

Shabad, Goldie. 1978. "Strikes in Yugoslavia: Implications for Industrial Democracy." Paper presented at the American Political Science Association meetings. Washington, D.C.

Shepard, Jon M. 1969. "Functional Specialization and Work Attitudes." *Industrial Relations* 8:184–95.

Sheppard, H. L., and N. Q. Herrick. 1972. *Where Have All the Robots Gone? Worker Dissatisfaction in the Seventies.* New York: Free.

Shirom, Arie. 1972. "The Industrial Relations Systems of Industrial Cooperatives in the United States, 1880–1935." *Labor History* 13 (Fall):533–51.

Shur, Shimon, et al. 1981. *The Kibbutz: A Bibliography of Scientific and Professional Publications in English.* Haifa: Institute for Research of the Kibbutz and the Co-operative Idea.

Siber, Ivan, et al. 1978. "Perceptions of Enterprise Power Structure." In Obradovic and Dunn, 1978.

Sirianni, Carman. 1982. *Workers' Control and Socialist Democracy: The Soviet Experience.* London: New Left Books/Verso.

———. 1985. "Rethinking the Significance of Workers' Control in the Russian Revolution." *Economic and Industrial Democracy* 6:65–91.

Slater, Philip. 1970. *The Pursuit of Loneliness.* Boston: Beacon.

Smith, Adam. 1937. *The Wealth of Nations* (1776). 2 vols. New York: Random House.

Smith, Stephen C. 1985. "Political Behavior as an Economic Externality." *Advances in the Economic Analysis of Participatory and Labor-Managed Firms* 1:123–36.

Stephens, Evelyn Huber. 1980. *The Politics of Workers' Participation.* New York: Academic.

Stojanovic, Svetozar. 1973. *Between Ideal and Reality: A Critique of Socialism and Its Future.* Oxford: Oxford University Press.

Street, John. 1983. "Socialist Arguments for Industrial Democracy." *Economic and Industrial Democracy* 4:519–39.

Stryjan, Yohanan. 1983. "Self-Management: The Case of the Kibbutz." *Economic and Industrial Democracy* 4:243–83.

Tannenbaum, Arnold, et al. 1974. *Hierarchy in Organizations.* San Francisco: Jossey-Bass.

Tannenbaum, Arnold; I. R. Weschier; and F. Massarik. 1961. *Leadership and Organization.* New York: McGraw-Hill.

Terkel, Studs. 1974. *Working.* New York: Pantheon.

Terrill, Ross. 1973. *R. H. Tawney and His Times.* Cambridge: Harvard University Press.

Thomas, Henk, and Chris Logan. 1982. *Mondragon: An Economic Analysis.* London: Allen & Unwin.

Thompson, Dennis. 1970. *The Democratic Citizen.* London: Cambridge University Press.

Thompson, E. P. 1968. *The Making of the English Working Class.* Harmondsworth: Penguin.

Tocqueville, Alexis de. 1845. *Democracy in America.* New York: Langley.

Tornquist, David. 1973. "Workers' Management: The Intrinsic Issues." In Hunnius, Garson, and Case, 1973.

Trotsky, Leon. 1959. *The Russian Revolution.* New York: Doubleday.

Tudor, B. A. 1972. "A Specification of Relationships between Job Complexity and Powerlessness." *American Sociological Review* 37:596–604.

U.S. Department of Health, Education and Welfare. 1972. *Work in America*. Washington, D.C.: U.S. Government Printing Office.

Valentin, Fin. 1979. "Self-Management-Strategy for Autonomy or Integration." In Burns, Karlsson, and Rus, 1979.

Valler, Ivan. 1973. "Production Imperatives and Communal Norms in the Kibbutz." In *Communes*, ed. Rosabeth Moss Kanter. New York: Harper & Row.

Vanek, Jaroslav, ed. 1974. *Self-Management*. Baltimore: Penguin.

Vejnovic, Milos. 1978. "Influence Structure in a Self-Managing Enterprise." In Obradovic and Dunn, 1978.

Verba, Sidney, and Norman H. Nie. 1972. *Participation in America: Political Democracy and Social Equality*. New York: Harper & Row.

Vroom, Victor H. 1960. *Some Personality Determinants of the Effects of Participation*. Englewood Cliffs, N.J.: Prentice-Hall.

———. 1964. *Work and Motivation*. New York: Wiley.

Wachtel, Howard M. 1973. *Workers' Management and Workers' Wages in Yugoslavia*. Ithaca: Cornell University Press.

Wajcman, Judy. 1983. *Women in Control: Dilemmas of a Workers' Cooperative*. New York: St. Martins.

Walton, Paul, and Andrew Gamble. 1972. *From Alienation to Surplus Value*. London: Sheed & Ward.

Whyte, William Foote. 1983. "Worker Participation: International and Historical Perspectives." *Journal of Applied Behavioral Science* 19:395–407.

Williams, Gwyn. 1960. "The Concept of Egemonia in the Thought of Antonio Gramsci." *Journal of the History of Ideas* 21:586–98.

———. 1975. *Proletarian Order: Antonio Gramsci, Factory Councils and the Origins of Italian Communism*. London: Pluto.

Wills, Gary. 1970. *Nixon Agonistes*. New York: New American Library.

Witte, John. 1980. *Democracy, Authority, and Alienation in Work*. Chicago: University of Chicago Press.

Woodward, Susan Lampland. 1977. "The Freedom of the People Is in Its Private Life: The Unrevolutionary Implications of Industrial Democracy." *American Behavioral Scientist* 20 (March/April):579–96.

Wright, Erik Olin. 1978. *Class, Crisis and State*. London: New Left Books.

Yassour, Avrahma, ed. 1977. *Kibbutz Members Analyze the Kibbutz*. Cambridge, Mass.: Institute for Cooperative Community.

Yuchtman, Ephraim. 1983. "Reward Distribution and Work-Role in the Kibbutz." In *The Sociology of the Kibbutz*, ed. Ernest Krausz. New Brunswick, N.J.: Transaction.

Zupanov, Josip. 1975. "Participation and Influence." In Horvat, Markovic, and Supek, 1975.

Zwerdling, Daniel. 1973. "Beyond Boredom." *Washington Monthly* 6:80–91.

———. 1978. *Workplace Democracy*. New York: Harper & Row.

———. 1979. "Employee Ownership." *Working Papers for a New Society* (May/June):14–21.

Index

Alienation:
  MacPherson on, 16–17
  Marx on, 15, 67–73, 112
  from others, 71–72, 87–90, 109–10
  political and economic, 140–47
  from product, 68–69, 74–75, 102–3
  from production process, 69–71, 76–84,
    103–9
  from self, 72–73, 90–97
  in socialist tradition, 15–17
  in state socialism, 231n
Allende, Salvadore, 160–62
Anarchists, 65, 134
Arendt, Hannah, 116, 160

Bachrach, Peter, 117, 240n
Blasi, Joseph, 113, 235n
Blauner, Robert, 69–70
Bluestone, Barry, 14, 225n
Blumberg, Paul, 73
Bowles, Samuel, 14
Braverman, Harry, 70, 231n
Buber, Martin, 116
Bukharin, Nikolai, 153, 164, 238n, 241n

Caja Laboral Popular, 100, 102
Capitalism:
  mediated, effects of workplace democracy
    in, 157–60
  unmediated, effects of workplace democ-
    racy in, 156–57
Carnoy, Martin, 14, 21
Case, John, 22
Chile, 160, 162

Class consciousness, theory of, 133–35,
  151–52
Class identification, 137–40
Coates, John, 22
Cohen, Joshua, 14
Cole, G. D. H., 18, 22, 117, 121–23, 129,
  171
Comisso, Ellen, 108
Council communists, 65

Dahl, Robert, 31, 117, 236n, 242n
Data analysis, 191–92
Data collection, 187–88
Democratic theory, 30–31, 62–64
  and participation in workplace, 115–18
Dewey, John, 18

Elden, J. Maxwell, 119, 122, 236n, 237n
Employee stock ownership plans, 24
Equality:
  in self-governing socialism, 176–77
  worker belief in, 46–47
Escalation, theory of, 21, 151
Espinosa, Juan, 22, 162

Gordon, David M., 14
Gorz, André, 22
Gramsci, Antonio, 134–35, 161, 166, 179,
  181, 238n, 240n
Grunberg, Leon, 60
Gunn, Christopher, 60, 240n, 242n

Haas, Ain, 158
Harrison, Bennett, 14, 225n

Library of Congress Cataloging-in-Publication Data

Greenberg, Edward S., 1942–
 Workplace democracy.

 Bibliography: p.
 Includes index.
 1. Plywood industry—Northwest, Pacific—Management—Employee participa-
tion—Case studies. 2. Producer cooperatives—Northwest, Pacific—Management—
Employee participation—Case studies. 3. Industrial management—Northwest, Pa-
cific—Employee participation—Case studies. I. Title.
HD5658.P622U554 1986   674′.834′068   86–47641
ISBN 0–8014–1921–2 (alk. paper)